GOD'S WORD
INTO ENGLISH

GOD'S WORD

INTO ENGLISH

DEWEY M. BEEGLE

William B. Eerdmans Publishing Co.
Grand Rapids, Michigan

ACKNOWLEDGMENTS

Grateful acknowledgment is made to the following for permission to reprint
copyrighted material from the publications indicated:

Eyre & Spottiswoode, Ltd., London, administrators on behalf of the Crown:
"Dedication to King James I," and "The Translators to the Reader," from the
Authorized King James Version, copyright in Great Britain by the Crown.

University of Chicago Press, Chicago: The Complete Bible: An American Translation, the Old Testament translated by J. Powis Smith and a group of scholars,
the Apocrypha and the New Testament translated by Edgar Goodspeed, copyright, 1923, 1931, and 1938 by the University of Chicago.

Moody Press, Chicago: The New Testament in the Language of the People,
by Charles B. Williams, copyright 1949 by Moody Bible Institute.

University of Pennsylvania Press, Philadelphia: The Literary Lineage of the
King James Bible, by Charles C. Butterworth, copyright 1941 by University of
Pennsylvania Press.

The Macmillan Company, New York (United States and dependencies) and
Geoffrey Bles Ltd., London (Great Britain and Canada): Letters to Young
Churches, by J. B. Phillips with an Introduction by C. S. Lewis, copyright ©
1947 and 1957 by The Macmillan Company and Geoffrey Bles Ltd., and The
Gospels, by J. B. Phillips, copyright © 1952 and 1957 by The Macmillan Com-
pany and Geoffrey Bles Ltd.

Thomas Nelson & Sons, New York: Revised Standard Version of the Bible,
copyright 1946 and 1952 by the Division of Christian Education of the National
Council of Churches, and An Introduction to the Revised Standard Version of
the New Testament, copyright 1946 by the Division of Christian Education of
the National Council of Churches.

Zondervan Publishing House, Grand Rapids: The Holy Bible—The Berkeley
Version in Modern English, Gerrit H. Verkuyl, editor-in-chief and translator of
the New Testament, copyright © 1958 and 1959 by Zondervan Publishing
House.

In memory of my father

BURTON L. BEEGLE
1892–1960

with deepest affection for the years of
sacrificial, loving example in seeking
first God's kingdom and righteousness

ACKNOWLEDGMENTS FOR ILLUSTRATIONS

The author is grateful to the following for granting permission to reproduce the illustrations indicated:

Trustees of the British Museum, London: Fig. 1 "Codex Sinaiticus before Binding," from *Scribes and Correctors of the Codex Sinaiticus* (1939) by H. J. M. Milne and T. C. Skeat; and Fig. 10 "Beginning of the Gospel according to John in the Lindisfarne Gospels."

Clarendon Press, Oxford: Fig. 2 "First Page of the Gospel according to John in Codex Sinaiticus," from *Codex Sinaiticus Petropolitanus* (1911) reproduced in facsimile by Helen and Kirsopp Lake.

Presses Universitaires de France, Paris: Fig. 3 "A Page in Codex Ephraemi Rescriptus," from *Fac-similés des plus anciens Manuscrits Grecs en Onciale et en Minuscule de la Bibliothèque Nationale du IVe au XIIe Siècle* (1892), by Henri Omont, photograph courtesy of Princeton University Press, from *Light From the Ancient Past* (1946 and 1959), by Jack Finegan.

Chester Beatty Library, Dublin: Fig. 4 "A Page in the Chester Beatty Papyri of Paul's Letters," from *The Chester Beatty Biblical Papyri* (1937), by Frederic G. Kenyon.

John C. Trever and *The Biblical Archaeologist*, New Haven: Fig. 5 "Dead Sea (Qumran) Isaiah Scroll 'A,'" from Vol. XI, September, 1948, photograph courtesy of John C. Trever.

S. H. Horn, Washington, D.C.: Fig. 6 "Siloam Inscription."

American Schools of Oriental Research, New Haven: Fig. 7 "Column 32 of the Isaiah Scroll," and Fig. 14 "Column 10 of the Habakkuk Commentary," from *The Dead Sea Scrolls of St. Mark's Monastery*, Vol. I (1950), photographs courtesy of John C. Trever.

Württemberg Bibelanstalt, Stuttgart: Fig. 8 "Hebrew Text of Ruth 3:5," and Fig. 9 "Hebrew Text of Ruth 3:12," from *Biblia Hebraica*, edited by Rudolf Kittel.

New York Public Library: Fig. 11 "Title Page of the First Edition of the King James Version."

American Bible Society, New York: Fig. 12 "2 Corinthians 8:14 in a 1611 Edition of the King James Version," and Fig. 13 "2 Corinthians 8:14 in a 1612 Edition of the King James Version."

Contents

Acknowledgments . . . . iv, vi
Preface ix
Chapter 1   Why Revise God's Word? 1
Chapter 2   The New Testament Text 9
Chapter 3   The Old Testament Text 34
Chapter 4   Languages Change 55
Chapter 5   Artistic Style and the Truth 73
Chapter 6   New Meanings for Biblical Words 90
Chapter 7   Alternative Translations 99
Chapter 8   One Word Corresponds to Many 105
Appendix A   A Chronology of Representative English Translations from Wyclif to the Present 121
Appendix B   "W. T. To the Reader"—Tyndale's Story of His Translation 123
Appendix C   "The Translators to the Reader"—the Preface to the King James Version 128
Appendix D   The Dedication to King James I 152
Appendix E   *Kethib, Qere,* and the Name "Jehovah" 155
Appendix F   More Recent Translations 158
Scriptural Index 209
General Index 214

An eight-page section of photographs follows page 52.

Preface

Since the beginning of the Reformation in 1517 the Bible has held a place of prime importance in Protestant Christianity. Luther, Calvin, and Wesley all stressed the necessity of knowing Scripture and also of putting its message into practice. How essential it is, then, to have translations which communicate God's Word effectively!

The immediate goal of this book is to indicate the essential translation features which enable the modern reader to understand most clearly the truths intended by God's messengers in the Old and New Testaments. The ultimate goal is that in learning the truth one may come into an ever more vital relationship to his Lord and Savior Jesus Christ.

The two basic means of accomplishing the immediate goal will be: (1) to review some highlights of a thrilling story—the story of how we got our English Bible, and (2) to give examples showing how translators of the past and present have dealt with the difficult problems involved in translating into English. Of necessity not all the translations available could be consulted, but the sampling should be sufficient in scope to illustrate the points in question.

While pastors, Sunday-school teachers, and theological students should find the material helpful, this book is designed primarily for the layman. At times the material will seem somewhat complex, but this very complexity will enable the reader to appreciate more profoundly the devotion and care with which God's servants have passed on the "Good News." We should not be ignorant of the fruits of their labors, and we dare not ignore the lessons which they learned and passed on to us.

One of the difficult portions of the story has been summarized in the text of the book and the more detailed discussion appears (for those who are interested) as an appendix. Scriptural and general indexes have also been provided for the convenience of the reader.

Teachers, colleagues, students, and friends (far too many to name individually) have aided and encouraged the writer. Deep appreciation is expressed to each of these.

DEWEY M. BEEGLE

New York City
April, 1960

Preface - Revised Edition

One of the purposes of *God's Word into English* was to help Christians understand the essential features of a good translation. This goal has been achieved in some measure, but the process of instruction is far from complete. A paperback edition will enable many more groups to use the book as a basis for study about translations.

Moreover, since the modern translation boom did not stop in 1960, it has become necessary to update the first edition. Rather than insert the data about new translations in the topical discussions of the original eight chapters, the new material has been assembled in "Appendix F." Each translation is considered separately with discussion, where relevant, of such matters as principles, text, style, clarity, and accuracy.

DEWEY M. BEEGLE

New York City
March, 1964

GOD'S WORD
INTO ENGLISH

Why Revise God's Word?

Since the turn of the century the names of Weymouth, Moffatt, Goodspeed, Williams, Verkuyl, and Phillips have become famous in the English-speaking world because of their association with translations of Scripture. While the increase in revisions and translations of God's Word has been quite remarkable (see Appendix A for a chronology of representative English translations) we are not justified in thinking that this phenomenon is limited solely to our time. Between 1525 and 1582 there were at least seven major translations or revisions of the English Scriptures and, strange as it may seem, between the publication of the King James Version in 1611 and the present time more than five hundred translations have been published in English: twenty-seven full Bibles, about seventy-five New Testaments, over one hundred and fifty publications having less than the full New Testament, and about two hundred and fifty translations in commentaries, often large portions of the Bible, serving as a basis for exposition of the meaning of Scripture.

Whereas these facts, if charted, show certain peak periods of translation activity they also indicate that ever since the start of the Reformation in 1517 there has been extensive interest in revising or translating God's Word. At the same time, however, there have always been those who asked, "Why is it necessary to revise God's Word?" This was true in 1611 for, although we are accustomed to thinking in terms of the superiority and supremacy of the King James Version, the translation faced real opposition. The preface (entitled "The Translators to the Reader"—see Appendix C) anticipated the difficulty by repeating the questions posed by the opposition:

Many men's mouths have been opened a good while (and yet are not stopped) with speeches about the translations made before: and ask what may be the reason, what the necessity, of the employment. Hath the Church been deceived, say they, all this while? Hath her sweet bread been mingled with leaven, her silver with dross, her wine with water, her milk with lime? . . . Was their translation good before? Why do they now mend it? Was it not good? Why then was it obtruded [presented] to the people?

The Reasons for Revision

These, or similar questions, are still being asked and it is imperative that satisfactory answers be given now as they were in 1611. Among the principal reasons for revising God's Word may be included the following: (1) the discovery of more accurate texts in Greek and Hebrew; (2) the continual change in the English language; (3) the renewed emphasis on readily intelligible translations; (4) the new information as to the meanings of Biblical terms; and (5) the improvements in the interpretation of passages.

More Accurate Texts

In John 1:18 most translations, including the King James Version, read, "the only begotten Son, which is in the bosom of the Father." On the other hand, some of the important manuscripts (handwritten copies) of the Greek New Testament discovered during the last century have "God" where most of the manuscripts have "Son." This striking testimony to the deity of Jesus Christ was considered by many scholars as a change introduced by a well-meaning, but overzealous, scribe. However, the recently published manuscript Bodmer II, dating from the second century A.D. (about 150 years earlier than the oldest manuscript of John's Gospel previously known), also has "God" in John 1:18. While no one can guarantee that this is the reading of the original manuscript of John's Gospel this early evidence increases the importance of the "variant reading" (use of a different wording) to the point where modern translations must include it, either in the text or in the footnotes. Even prior to the discovery of Bodmer II the footnotes of the American Standard Version (1901) and the Revised Standard Version (1946) indicated that "many (other) ancient authorities read *God*."

Translating the standard Hebrew text of Isa. 33:8 word for word, the King James Version reads, "The highways lie waste, the wayfaring man

ceaseth: he hath broken the covenant, he hath despised cities, he regardeth no man." This translation has puzzled many readers because it
appears that "he" who is breaking, despising, and not regarding is the
"wayfaring man," but such is not the case. An unnamed enemy has
broken his word with the result that such a lawless state of affairs exists
in Palestine the merchant or traveler journeys on the regular routes at
the risk of his life. In order to help clarify the passage the American
Standard Version adds words in italics: "The highways lie waste, the
wayfaring man ceaseth: *the enemy* hath broken the covenant, he hath
despised cities, he regardeth no man."

The King James and American Standard Versions were dependent
on the available Hebrew manuscripts, all of which read עָרִים *'arim*
"cities," but Bible scholars had occasion to wonder about this reading
because the Assyrian kings whose conquering armies destroyed cities
in Palestine did not do so because they "despised cities." There had to
be some other explanation to account for this word. The answer was
forthcoming in 1947 for in the spring of that year an Arab Bedouin
discovered a cave in the cliffs overlooking the northwestern rim of the
Dead Sea in Palestine. There was found a number of large jars, some
of which contained ancient scrolls (a continuous roll of leather or paper
as contrasted with a book which has leaves or sheets). Little did he
realize that his marvelous find would lead to a series of cave discoveries
producing hundreds of priceless fragments and scrolls.

One of the manuscripts from Cave 1 was a leather scroll in Hebrew
containing the entire book of Isaiah. Information gained subsequent to
the discovery has shown that it dates from the second or first centuries
B.C., and that it was no doubt hidden in the cave by its owner in A.D.
68, just before the Roman armies swept into southern Palestine. This
very early Hebrew manuscript, preserved through the centuries by the
hot, dry climate of the Dead Sea area, reads עֵדִים *'edim* "witnesses,
treaties" in the difficult passage in Isa. 33:8. With this new variant
reading available the Revised Standard Version was able to improve
the sense of the passage by translating, "The highways lie waste, the
wayfaring man ceases. Covenants are broken, witnesses are despised,
there is no regard for man." The parallelism of the verse could be
indicated even more clearly by translating, "Covenants are broken,
treaties are despised. . . ." Ignoring the vowels, which were not indicated fully in the Hebrew manuscripts until after A.D. 600, the change
from the original reading עדים to ערים is easily explained. Some
scribe mistaking the ד "d" for an ר "r" (two very similar consonants
which were continually being confused) copied the wrong word.

The examples from John 1:18 and Isa. 33:8 are illustrative of the many places in which textual research and discovery have blessed us with passages of greater historical and spiritual value. We who believe in the inspiration of God's Word should ever be grateful, for we have everything to gain by endeavoring to discover the most accurate Greek and Hebrew texts.

Change in the English Language

As long as a language continues to be a means of communication between human beings it is of necessity a living, dynamic thing, continually in flux or change. For this reason many verses which were readily understood in 1611, for example, cause the modern reader difficulty or embarrassment. In 1 Thess. 4:15 the King James Version reads, "we which are alive *and* remain unto the coming of the Lord shall not prevent them which are asleep." The difficulty arises because in our time "prevent" means "to hinder," whereas in 1611 it meant (as in Latin from which it came) "to go ahead of."

The King James translation of Rom. 1:13, "oftentimes I purposed to come unto you, (but was let hitherto)," is quite accurate if the reader understands "let" to mean "hindered," but aside from the tennis expression "a let ball" (that is, "a hindered ball," now often changed to "a net ball") the meaning is obsolete. This came about because the Old English word "laet," meaning "to loose, allow, permit," was gradually pronounced and spelled "let," and in time it displaced "let = hinder." Accordingly, present-day readers are inclined to misinterpret the King James Version in Rom. 1:13.

These misleading words of the King James Version have, at times, the additional disadvantage of suggesting to modern readers or hearers uncouth, even obscene, situations which are devastating to any real understanding of the passage. Song of Sol. 5:4, for example, reads, "My beloved put in his hand by the hole *of the door,* and my bowels were moved for him." The American Standard Version improves the sense tremendously simply by changing "bowels" to "heart," but the Revised Standard Version improves still more by translating, "My beloved put his hand to the latch, and my heart was thrilled within me."

Sometimes misunderstandings result from a change of order of words in English. The King James of Matt. 26:27 reads, "And he took the cup, and gave thanks, and gave *it* to them, saying, Drink ye all of it." Most readers interpret Jesus' command to mean, "You, drink all of the cup," but the Greek text and the King James translators mean, "All of you, drink from the cup." The expression "ye all" meant, accordingly, much the same as the American idiom "you all."

While some of us may be reluctant to relinquish old words and expressions which have acquired special meaning, we must bear in mind that the revision of these archaisms is a genuine attempt to be true to the Greek text (the same goal which the King James translators had) by restoring for the modern reader the precise meaning intended.

Renewed Emphasis on Intelligibility

Another important reason for revision of God's Word is the increased demand by the common people that a translation be as intelligible as possible. A case in point is the idiomatic phrase "children of the bride-chamber" which occurs in the King James Version in Matt. 9:15, Mark 2:19, and Luke 5:34. But the expression is meaningless to (or grossly misinterpreted by) the average reader, so most of the translations made in the twentieth century have striven for intelligibility by reading "wedding guests" or "friends of the bridegroom." While the text of the American Standard Version has "sons of the bridechamber," a footnote explains, "That is, *companions of the bridegroom*."

Because Paul tended to write with long, involved sentences his letters pose a real difficulty for all those making translations into English. The King James translators tried to keep the longest sentence, Eph. 1:3–14, as one unit by the free use of colons and semicolons, but this was hardly necessary. Inasmuch as English tends to employ shorter, more concise sentences most modern translations (for example, C. B. Williams, Verkuyl, Revised Standard Version, and Phillips) have broken this paragraph-sentence into smaller units.

The King James Version, following the word order of the Greek text in John 1:14, translates, "And the Word was made flesh, and dwelt among us, (and we beheld his glory, the glory as of the only begotten of the Father,) full of grace and truth." The translators employed parentheses to show that "full of grace and truth" did not modify "Father," but readers continue to misinterpret the passage. It is much better, therefore, to rearrange the English sentence so as to indicate clearly the intent of the Greek; for example, Goodspeed (1923) translates, "So the Word became flesh and blood and lived for awhile among us, abounding in blessing and truth, and we saw the honor God had given him . . . ," while the Revised Standard Version has, "And the Word became flesh and dwelt among us, full of grace and truth; we have beheld his glory . . . ."

Once again we must realize that the purpose of such revisions is to convey with greater clarity the real message which God's Word has for each of us. While modern translators have improved on the intelligibility of some parts of the King James Version this is not to say that the King James translators were indifferent to the matter of intelligibility. They stated most emphatically their concern that "the Scripture may speak like itself, as in the language of Canaan, that it may be understood even of the very vulgar" ("vulgar" in this context meant the common people).

New Meanings for Biblical Terms

The reader may wonder how new meanings can be given to words which were used in certain specific ways by people two thousand or more years ago. Actually the meanings for these Biblical terms are ancient; it is only our understanding of the meaning which is new. We came by this information through tens of thousands of written documents discovered in. Bible lands during the last seventy-five years. The most important of these new sources of information have been the thousands of papyrus (ancient type of paper) fragments and scrolls ranging all the way from love letters to grocery lists.

There are almost five thousand different Greek words used in the Greek New Testament, and prior to the discovery of the papyri over five hundred of these words were classified as "Biblical" words because, either they were found only in the New Testament, or they were employed with different meanings from those commonly found in the classical Greek writings. Some good illustrations are to be found in Paul's letters to the church at Thessalonica. There he uses the Greek adjective *ataktos* (1 Thess. 5:14), the adverb *ataktos* (2 Thess. 3:6, 11), and the related verb *atakteo* (2 Thess. 3:7). The King James and American Standard Versions, on the basis of the scholarly opinion then current, translated these words "unruly, disorderly, walk or behave disorderly." The papyri, however, indicate that the words, as Paul used them, meant "idle, idleness, be idle," and so the Revised Standard Version translates, "admonish the idle" (1 Thess. 5:14), "we command you . . . that you keep away from any brother who is living in idleness" (2 Thess. 3:6), "we were not idle" (2 Thess. 3:7), and "we hear that some of you are living in idleness" (2 Thess. 3:11).

Hindsight is always better than foresight, but it is interesting that scholars did not seize onto the clue in the context of 2 Thess. 3:11 where the King James Version translates, "For we hear that there are some which walk among you disorderly, working not at all, but are busybodies." Now we know that the expression "working not at all" was Paul's way of emphasizing and clarifying the preceding word which meant "in idleness," not "disorderly."

In Gal. 6:2 the King James and American Standard Versions translate, "Bear ye one another's burdens, and so fulfil the law of Christ," but in verse 5 of the same chapter they have, "For every (each) man shall bear his own burden." Many readers of these translations have pondered, with good reason, what Paul could have meant by this apparent contradiction. The more recent translations, however, have been careful to remove the difficulty by indicating in the English translation of verse 2 that Paul used the Greek word *baros* "burdens, weight," those excessively heavy burdens which come upon all of us at times, whereas in verse 5 he employed the Greek word *phortion* "load," the legitimate tasks and responsibilities of our normal life.

An Old Testament illustration of new meanings is found in the section 1 Sam. 13:19–21 where the writer explains why there were no swords or spears in the hands of the people who accompanied Saul and Jonathan in their attack against the Philistines at Michmash. The King James Version translates this unit as follows:

19 Now there was no smith found throughout all the land of Israel: for the Philistines said, Lest the Hebrews make *them* swords or spears:

20 But all the Israelites went down to the Philistines, to sharpen every man his share, and his coulter, and his axe, and his mattock.

21 Yet they had a file for the mattocks, and for the coulters, and for the forks, and for the axes, and to sharpen the goads.

The American Standard Version has the same, except it changes "sharpen" to "set." A footnote suggests an alternative translation, but the note concludes, "The Hebrew text is obscure."

In both translations the Hebrew words *happeṣira pim* were taken to mean "sharpener of mouths (edges)," that is, "a file," but one wonders why mention should be made of "a file" when verse 20 says, "all the Israelites went down to the Philistines, to sharpen every man his share . . . ." The obscurity was removed by the archaeological discovery of a small weight (inscribed *pim* or *payim*) equal to two-thirds of a shekel. On the basis of this new evidence, plus the fact that Hebrew *happeṣira* could mean "the charge," the Revised Standard Version translates in 1 Sam. 13:21, "and the charge was a pim for the plowshares and for the mattocks, and a third of a shekel for sharpening the axes and setting the goads."

Many other obscure passages have been made intelligible by meanings derived from newly discovered ancient documents, so it is quite right and proper that students and readers of the Bible should desire revisions which impart more of the divinely intended truths of God's Word.

Improved Interpretations

Not all revisions are due to changes in language or to new findings in regard to the text or meanings of words. There are some which stem from the suggestions of Biblical scholars in an attempt to interpret the meaning of a specific passage in the light of the total teaching of the chapter and book. John 1:9, for example, reads in the King James Version, "*That* was the true Light, which lighteth every man that cometh into the world." This is a possible interpretation because the Greek does not make it clear whether the expression "coming into the world" goes with "every man" or "the true Light." The vast majority of the twentieth-century translators (realizing that the *important message* in the Gospel of John is not the coming of man into the world, but the coming of the true Light, the God-man Jesus Christ) have followed the alternative possibility (also permitted by Greek grammatical usage) in translating, "The true Light, which enlightens (illumines, shines on) every man, was coming into the world."

The Freedom of Truth

Jesus said to some who believed on him, "If ye continue in my word, *then* are ye my disciples indeed; and ye shall know the truth, and the truth shall make you free" (John 8:31–32). But in spite of the fact that this is one of the most significant statements of Scripture and that it was spoken by our Lord, many today are hesitant to act on the basis of this divine declaration. They have learned that there is the possibility of danger in freedom and so to minimize the hazards they have not always zealously sought the truth. But notice the condition for true freedom—"if ye continue in my word." As long as we determine to know Christ's "word," and to live by it, we need have no fear of knowing and following "the truth." It stands to reason that if the more recent translations and revisions are capable, for the most part, of enlarging our understanding of "the truth" and helping us to know more accurately Christ's "word," then they are worthy of our study and prayerful reading.

It is to fulfill this purpose that the following chapters have been written—that we may know the truth, and by that discovery come into an ever more vital relationship to our Lord and Savior Jesus Christ.

2

The New Testament Text

One of the choice verses in God's Word is 1 John 3:1. The King James Version translates it, "Behold, what manner of love the Father hath bestowed upon us, that we should be called the sons of God: therefore the world knoweth us not, because it knew him not." In the English Revised Version (1881) and the American Standard Version (1901) the middle portion of this verse reads, "that we should be called children of God; and *such* we are. For this cause the world knoweth us not." John, speaking for himself, his readers, and us, declares that we are not only "called children of God," but "such we are." Almost all of the subsequent translations have included these reassuring words. Weymouth (1903) and Charles B. Williams (1937) translated the additional clause, "and that is what we are." Goodspeed (1923) has, "for that is what we are," Kingsley Williams (1949) translates, "and that we are," while the Revised Standard Version reads, "and so we are." Moffatt (1913) translates the addition as a complete sentence, "And such we are," as does Verkuyl (1945), "And we are." Phillips (1947) rephrases the passage by translating, "Here and now we *are* God's children."

"But how is it," many have asked, "that the twentieth-century translations have these words whereas they are missing in the King James Version?" This good question goes right to the heart of the problem concerning the Greek text of the New Testament. It is obvious that

9

every translator must have some text in front of him to translate. It so happened that the Greek text which the King James translators used as their source was compiled from manuscripts which date largely from the thirteenth to the fifteenth centuries A.D. Since 1611, however, a number of Greek manuscripts have been found dating back as early as the third and fourth centuries, with a few even going back to the second century. While we do not have the original writings (often called the "autographs") which came from the hands of the New Testament authors, these early manuscripts enable the textual scholars to discover a Greek text which is very close to, if not, the original.

Using, as a matter of convenience, the type of lettering employed in our modern editions of the Greek text, the longer passage in 1 John 3:1 (with an English transliteration and a literal English translation inserted underneath) appears as follows:

ἵνα	τέκνα	θεοῦ	κληθῶμεν
hina	tekna	theou	klethomen
that	children	of God	we should be called

καὶ	ἐσμέν	διὰ	τοῦτο
kai	esmen	dia	touto
and	we are	on account of	this

This was most certainly the wording in John's original letter. His letter served as a master copy from which a number of copies were made. These, in turn, most likely served as master copies for still other copies. In this general way the letter was preserved and transmitted down through the centuries.

Somewhere in this process a scribe or copyist after writing κληθωμεν looked back at the manuscript from which he was copying, and, getting his eye on the -μεν of εσμεν (thinking it was the -μεν of κληθωμεν), went on to copy δια τουτο. In doing so he passed over και εσμεν. Once these words were omitted all copies made from the defective copy shared the deficiency. Happily for us, scholars were able to discover early manuscripts which retained the long-lost original words. In times of testing and doubt they come as a gracious testimony of assurance that we are indeed "children of God."

Matthew 6:1

The example in 1 John 3:1 illustrates the probability of increased scribal mistakes when words or groups of words close together ended or began with the same letters. Eyes are inclined to pick up the same letters in a nearby location. In addition to "mistakes of the eye," however, there are also "mistakes of the mind." Because of continual copying scribes came to feel that they knew certain passages by heart and as a result they tended to rely on their memory instead of consulting the copy in front of them. This is apparently the reason for a different wording in Matt. 6:1. The King James Version translates, "Take heed that ye do not your alms before men, to be seen of them," but the earliest and most accurate Greek manuscripts have "righteousness" instead of "alms," and practically all of the twentieth-century translations follow this wording.

If we consult this portion of the Sermon on the Mount we will observe that Jesus begins a section on almsgiving in 6:2. In 6:5 he commences the section on prayer, and in verse 16 he speaks about fasting. When we look at the unit as a whole (6:1–18) we can readily see that verse 1 serves as an introduction with the word "righteousness" being used in the sense of "righteous acts." This is a most fitting classification or heading for the religious acts of almsgiving, prayer, and fasting.

How did the word "alms" get into verse 1? Apparently a scribe, remembering that the first topic of the unit dealt with almsgiving, wrote ἐλεημοσύνην *eleemosunen* "alms" instead of copying δικαιοσύνην *dikaiosunen* "righteousness" which was in the text before him. It is also possible that the similar endings contributed to the scribal change.

1 John 5:18

A passage which has perplexed a number of people is the King James Version translation of 1 John 5:18 which reads, "We know that whosoever is born of God sinneth not; but he that is begotten of God keepeth himself, and that wicked one toucheth him not." In verses 13–17 John has been dealing with matters pertaining to those "that believe" (verse 13) and so the expression "whosoever is born of God" (verse 18) is also a reference to "believers." The perplexity arises from the translation "he that is begotten of God keepeth himself." It seems to teach that a "believer" is able to "keep himself," but this is a strange doctrine when compared with the New Testament emphasis on faith and dependence on Christ.

The difficulty is twofold. In the first place, the King James translation "he that is begotten" is a mistranslation which goes back all the way to the translation of William Tyndale in 1525. Translating the Greek correctly the American Standard Version reads, "he that was begotten," thereby making it possible for the reader to understand that Christ is referred to. But this is only a partial solution for one is still puzzled why, in a verse concerning believers, John would bring in the idea that "Christ keeps himself."

The answer to the second part of the difficulty is to be found in a different Greek word. While the majority of manuscripts have ἑαυτόν *heauton* "himself," some early manuscripts have αὐτόν *auton* "him." Although the change in form is very slight the difference in meaning is highly significant. The American Standard Version recognized this different wording by means of the footnote, "Some ancient authorities read *him*," but the first translation to accept the new reading into the text was that of Weymouth. He translated, "We know that no one who is a child of God lives in sin, but He who is God's Child keeps him, and the Evil one cannot touch him." The capital "He" and "Child" informed the reader that Christ was meant. Such a translation makes it clear, furthermore, that according to John the Christian does not "live in sin" and "the Evil one cannot touch him" because Christ "keeps him."

Moffatt, Verkuyl, and the Revised Standard Version also employ the capital "He" to bring out the contrast between Christ and the believer. Kingsley Williams achieves the same result by translating, "We know that any man that is a child of God does not sin; he that was born God's Child keeps him, and the evil one does not take hold of him." While Charles B. Williams has, "We know that no one who is born of God makes a practice of sinning, but the Son who was born of God continues to keep him, and the evil one cannot touch him," Phillips translates, "We know that the true child of God does not sin, he is in the charge of God's own Son and the evil one must keep his distance."

Once again we can be thankful for the new textual information which manuscript discoveries have given us, for with it translators have been able to remedy a very small mistake made by some faithful, but perhaps tired, scribe when he wrote ἑαυτόν instead of copying αὐτόν which was in the text before him.

Romans 8:28

Without doubt one of the most quoted verses in God's Word is Rom. 8:28. The King James Version reads, "And we know that all things work together for good to them that love God, to them who are called according to *his* purpose." Some Greek manuscripts discovered since 1611 have ὁ θεός *ho theos* "God" inserted into the text, so that instead of the verse reading "all things work for good," it says "God works for good in all things." But before we can consider the textual evidence for these two Greek readings it will be necessary to relate some interesting facts about the age, discovery, and characteristics of a number of the oldest texts.

Early Greek Manuscripts

The manuscript or codex (a technical term for a document with pages, as contrasted with a roll or scroll) which textual experts have generally considered the best over-all is Codex Vaticanus, known technically as Codex B. It was in possession of the Vatican Library in Rome when the library was first catalogued in 1475. How it happened to get there and how long it had been there no one knows. In 1809 it was taken to Paris as part of Napoleon's war booty, but it was returned in 1815. The codex originally contained the entire Greek Bible (Old Testament, Apocrypha—books rejected from the Protestant Scriptures, and the New Testament), but the first part of Genesis, some of the Psalms and all the New Testament after Heb. 9:13 had been lost. The leaves are vellum (fine parchment made from calf, goat, or sheep skins) and measure about 10″ square with three columns of text, each column having forty-two lines. The writing is in capital (so-called *uncial*) letters with no separation between words and almost no punctuation marks. The style of handwriting and the lack of punctuation and ornamentation date the manuscript about A.D. 350.

Another manuscript from about the same time is Codex Sinaiticus. It was found in May, 1844, in the Monastery of St. Catherine near Mount Sinai, whence its name. The discoverer, Lobegott ("Praise God") Konstantine Tischendorf, tells the thrilling story of his great find in the following words:

It was in April, 1844, that I embarked at Leghorn for Egypt. The desire which I felt to discover some precious remains of any manuscripts, more especially Biblical, of a date which would carry us back to the early times of Christianity, was realized beyond my expectations. It was at the foot of Mount Sinai, the convent of St. Catherine, that I discovered the pearl of all my researches. In visiting the library of the monastery, in the month of May, 1844, I perceived in the middle of the great hall a large and wide basket full of old parchments; and the librarian, who was a man of information, told me that two heaps of papers like this, mouldered by time, had been already committed to the flames. What was my surprise to find amid this heap of papers a considerable number of sheets of a copy of the Old Testament in Greek, which seemed to me to be one of the most ancient that I had ever seen. The authorities of the convent allowed me to possess myself of a third of these parchments, or about forty-three sheets, all the more readily as they were destined for the fire. But I could not get them to yield up possession of the remainder. The too lively satisfaction which I had displayed, had aroused their suspicions as to the value of this manuscript. I transcribed a page of the text of Isaiah and Jeremiah, and enjoined on the monks to take religious care of all such remains which might fall in their way.

On my return to Saxony there were men of learning who at once appreciated the value of the treasure which I brought back with me. I did not divulge the name of the place where I had found it, in the hopes of returning and recovering the rest of the manuscript. . . .

Having set out from Leipzig in January, 1853, I embarked at Trieste for Egypt, and in the month of February I stood for the second time in the convent of Sinai. This second journey was more successful even than the first, from the discoveries that I made of rare Biblical manuscripts; but I was not able to discover any further traces of the treasure of 1844. . . .

By the end of the month of January [1859] I had reached the convent of Mount Sinai. The mission with which I was entrusted [by the Emperor of Russia] entitled me to expect every consideration and attention. The prior, on saluting me, expressed a wish that I might succeed in discovering fresh supports for the truth. His kind expression of good will was verified even beyond his expectations.

After having devoted a few days in turning over the manuscripts of the convent, not without alighting here and there on some precious parchment or other, I told my Bedouins, on the 4th of February, to hold themselves in readiness to set out with the dromedaries for Cairo on the 7th, when an entirely unexpected circumstance carried me at once to the goal of all my desires. On the afternoon of this day I was taking a walk with the steward of the convent in the neighborhood, and as we returned towards sunset, he begged me to take some refreshment with him in his cell. Scarcely had he entered the room when, resuming our former subject of conversation, he said, "And I, too, have read a Septuagint, i.e., a copy of the Greek translation [of the Old Testament] made by the Seventy"; and so saying, he took down from the corner of the room a bulky kind of volume, wrapped up in a red cloth, and laid it before me. I unrolled the cover, and discovered, to my great surprise, not only those very fragments which, fifteen years before, I had taken out of the basket, but also other parts of the Old Testament, the New Testament complete, and, in addition, the Epistle of Barnabas and a part of the Pastor of Hermas. Full of joy, which this time I had the self-command to conceal from the steward and the rest of the community, I asked, as if in a careless way, for permission to take the manuscript into my sleeping-chamber, to look over it more at leisure. There by myself I could give way to the transport of joy which I felt. I knew that I held in my hand the most precious Biblical treasure in existence—a document whose age and importance exceeded that of all the manuscripts which I had ever examined during twenty years' study of the subject. I cannot now, I confess, recall all the emotions which I felt in that exciting moment with such a diamond in my possession. . . .

Tischendorf designated his discovery as Codex Aleph (ℵ), the first letter of the Hebrew alphabet, an expression of the great confidence which he had in the accuracy of the codex. He presented the manuscript (Fig. 1) to the Emperor of Russia and it stayed in Leningrad (known earlier as St. Petersburg and Petrograd) until 1933 when it was sold to the British Museum for almost $500,000. The vellum leaves are about 15″ by 14″ with four columns to a page and 48 lines to a column (Fig. 2). There is some reason to believe that Codex Vaticanus and Codex Sinaiticus are two of the fifty vellum Bibles ordered by Emperor Constantine from Eusebius of Caesarea in A.D. 332, but there is no conclusive proof of this theory.

Codex Alexandrinus, designated as Codex A, is a vellum manuscript of the whole Greek Bible which was copied in Alexandria, Egypt, about A.D. 425. Its leaves are approximately 12½″ by 10½″ with two columns (varying from 46 to 52 lines each) on every page. Cyril Lucar, Patriarch of Alexandria, apparently took the manuscript with him when he was made Patriarch of Constantinople in 1620. The codex, presented by Lucar to the king of England, was placed in the Royal Library in 1628, some seventeen years after the publication of the King James Version.

An exceedingly interesting manuscript is Codex Ephraemi Rescriptus, known as Codex C. It is called a *palimpsest* (that is, a rewritten document). Originally the vellum sheets contained a copy of the Greek Bible dating from about A.D. 450, but because of the scarcity of vellum in the twelfth century the writing was scraped off and the sheets reused for a Greek translation of the sermons and theological discourses of Ephraem of Syria, a leader in the Syrian Church in the fourth century A.D. The late Prof. A. T. Robertson, Southern Baptist Theological Seminary, Louisville, Kentucky, once commented, "It is not the only time that sermons have covered up the Bible, alas."

The original writing of Codex C was not completely obliterated because the pores of the skin still contained some of the ink. By means of ultraviolet ray photographs the original text has been made fairly legible

(Fig. 3). Unbelievable as it may seem, Tischendorf, prior to his discovery of Sinaiticus, was able, without the aid of our modern techniques, to decipher and publish (but not without some errors) the whole New Testament of the manuscript. The early history of the codex is unknown, but by the sixteenth century it was in the possession of the de' Medici family in Italy. Toward the end of that century it was brought to France and it is now part of the collection in the Bibliothèque Nationale, Paris.

One of the most sensational discoveries relating to the Greek text occurred about 1930. A number of papyri (manuscripts on papyrus, the ancient type of paper) which had been preserved for centuries by the hot, dry sands of Egypt were found by some natives of the country. Local dealers sold the greater part of the collection to Chester Beatty of London, so that in 1931 these invaluable documents came to the attention of the world. One unit of the Beatty Papyri was a collection of Paul's letters, designated as Codex p[46] (Fig. 4), which the experts date about A.D. 200, a full century and a half before Codex Vaticanus and Codex Sinaiticus. With thrilling discoveries such as this and the more recent Dead Sea Scrolls there is every reason to expect manuscript finds which are even closer to the time of the original writings.

Manuscript Evidence Evaluated

Returning to our consideration of Rom. 8:28, we may now note the manuscript evidence for the different Greek readings. The manuscripts which include the word "God" (and thus translated "God works for good in all things") are: Beatty Papyrus p[46], Codex Vaticanus, and Codex Alexandrinus. Those manuscripts which have "all things work for good" are: Codex Sinaiticus, Codex Ephraemi Rescriptus, and the hundreds of manuscripts which date from the ninth to the fifteenth centuries. From the standpoint of quantity or numbers it would appear, at first glance, that the better wording would omit θεός "God."

This would definitely be our choice if we followed the thinking of the King James translators, for example, because from about A.D. 1516 to 1831 the common method for finding the most accurate text was to accept the wording which had the support of the majority of the manuscripts. But the early textual scholars did not realize that to argue in favor of the majority was placing too much emphasis on quantity and not enough on quality. There are times when a few good manuscripts have the correct reading while the majority are wrong. If out of ten manuscripts eight were copied from a single manuscript (let us suppose Codex A) while the remaining two were copied from *a more accurate manuscript* (such as Codex B), then the basis for determining the relative merit of the copies would be the quality of their respective sources, and not the fact that the eight outnumbered the two in quantity. In other words, the readings or wording of manuscripts 9 and 10 would, on the average, be more accurate than the manuscripts 1 through 8.

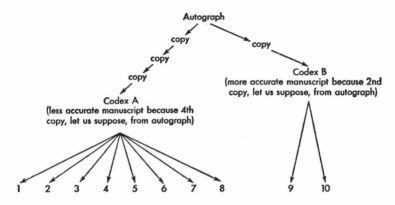

Diagram Illustrating the Superiority of Manuscript Quality.

Therefore, in the case of Rom. 8:28 the decision as to the more accurate wording must be made on the basis of the "best" manuscripts. Are Sinaiticus and Ephraemi Rescriptus more accurate than p[46] (Beatty Papyrus), Vaticanus, and Alexandrinus? Some twentieth-century translators have thought so, among whom are the American Standard revisers, Weymouth, Charles B. Williams, and Phillips. On the other hand, Goodspeed, the Revised Standard Version, and Kingsley Williams accept the alternate wording, feeling that p[46] more likely represents the original text of Paul.

Verkuyl accepts the Greek wording which omits "God," but he adds "He" which results in the meaning of the alternative reading: "But we know that for those who love God, for those called in agreement with his purpose, He cooperates in all things for what is good." Few of those who prefer the traditional wording believe that "all things" automatically "work for good." The truth is, all things *do not* work for good unless God steps in. So from the standpoint of textual evidence, as well as meaning, it would appear that "God works for good in all things" is the more accurate, explicit reading.

1 John 5:7–8

With the exception of the brackets, inserted to show clearly the passage to be discussed, the King James Version translation of 1 John 5:6–8 reads as follows:

6 This is he that came by water and blood, *even* Jesus Christ; not by water only, but by water and blood. And it is the Spirit that beareth witness because the Spirit is truth.

7 For there are three that bear record [in heaven, the Father, the Word, and the Holy Ghost: and these three are one.

8 And there are three that bear witness in earth,] the spirit, and the water, and the blood: and these three agree in one.

The words within brackets are found in all the English translations from John Wyclif (A.D. 1382) through the King James Version. The main textual evidence is from the Latin.

Latin Translations

During the first and second centuries A.D. the Latin-speaking peoples of the Roman Empire, especially around Carthage and Hippo in North Africa, made translations from the existing Greek manuscripts. These Latin versions, known as Old Latin, not only contained some of the mistakes from the Greek sources, but as they were passed on and recopied they acquired their own scribal changes. Jerome (A.D. 347–419) spoke out frankly concerning "the mistakes introduced by inaccurate translators, and the blundering alterations of confident but ignorant critics, and further, all that has been inserted or altered by sleepy copyists." Because of the wide diversity of readings in the Latin translations Jerome referred mostly to the Greek manuscripts available in order to make, at the request of the Pope, a more accurate Latin translation.

However, in making this drastic revision he changed many of the sweet-sounding phrases of the Old Latin and as a result his translation was vigorously opposed. After some time, Jerome, his patience worn thin, called his opponents "two-legged donkeys," and he said of them, "I could afford to despise them if I stood upon my rights; for a lyre is played in vain to an ass. If they do not like the water from the pure fountainhead, let them drink of the muddy streams."

But time was in Jerome's favor and his Latin translation won the day, overcoming all opposition. In fact, it was the supreme translation of the Western Church for over a thousand years. At the Council of Trent (April, 1546) the leaders of this Western branch of Christendom, centered at Rome, proclaimed Latin as the language of divine revelation, relegating Greek to a subordinate position. Jerome's revision was known officially, from that time on, as the Vulgate (Common) Edition of the Latin. Where the Greek manuscripts differed from the Vulgate the Greek was invariably considered incorrect. This judgment implied that Jerome had translated from the original Greek manuscripts, but this, of course, was not the case. Although he worked diligently to discover the original text, he did not succeed completely.

The earliest evidence for the Trinity passage in 1 John 5:7-8 comes from the Latin Fathers Ithacius and Priscillianus, both from the fourth century. It also occurs in the Sixtine (1590) and Clementine (1592) editions of Jerome's Latin Vulgate.

Minuscule Manuscripts

The only Greek texts to include the Trinity passage are the *minuscule* (small lettered) manuscripts 61, 629, and 88. The *uncial* or capital-letter style of writing employed in the early Greek manuscripts was fairly slow and tedious. About the ninth century A.D. a very attractive, smooth-flowing type of handwriting was developed which made it possible for the scribes to connect many letters without raising the pen (two-column text in Fig. 3). This minuscule type of writing gradually replaced the uncial or printing style so that the vast majority of the Greek manuscripts from the ninth through the fifteenth centuries are minuscules. Other features of these manuscripts are the word divisions, punctuation marks, and in some instances highly decorative illustrations. From a textual point of view, however, the minuscules generally have a less accurate type of Greek text, so the witness of manuscripts 61, 629, and 88 is of little worth.

Origin of the Trinity Passage

In A.D. 325 the Emperor Constantine called a General Council of the Church to be held at Nicaea in Asia Minor. The chief point at issue during this Council was the doctrine of the Trinity. Much of the debate which ensued over this crucial point has been preserved for us, but nowhere is the Trinity passage of 1 John 5:7-8 quoted as Biblical support for the doctrine. It is impossible that such a wonderful proof text could have gone unnoticed. Only one conclusion is possible: the passage was not known in A.D. 325.

Then how did it get into some copies of 1 John? This is quite difficult to determine, but one thing is sure—it appeared first of all in the Latin. Probably some scribe on seeing the reference to three witnesses made a marginal note to the effect that this was symbolic of the Trinity: the

Father, the Word, and the Holy Spirit. At some later period another scribe copied this marginal note into the text of his Latin copy on the assumption that the previous scribe, accidentally omitting the passage, had put it in the margin after detecting his mistake.

That such well-intended additions were actually made to the text is clearly shown from available manuscripts. There are several examples, but perhaps the most startling is found in 2 Cor. 8:4. The words "that we would receive," found in the King James Version, are based on a variant reading in some of the late minuscule manuscripts. With respect to this addition, the scribe of one of these manuscripts explained in a marginal note in Greek, "thus it is found in many of the copies." Some time later a very sleepy or dullheaded scribe transferred the explanatory note right into the text of his copy, making nonsense out of Paul's original statement.

Greek Text of Erasmus

The addition of the Trinity passage in the Latin manuscripts seems to have had little effect on the Greek, for all the manuscripts, except the three noted previously, omit it. Consequently, when the scholar Erasmus published in 1516 the first edition of the Greek text it did not have the Trinity passage. He had only eight manuscripts (none of them containing the entire New Testament) for his sources, the earliest dating from about A.D. 1000. The only copy of Revelation which he had available lacked verses 22:16-21. Rather than leave a blank at the end of his Greek edition he translated the Latin Vulgate of these verses back into Greek, adding them as the conclusion of his text.

Furthermore, Erasmus had a competitor, Cardinal Ximenes of Spain, and in his attempt to publish sooner than Ximenes he hurried too fast, with the result that his text was not as good as it could have been. Nevertheless, his edition was an immediate sensation. It was revised twice (1519 and 1522) and became the standard Greek text.

Erasmus had claimed that his 1516 edition was the true text, but on being questioned about the omission of the passage in 1 John 5:7-8 he replied that he would print the words in his Greek text if anyone could produce a Greek manuscript having them. Someone found such a manuscript (apparently written in the early sixteenth century), but there has always been some suspicion that such a newly copied manuscript had been made in order to compel Erasmus to include the passage. We will never know if Erasmus had any misgivings about the manuscript. If so, he repressed them, for he included the words, true to his promise, in his third edition (1522).

Greek Texts of Stephanus and Beza

The Trinity passage remained in the editions of the Greek text by Robert Estienne (Stephanus), a Paris printer, who, on the basis of a few additional manuscripts, revised the 1522 edition of Erasmus and published his own Greek text in 1546, 1549, 1550, and 1551. The 1551 edition was the first New Testament to give the verse divisions which we have in our present Bibles.

Theodore Beza, the scholar associated with John Calvin at Geneva, published nine editions of the Greek New Testament from 1565 to 1604, all of which were based on Stephanus and contained the Trinity passage. Beza had a manuscript, named Codex Bezae in his honor and known technically as Codex D, which dates from the sixth or late fifth century. It is a curious manuscript in that it is bilingual; the left page is in Greek and the right in Latin, both having one column to a page. Codex D contains only the Gospels and Acts, however, so it had no bearing on the Trinity passage. But even where he could have Beza made little use of it. Being ignorant of its age and value, he was suspicious of its numerous different wordings.

The first rule set forth by King James I for the translators of the Bible which was to bear his name read, "The ordinary Bible read in the Church, commonly called the *Bishops Bible,* to be followed, and as little altered as the Truth of the original will permit." The "original" noted in this rule was Beza's Greek text of 1604. In was in this manner, then, that the well-known Trinity passage was retained in the King James Version.

Modern Translations of 1 John 5:7-8

Because the Greek evidence for the Trinity passage was so slight the American Standard Version, Moffatt, Goodspeed, the Revised Standard Version, Phillips, and Kingsley Williams felt free to omit the words without so much as a footnote to inform the reader. Weymouth and Charles B. Williams omit the variant reading, but include a footnote of explanation. Verkuyl includes the passage in the text within parentheses; however, a footnote explains, "True as the insertion is, of Father, Word, and Holy Spirit, it is not needed; for such is the clear teaching of the whole New Testament."

Goodspeed omits the number "7" so the careful reader can detect that something has dropped out, but Moffatt, the Revised Standard Version, and Kingsley Williams, following the lead of the American Standard Version, take the last part of the 6th verse and number it "7" while shifting the number "8" back to what is the beginning of verse 7 in the King James Version. The result, according to the American Standard Version, is:

> 7 And it is the Spirit that beareth witness, because the Spirit is truth. 8 For there are three who bear witness, the Spirit, and the water, and the blood: and the three agree in one.

Thus, in the four translations noted all hints of deletion or omission are removed.

One can readily understand how a person who loved God's Word and did not know the facts which we have been considering would be startled, and even indignant, at these twentieth-century translations for omitting this time-honored passage. But when one accuses the translators of deliberately removing the words in order to do away with the doctrine of the Trinity then he is going too far. We know that they had other reasons for doing so—the unquestionable textual facts gleaned from the research of the last century.

Furthermore, the Biblical basis for the doctrine of the Trinity is interwoven throughout many verses in the New Testament. These passages, included in all our modern translations, must be the source material for formulating the doctrine of the Trinity just as they were for Athanasius and his followers when they first set down the orthodox view of the Trinity at Nicaea in A.D. 325. When we come to understand that our belief in the Trinity does not rest solely on the King James rendering of 1 John 5:7-8, then the omission ceases to be a concern and we can feel free to follow the truth all the way; to recognize that the original copy of 1 John did not contain the Trinity passage.

Matthew 6:13

Another variant reading which has caused some concern in evangelical circles is that found in Matt. 6:13. In all the Protestant English translations from Tyndale through King James the prayer which Christ taught his disciples concludes with the doxology, "For thine is the kingdom, and the power, and the glory, for ever. Amen." A slight modification of this doxology is found in the non-Biblical book *The Teaching of the Apostles*, known also as the *Didache*. This liturgical document, composed apparently with a view to standardizing the worship and practices of the Christian churches, dates from about A.D. 130 and is, therefore, an early witness to the existence of the doxology. In addition the doxology appears in varying form in three Old Latin manuscripts and one Syriac manuscript. Syriac, a sister language of the Aramaic which Jesus spoke, was one of the main languages at Antioch where the followers of Christ were first called Christians. Here and elsewhere in Syria during the first and second centuries A.D., Syriac translations, known technically as Old Syriac, were being made. A later translation, called the Peshitto (meaning "Simple") edition, became the standard text from the fourth century on.

The form of the doxology as given in the King James Version is found in one ninth-century Greek manuscript and in most of the Greek minuscule texts from the twelfth century on. With the exception of the manuscripts noted above, however, all the early Greek and Latin texts omit the doxology. Jerome's Latin Vulgate did not have it, so all the translations based on the Vulgate lack it: for example, John Wyclif's English New Testament of 1382, and the Rheims New Testament (1582) which later became a part of the Douay Bible, the traditional English translation for the Roman Catholic Church.

How, then, did this conclusion to the prayer get into the Gospel of Matthew? In the more accurate Greek texts the prayer ends with the petition, "Deliver us from evil (or the evil one)." Perhaps this seemingly abrupt conclusion caused someone with a liturgical sense to add a fitting doxology. It is generally recognized that the source was David's prayer of praise as given in 1 Chron. 29:10–13. Verse 11 of this prayer reads:

Thine, O LORD, is the greatness and the power, and the glory, and the victory, and the majesty; for all that is in the heavens and in the earth is thine; thine is the kingdom, O LORD, and thou art exalted as head above all.

The doxology, as indicated by the *Didache,* appeared first in the liturgy of the Church. Its familiarity to some scribes most likely resulted in its being copied unconsciously, or even possibly intentionally, into some manuscripts of Matthew.

Verkuyl retains the doxology in the text within parentheses, but there is a footnote to alert the reader to the textual problem. On the other hand, the American Standard Version, Weymouth, and the Revised Standard Version read it in the footnotes along with an explanatory note. Moffatt, Goodspeed, Charles B. Williams, Phillips, and Kingsley Williams have no footnote of explanation even though they omit the doxology from their texts and footnotes.

It is clear from the evidence that originally Jesus' model prayer (commonly, but less accurately, known as the Lord's Prayer) did not have this conclusion. The Roman Catholics have never used the doxology in their worship services so the omission causes no difficulty for them, but what about the Protestant churches? Should they drop it as well? This is hardly practical nor is it necessary because the Protestant Church has not, and does not now limit its worship solely to the Scriptures. Hymns, sermons, and prayers vary from God's Word even though they derive their inspiration and much of their content from it. Accordingly, Protestant Christians will no doubt continue to use the doxology in worship even though it is certain that Jesus did not employ it in teaching his disciples how to pray.

Story of the Adulterous Woman

The account of the tender manner in which Jesus dealt with the adulterous woman (John 7:53–8:11) has become a favorite of Bible readers the world over. For this reason it always comes as a shock to those who learn for the first time that there is some question concerning the textual basis for this story.

Textual Evidence for John 7:53–8:11

The unit John 7:53–8:11 appears in manuscripts of the Palestinian Syriac translation (dating from the sixth century), and the fact that it is quoted in the Syriac *Teaching of the Apostles* would indicate knowledge of the story as early as the third century. It also appears in about six of the Old Latin manuscripts. The fourth-century Latin Fathers (Ambrose, Jerome, and Augustine) considered the account authentic and Jerome included it in his Latin Vulgate.

Eusebius, the Church historian of the fourth century, related that in the work of Papias, a second-century Church Father, there was a story about a woman accused before the Lord of many sins, a story which was also contained in the *Gospel according to the Hebrews*. If the story referred to by Eusebius is that of the adulterous woman, then this is even earlier evidence for its existence.

The most crucial evidence, however, comes from the Greek. In 1956 a well-preserved manuscript containing the first fourteen chapters of John's Gospel was published by the Bodmer Library in Geneva, Switzerland. While the publication was at the printer's the Library acquired the remaining chapters of the Gospel, although the pages were broken into a number of fragments. The discovery of this remarkable manuscript, known as Bodmer II, is the greatest New Testament textual find since the Chester Beatty Papyri, and the date of the papyrus, about A.D. 200, ranks it with the earliest of the Beatty Papyri. It is highly significant, therefore, that this earliest complete text of John's Gospel does *not* have the account of the adulterous woman, for it adds its testimony to that of Codex Vaticanus and Codex Sinaiticus which also do not include the story.

In 1906 a Greek manuscript of the four Gospels was discovered in Cairo, Egypt. This fifth-century document was purchased by Charles L. Freer of Detroit and is now displayed in the Freer Gallery of Art, Washington, D.C., whence the name Washington Codex and the designation Codex W. At one time the Gallery made available to visitors some postcards with a photograph of the Greek text of Codex W beginning at John 7:46. The back of the card, noting that the text was from Chapter 8 of John's Gospel, quoted in abbreviated fashion the King James translation of the account concerning the adulterous woman. The Gallery officials learned, much too late and much to their embarrassment, that not one word of the story was to be found in the Greek text of the Washington Codex. This colossal textual error could have been avoided had the person who made up the card known that (with the exception of the bilingual manuscript Codex Bezae) no Greek manuscript prior to the ninth century has the story, and that none of the Church Fathers who wrote in Greek commented on this passage until the twelfth century, although many of them made reference to the passages which immediately precede and follow it.

In many of those Greek manuscripts which have the story it is marked so as to inform the reader that it is an insertion. While the account generally appears after John 7:52, it also occurs in other locations. Minuscule manuscript 225 has the story after John 7:36, and Codex 1 along with a few others has it after John 21:24. The minuscules 13, 69, 124, and 346 (recognized by Ferrar as belonging together and so known as "Family 13") have the story, surprisingly as it may seem, after Luke 21:38.

The manuscripts which have the account of the adulterous woman vary so much from each other in wording that there are at least sixty different readings. This is an average of five variants for each verse of the twelve-verse unit—a much higher average than is found in the rest of John's Gospel. Such obvious uncertainty of placement and wording of the story indicate that it was not in the original or autograph copy of the Gospel.

How did it get into the manuscripts? Once again it is impossible to say, but most certainly it appeared first in the Latin translations, just as in the case of the Trinity passage in 1 John 5:7–8. The source of the story could have been Papias or the apocryphal *Gospel according to the Hebrews* which while similar to the Gospel of Matthew was nevertheless rejected from having a place in the New Testament Canon or Scriptures. At any rate, the story gradually found its way into some Greek manuscripts, eventually appearing in most of them after the tenth century.

Modern Translations and John 7:53–8:11

On the basis of this textual evidence the American Standard Version enclosed the story within brackets, even though it is up in the text or main part of the translation, and added the footnote, "Most of the ancient authorities omit John 7.53–8.11. Those which contain it vary much from each other." Weymouth, Moffatt, Kingsley Williams, and Verkuyl retain it in the text within brackets or parentheses, but each has a footnote to inform the reader that there is some question about the passage. Verkuyl's note reads, "Although 7:53–8:11 is not in older found manuscripts, the incident has such a Christlike ring to it, the omission of it would be a great loss. We accept it as a true report."

The Revised Standard Version omits the story from the text, but a footnote gives the story in small print as well as the reason for its omission from the text. Charles B. Williams omits the section entirely, both in text and footnotes, but there is a note alerting the reader to the omission. Goodspeed omits the story completely and has no footnote of explanation. Phillips has it in the text without any brackets, but he adds the interesting note:

> This passage has no place in the oldest manuscripts of John, and is considered by most scholars to be an interpolation from some other source. Almost all scholars would agree that, although the story is out of place here, it is part of a genuine apostolic tradition.

The Message of John and 7:53–8:11

In addition to the decisive textual evidence there is also the valuable information which comes from comparing the unit 7:53–8:11 with the rest of the Gospel. For example, the style and vocabulary of the story in Greek are quite different from that which John employs in the rest of the book. In addition, John, unlike the other three Gospel writers, does not classify the types of sin and go into details regarding Jesus' dealings with specific sins and sinners. Rather he is concerned throughout the book to illustrate the themes of belief and unbelief. To him the ultimate sin, the source of all specific sins, is unbelief. For this reason the story of the adulterous woman does not contribute to John's account.

On the contrary, it seems to disrupt the context. In John 7:37 we read, "On the last day of the feast, the great day, Jesus stood up and proclaimed, 'If any one thirst, let him come to me and drink.'" The feast referred to was the Feast of Tabernacles or Booths (Lev. 23:39–43) which began on the 15th of Tishri, the seventh month of the Jewish calendar, and lasted for seven days. The feast normally coincides with the end of our month September and the beginning of October.

One of the outstanding features of this joyous harvest festival was the pouring of water at the morning services in the Temple. A specially appointed priest drew water in a golden pitcher from the Pool of Siloam and carried it in solemn procession to the Temple. There the high priest poured the pitcher of water into a basin at the foot of the altar. Wine from another pitcher was also poured into the basin and the mixture of water and wine flowed through pipes down into the Brook Kidron. On the last day of the feast during the pouring of water, symbolic of abundant rain and spiritual blessing, the priests sounded trumpets, the Levites sang, and the people chanted Pss. 113–118. Because of the words "Save now" (Hebrew *hoshianna*) in Ps. 118:25, the last day of the feast was known as *The Day of the Great Hosanna*. It was on this occasion that Jesus stood up and proclaimed, "If any one thirst, let him come to me and drink."

The other outstanding feature of the Feast of Booths was the brilliant illumination of the outer court of the Temple where the golden lamps and the torches in the hands of many worshipers permitted celebration of the feast into the night. Amid the brilliant illumination and the chanting of Psalms and prayers for deliverance Jesus declared, "I am the light of the world; he who follows me will not walk in darkness, but will have the light of life" (John 8:12). How meaningful these declarations of Jesus become when we understand their setting! But if the unit 7:53–8:11 remains in the text of John's Gospel then both the incident of the adulterous woman and the discourse on "light" occur at the Temple *on the day after the feast has closed,* for 8:2 reads, "Early in the morning he came again to the temple."

Although the story of the adulterous woman appears to be an authentic event in the life of Jesus, one which Christians will not want to forget, from the standpoint of textual evidence and of theological relevance it does not belong in the text of John's Gospel.

Conclusion of Mark's Gospel

One more long textual unit which has been a cause for concern is Mark 16:9–20. It is found among others in the following Greek manuscripts or codices: Ephraemi Rescriptus, Bezae, Washington, Regius (an eighth-century document now in Paris), Theta or "Koridethi Gospels" (a ninth-century manuscript now in Tiflis, U.S.S.R.), and the mass of the minuscules. There is indication that the second-century Church Fathers Justin Martyr, of Ephesus in Asia Minor, and Irenaeus, Bishop of Lyons in Gaul, quoted from these verses. Also some of the Old Latin and Syriac manuscripts have this passage.

The most important manuscripts which do not have Mark 16:9–20 are: the Greek codices Vaticanus and Sinaiticus, the valuable Old Latin document "k" and the early Syriac manuscript discovered at Mount Sinai in 1892 by Agnes S. Lewis. Furthermore, the Church Fathers Clement of Alexandria (late second century), Origen (third century), and Eusebius (fourth century) do not quote from this passage.

Another textual factor to consider, however, is the much shorter ending to Mark which is found after 16:8 in the following manuscripts: Codex Regius, Codex Psi (eighth-century manuscript in Mt. Athos, Greece), the uncial codices 099 and 0112, the minuscule 579, the Old Latin "k" and the margin of the Harklean Syriac (seventh century). This different conclusion for Mark's Gospel reads, according to the Revised Standard Version, "But they reported briefly to Peter and those with him all that they had been told. And after this, Jesus himself sent out by means of them, from east to west, the sacred and imperishable proclamation of eternal salvation." The style and language of this ending differs quite evidently, even in the English translation, from the rest of Mark and indicates that it is a much later addition.

Some manuscripts, most notably Codex Regius, have both of the endings. Presumably the scribes of these documents knew that there were two different endings for the Gospel of Mark and not being sure which to prefer they included them both.

Modern Translations and Mark 16:9–20

The American Standard Version includes these verses in the text, but it separates them from verse 8 with a blank line. Also a footnote reads, "The two oldest Greek manuscripts, and some other authorities, omit from ver. 9 to the end. Some other authorities have a different ending to the Gospel." Weymouth has the longer ending in the text enclosed within brackets with a footnote informing the reader that other manuscripts omit it. Charles B. Williams has it in the text separated slightly from verse 8 where a footnote alerts the reader. Verkuyl puts the ending in the text within parentheses, followed by the explanatory note:

> The ending with "for" in the eighth verse, which is that way in the Greek, suggests an abrupt breaking off as if a leaf in Mark's writing had been mislaid. What follows is strictly in agreement with the other Gospels but contains nothing we would not otherwise possess.

Phillips does not have a footnote, but he includes the longer unit in the text under the heading, "AN ANCIENT APPENDIX."

Three of the modern translations consider both endings. Moffatt includes the longer one in the text under the heading (a) and the shorter one under (b). After verse 8 a footnote reads, "The following appendix represents a couple of second century attempts to complete the gospel . . . ." Goodspeed has no footnote; however, he has the short ending in the text under the caption "AN ANCIENT APPENDIX," followed by verses 9–20 under the heading, "ANOTHER ANCIENT APPENDIX." At the end of verse 8 the Revised Standard Version has a footnote reading, "Other texts and versions add as 16.9–20 the following passage:" and then follows in fine italic print the translation of the unit. After this appears another note in which the shorter reading, noted previously in this chapter, is added.

Colossians 1:14

There are many more variant readings in the New Testament Greek text which could demand our attention, but there is space to treat only one more type of textual difficulty.

In Col. 1:14 the King James Version reads, "In whom we have redemption through his blood, *even* the forgiveness of sins." The only textual evidence for the phrase "through his blood" is in a few late minuscule texts, the Harklean Syriac, and the Clementine edition of the Latin Vulgate. All of the early and reliable manuscripts omit these words. Because of this overwhelming textual evidence practically all the modern translations omit the phrase from the text. Furthermore, they do not include it in the footnotes, nor do they have a footnote to explain its absence. Verkuyl, the notable exception, includes the words "through his blood" in the text within parentheses, but he has no footnote of explanation.

"What, then," we ask, "is the source of this phrase in Col. 1:14?" Unquestionably it is to be found in Eph. 1:7 which reads, according to all the manuscripts, "In whom we have redemption through his blood, the forgiveness of sins, according to the riches of his grace." The addition in Colossians can be accounted for in two ways, but it is impossible to say which was actually the case. On the one hand, instead of working directly from the source in front of him, a scribe, because of the similar text in Col. 1:14, started copying Eph. 1:7 from memory. Whereas this would be an unintentional mistake, some scribe, on the other hand, could have deliberately inserted the words into his copy of Colossians, reasoning that they must have originally been in Col. 1:14, just as they were in Eph. 1:7, but that the manuscript of Colossians from which he was copying had accidentally lost them.

This well-meaning scribal tendency to harmonize (make passages alike) was very common, and numerous illustrations could be given from the New Testament, the Gospels especially, but one passage will do. In Luke 11:2–4 in the King James Version the words "Our," "which art in heaven," "Thy will be done, as in heaven, so in earth," "but deliver us from evil" do not occur in the most accurate manuscripts of Luke's Gospel. These additions are from Matt. 6:9–13 where the fuller account of the prayer is given. Some conscientious scribe or scribes assumed that Luke had to agree with Matthew, therefore the additions were made.

Of course, this tendency to harmonize, whether on the part of the ancient scribe, or the modern reader, is founded on a false assumption. It is quite possible for two letters by the same author to have similar passages, but this is not to say that he has to use identical wording. The emphasis in Col. 1:14 and Eph. 1:7 is on the "forgiveness of sins," not the means by which forgiveness is obtained. Because one letter explains that forgiveness comes "through the blood" is no reason why the other must say the same.

One further lesson to be learned from Col. 1:14 is the danger in arguing from silence. Because a translation omits certain words or phrases the reader is not justified in attributing the omission to disbelief on the part of the translator. In the case of Col. 1:14 the textual evidence makes it certain that Paul did not include the words "through his blood" in his original letter. Would anyone dare say that because Paul omitted these words he did not believe in "the blood" as the means of forgiveness? It is equally dangerous to attribute ulterior motives to the twentieth-century translators because they attempt to put into English what, according to our best textual evidence, the New Testament authors wrote.

Textual Changes and Revelation 22:18–19

One further matter concerning textual changes is the warning of Rev. 22:18–19 which the King James Version translates as follows:

18 For I testify unto every man that heareth the words of the prophecy of this book, If any man shall add unto these things, God shall add unto him the plagues that are written in this book:

19 And if any man shall take away from the words of the book of this prophecy, God shall take away his part out of the book of life, and out of the holy city, and *from* the things which are written in this book.

How can we reconcile changes in the New Testament text in the light of this clear warning? In the first place, it should be noted that when the book of Revelation was finished it circulated as a separate book for some time, so that initially these warnings against addition and omission applied just to the text of Revelation. Only when the book was placed at the close of the collection of books which we call the New Testament could any reader apply the warnings to the rest of the New Testament. This, of course, is equally true of the Old Testament.

In the second place, however, we must consider the meaning back of the warning. It was placed there to protect the wording of the original text. When, on the basis of textual evidence, twentieth-century translators change a passage in Revelation or any other book of the Bible they do not fall under the penalty of the warning because they are attempting to discover the original wording. Rev. 22:18–19 causes difficulty only when we assume that the King James Version represents the original wording of the Bible. Our investigations of this chapter, however, have shown that this assumption is not always so.

The Received Text

The Greek text employed by the King James translators was, as noted previously, the 1604 edition of Beza. This same text was reprinted in 1624 and 1633 by the Elzevir brothers of Holland. The preface of the 1633 edition claimed that the reader now had the text "received by all," so this edition came to be known as the *Textus Receptus* or "Received Text." There was little difference between the Greek texts of Elzevir and Erasmus, for, as we have seen, Elzevir printed Beza who had reprinted Stephanus who had in turn reprinted Erasmus. Therefore, from a practical point of view, all the Greek texts from Erasmus through Elzevir can be classified together as the "Received Text."

This type of Greek text has been classified as the Byzantine text because it is *substantially* the same as the standard Greek text which came into being during the fifth century A.D. at Byzantium (Constantinople, modern Istanbul), the center of the Eastern branch of Christendom. This type of text has also been called the *Koine* (Common) text because the vast majority of the known manuscripts (now in excess of 4600) have this type of Greek.

By "type" of Greek text we mean similarity in wording. In all the centers of the early Church (Caesarea in Palestine, Antioch in Syria, Byzantium in Asia Minor, Alexandria in Egypt, Rome in Italy, etc.) copies of New Testament books were made. Scribes in one locality made some mistakes in different passages from those in the other centers. These peculiar readings tended to be copied into many other copies, so that in time a more or less uniform text developed for each locality with most copies of the New Testament books in that region having the same type of readings, mistakes and all. Working backwards, on the basis of the rule "similarity in reading or wording implies similar origin," textual scholars employed these similarities to group various manuscripts. By this process they have been able to determine that the "Received Text" was standardized at a much later period than the so-called Western, Neutral (Egyptian), or Caesarean types of text which are represented by the earlier Greek manuscripts.

When the New Testament Revision Committee of the English Revised Version was attempting to discover and compile the Greek text which was to be the basis for its translation it found that the "Received Text" used by the King James translators was mistaken in more than 5000 readings, counting each rejected reading as one, whether it contained one word or several. Now most of these are inconsequential from the standpoint of theological meaning, but it illustrates why there are so many differences between the King James Version and the twentieth-century translations.

On the other hand, we must bear in mind that the "Received Text" is not a bad or heretical text. It is a *substantially* correct text. One of the best modern editions of the Greek text is that published in 1882 by B. F. Westcott and F. J. A. Hort. Proof copy of this text was available to the translators of the English Revised Version New Testament (1881), and it influenced their translation considerably. The American Standard Version represents, with minor revision, the same Greek text back of the English Revised Version. Yet Hort, the co-editor of this very influential Greek text, wrote the following statements concerning the "Received Text":

With regard to the great bulk of the words of the New Testament, as of most other ancient writings, there is no variation or other ground of doubt, and therefore no room for textual criticism. . . .

The proportion of words virtually accepted on all hands as raised above doubt is very great; not less, on a rough computation, than seven-eighths of the whole. The remaining eighth, therefore, formed in great part by changes of order and other comparative trivialities, constitutes the whole area of criticism. . . .

. . . we find that, setting aside differences of orthography [spelling], the words in our opinion still subject to doubt only make up about one-sixtieth of the whole New Testament. . . . what can in any sense be called substantial variation is but a small fraction of the whole residuary variation, and can hardly form more than a thousandth part of the entire text.

The only reason Hort or any modern translators revised the "Received Text" is because the recent manuscript discoveries reproduce more accurately the original wording in the very important "thousandth part" of the New Testament. The King James Version and the "Received Text" have served us well. We leave the "good" only because of something "better."

3

The Old Testament Text

In attempting to find the most accurate Old Testament text we encounter a far more complex problem than that which faced us in the case of the Greek New Testament. There we had the benefit of thousands of textual sources (Greek manuscripts, translations such as the Syriac and Latin, and writings of the Church Fathers) some of which go back within a century or so of the original writings.

Hebrew Scrolls and Script

In contrast to the wealth of information concerning the New Testament text, the Old Testament sources are relatively few in number and they are further removed from the originals. Up to the time of the discovery of the Dead Sea (Qumran) Scrolls, 1947 and following, there were only about eight hundred manuscripts of the Old Testament, the earliest (Codex Cairensis) dating from A.D. 895. Some others date from the tenth century, but most of them were copied during the twelfth through the fourteenth centuries A.D.

The original Old Testament books were written on parchment (or possibly papyrus) in the form of a roll or scroll (Fig. 5). The language was Hebrew, except for a few passages (mostly in Daniel and Ezra) in Aramaic, a Semitic language related to Hebrew. Inasmuch as these languages were written from right to left, just the opposite from English, the reader began at the first column to the right of the scroll.

After finishing it he moved to the second column, rolling up the scroll with his right hand while unrolling with his left.

From ancient times to about the third century B.C. the Hebrew Scriptures were written in the Old Hebrew (Canaanite) script, illustrated by such famous inscriptions as the Gezer Calendar, about 925 B.C., the Mesha or Moabite Stone, about 835, and the Siloam Inscription (Fig. 6), about 700.

In Palestine, after the Babylonian Exile, Aramaic (the language of commerce and diplomatic exchange during the time of the Assyrian, Babylonian, and Persian Empires) gradually displaced Hebrew as the language of the common people. Jewish scholars and scribes, however, continued to use Hebrew and many copies of the Hebrew Scriptures were written in the Old Hebrew script, but increasingly from the fourth to the second centuries B.C. the square script, used formerly for Aramaic, became the common script for Hebrew as well. This was so in the time of Jesus because his statement concerning the "jot" (Matt. 5:18) was a reference to the letter ׳ *yod*, the smallest letter of the Hebrew alphabet in the square script, a condition which did not prevail in the Old Hebrew script.

The earliest Hebrew writings consisted solely of consonants and apparently the people were able to communicate effectively. We could get used to this style of writing, just as the Hebrews did, but it is obvious that such a system has a greater possibility of being misunderstood because there is no guarantee that the reader will supply the same vowels the writer intended: for example, the English consonants *bt* could represent the words "bat, bet, bit, but, bait, beat, beet, boat, boot, bout, bate, bite, abate, abet, about" etc. Although the context would, as a general rule, enable the reader to select the right word, there would be situations in which two different words made equally good sense and then he would be at a loss to determine what the author definitely intended.

Unlike the Greek uncial manuscripts in which all the words were run together with no separation or dividing marks between words, sentences, and paragraphs, Hebrew seems always to have been written with a word divider or slight space between words or short phrases. Word dividers were used regularly in the Ostraca (pieces of pottery with inscriptions in ink) of Samaria, about 775 B.C., and frequently in the Lachish Ostraca, about 588. Apparently this was necessary because vowelless script with no word division would have resulted in word puzzles instead of effective communication.

At a later period in the history of the Hebrew language some of the consonants (known technically as *matres lectionis* "mothers of reading") were used to indicate vowels, thereby assisting the reader and speeding up the reading process. The two letters used most often in this manner were the "y" ‎י *yod* for the long vowels "i" and "e," and the "w" ‎ו *waw* for the long vowels "o" and "u." The Dead Sea Scrolls from Cave 1 indicate that in the second and first centuries B.C. and even in the time of Christ both types of spelling were employed, the fuller type (with some vowels indicated by consonants) presumably for the common person who was not as well educated as the scribes and scholars. Whereas the complete Isaiah Scroll found in Cave 1 has the full spelling with many uses of consonants as vowels, the text of the incomplete scroll of Isaiah, also found in Cave 1, has the shorter spelling.

Interchange of Similar Letters

As the Hebrew manuscripts were copied and handed down from generation to generation it was inevitable that some scribal slips would occur. The most common mistake was that of confusing similar letters. In the Old Hebrew script at least four pairs of letters tended to be interchanged, and in the square script six pairs of letters were likely to be confused.

The most common interchange was that between ‎ד "d" and ‎ר "r." In Isa. 33:8, a passage discussed in Chapter 1, the original form ‎עדים "witnesses, treaties" became ‎ערים "cities" because of the confusion of "d" and "r." The name ‎דדנים "Dodanim" in Gen. 10:4 appears in an identical context in 1 Chron. 1:7 as ‎רודנים "Rodanim." These two names, taken from the standard Hebrew text in use today, also illustrate the difference in spelling. While both have ‎י to represent the vowel "i," only the form in 1 Chron. 1:7 has ‎ו to represent the letter "o."

Two more examples of this interchange occur in the unit 2 Sam. 8:11–14 which the King James Version renders:

11 Which also king David did dedicate unto the LORD, with the silver and gold that he had dedicated of all nations which he subdued;

12 Of Syria, and of Moab, and of the children of Ammon, and of the Philistines, and of Amalek, and of the spoil of Hadadezer, son of Rehob, king of Zobah.

13 And David gat *him* a name when he returned from smiting of the Syrians in the valley of salt, *being* eighteen thousand *men*.

14 And he put garrisons in Edom; throughout all Edom put he garrisons, and all they of Edom became David's servants. And the LORD preserved David whithersoever he went.

These events in David's life are also recorded in 1 Chron. 18:11-13, but there "Syria" (verse 12) becomes "Edom," and "Syrians" (verse 13) becomes "Edomites." The title to Ps. 60 attributes the psalm to David and it mentions the killing "of Edom in the valley of salt." The reference to "garrisons in Edom" occurs in 1 Chron. 18:13 as well as 2 Sam. 8:14, therefore it is certain that David's military activities recorded in these two passages took place largely in Edom (to the southeast of Palestine), not Syria (to the northeast).

But how did this change occur in the Hebrew text of 2 Samuel? There could have been some influence from 2 Sam. 8:6, just above the passage being discussed, which the King James Version translates, "Then David put garrisons in Syria of Damascus: and the Syrians became servants to David *and* brought gifts." The most likely answer, however, is the similarity of the forms in Hebrew. In the King James Version "Syria" is a translation for אֲרָם, literally "Aram." The Hebrew for "Edom" is the similar form אֱדוֹם. Some scribe, confusing "d" for "r," copied the wrong word in 2 Sam. 8:12 and 13.

The American Standard Version retains "Syria" in the text with the footnote "Heb. *Aram*," and in verse 13 it has "Syrians" in the text with the note, "*Edom*, in 1 Chr. 18.11, 12; Ps. 60. title." On the other hand, the Old Testament texts in Moffatt (1924), American Translation (1927), the Revised Standard Version (1952), and the Berkeley Version (1959) translate "Edom" in verse 12 and "Edomites" or "troops of Edom" in verse 13 *without a footnote* to explain they have not followed the Hebrew text. The one exception is the note on verse 13 in the Revised Standard Version where credit for "Edomites" is given to the Greek translation of the Old Testament.

Inversion of Letters

The tendency for Hebrew manuscripts to omit most of the vowels made it easier for scribes to invert consonants while in the process of copying a text. An excellent example is found in Ezek. 42:16 where most of the Hebrew manuscripts and the standard Hebrew text have אַמּוֹת "cubits," thus reading, "He measured the east side with the measuring reed, five cubits reeds, with the measuring reed round about." It so happens that the word "cubits," clearly a mistake, should have read מֵאוֹת "hundreds," but a scribe accidentally inverted the first two letters. The twentieth-century translations interpret the word as "hundreds," ignoring the consonantal Hebrew text, but none of them has a footnote so informing the reader.

Double Writing

Writing a letter, group of letters, a word, or group of words twice (known as *dittography*) was another type of scribal error. An extensive illustration is found in Isa. 38:20 of the complete Isaiah Scroll. After starting to copy what in our present Hebrew texts is verse 20 (the numbering of verses did not occur prior to the sixteenth century A.D.) the scribe let his eye return, for some unknown reason, to the beginning of verse 19, and so he recopied, almost letter for letter, all of verse 19 and part of 20 (see Fig. 7 where the reduplicated words are enclosed within brackets).

Single Writing

The opposite of "double writing" was "single writing" (known as *haplography*) where the scribe omitted one of two letters, words, or groups of words which occurred together. The standard text of Isa. 38:11 has יְהֹ יְהֹ "LORD, LORD," but the Isaiah Scroll, for example, has only יְהֹ (Fig. 7—within the circle).

Closely related to "single writing" is the situation (known as *homoeoteleuton*) in which two units of text close with the same word or words. An excellent example of this also is found in the Isaiah Scroll. The standard text of Isa. 38:20 ends with בֵּית יְהֹוָה "the house of the LORD," and verse 22 closes with the same words. The scribe of the Isaiah Scroll finished copying verse 20, but on returning to the text in front of him he picked up בֵּית יְהֹוָה in verse 22 instead of 20 with the result he omitted verses 21 and 22. Some other scribe noticed the mistake and copied the two verses (using a more pointed pen and more crowded letters) into the space remaining on the line where verse 20 concluded, and then on down the margin of the column (Fig. 7—within parentheses).

Another omission, not corrected by later scribes, also occurs in 4:5–6 of the Isaiah Scroll. The scribe copied about half of verse 5, through the word יוֹמָם "by day, in the daytime," and in going back to his source he got his eye on the same word in verse 6, so he omitted the last half of verse 5 and part of verse 6. Just by consulting our English translations (where they consistently translate the Hebrew the same) it is possible to understand how easily this scribal mistake took place.

The Masoretic Text

In the first century A.D. and on into the second the Jews of Palestine made a special, but not completely successful, attempt to standardize the Hebrew text of the Old Testament. A normative text was selected and insofar as possible all available manuscripts were either corrected to agree with it or destroyed. One of the leading figures in this concern was Rabbi Aqiba (about A.D. 55–137). In order to guarantee the accurate transmission of this normative Hebrew text the words and even the letters of the new manuscripts were counted. Faulty copies were corrected or destroyed.

This faithful preservation of the consonantal Hebrew text is something for which we can be very thankful. Had similar means of protecting the text been in force from the time of the earliest Old Testament writings the problem of recovering the original Hebrew text would be much less difficult.

The refined process of copying and handing on Hebrew manuscripts continued essentially unchanged until a great innovation about A.D. 600. At this time the Jewish scribes borrowed, from Syriac so it appears, the idea of indicating by various signs all the vowels needed to read the Scriptures aloud. This was simply carrying out in a thoroughgoing manner the old idea which resulted in a few of the Hebrew consonants being used as long vowels. It seems odd that this addition of vowels, called "pointing" by the Jewish scribes, was so long in coming, but to the average Jew the consonantal Hebrew text was sacred, and to add anything was considered a sacrilege. As late as the eleventh century A.D. the controversy continued, the pious Jews still claiming that the vowels were a desecration of the Hebrew text because God had not given them when he revealed the Law to Moses on Mount Sinai. We know, of course, that when God "spoke" to Moses, whether orally or through the mind, vowels were a part of that revelation. These vowels and those of the other Hebrew writings, omitted from the manuscripts, had to be preserved generation after generation in the minds and on the lips of Israel's devout.

Because of the centuries of separate oral transmission of the vowels the scholars of Palestine and Babylonia, areas of Jewish culture and learning, differed as to the pronunciation of certain Hebrew words, so it is little wonder that their "pointings" varied as well. By A.D. 900, however, the scribes of Tiberias in northern Palestine had worked out a complicated system of vowel pointing which was to supersede all previous efforts.

During the next half-century the two outstanding Tiberian families, *ben Asher* and *ben Naphtali*, known as Masoretes (or Massoretes), vied with each other in the attempt to produce the most accurate Hebrew text. This renewed effort at standardization was necessary because variant readings had persisted in oral tradition and in manuscripts which Rabbi Aqiba and his followers had not found and altered. It was not until the twelfth century, when Maimonides (the great Jewish scholar of Spain) decided in favor of the ben Asher text, that the issue was settled. All the English translations made directly from the Hebrew, including the twentieth-century versions, have been based *essentially* on this text of ben Asher (see Figs. 8 and 9 for examples of Kittel's edition of this text), known commonly as the Masoretic text (MT).

Kethib and Qere

One of the most interesting features of the Masoretic text is the manner in which the scribes preserved traditional readings which varied from the standard text. As noted previously, the consonantal text gradually acquired a sacredness which prohibited any scribe from tampering with it. This consonantal text, known as the *Kethib* "written," could not be changed, so the Masoretic scribes developed a clever system to get around the traditional restrictions. It consisted of putting the variant consonants out in the margin and calling them *Qere* "to be read." Because the vowels, being added later, did not have the sacredness of the consonants, the Masoretes felt it was proper to put the vowels for the new consonants (the *Qere* in the margin) with the old consonants in the text (the *Kethib*). This, of course, resulted in some impossible forms (see Appendix E for an illustration and a discussion of the name "Jehovah").

Masoretic Changes

In some instances the Masoretic scribes intended the variant readings of their *Kethib-Qere* system as corrections or improvements of the Hebrew text.

In Ezek. 42:16, noted previously in this chapter, the inversion of consonants required correction by the Masoretes. What the scribes did was to put the correct consonants in the margin and let the reader reconstruct the correct word mentally by placing the proper consonants with the vowels in the text.

In Ruth 3:5 the consonantal text reads, "And she said, 'All that you say I will do.'" The scribes felt, probably on the basis of some variant reading, oral or written, that the word אֵלַי *'elay* "to me" should be inserted after "say." The vowels "e" and "a" were put into the text, but no new consonants could be added, so these they wrote in the margin with the explanation "read, but not written." The oddity of vowels all by themselves (Fig. 8—within the circle) would compel the reader to supply the necessary consonants from the margin. The texts of the King James and Berkeley Versions and the margin of the American Standard Version follow the Masoretic insertion, but the texts of the American Standard, Moffatt, American Translation, and the Revised Standard Versions drop it.

A similar type of correction is found in Jer. 31. In the consonantal text verses 27 and 31 begin, "Behold, days are coming," but in verse 38 the text lacks "are coming" (Hebrew בָּאִים ba'im). The Masoretes inserted the vowels "a" and "i" into the text by themselves, placing the consonants in the margin. This obvious correction is found in all the translations in English.

Ruth 3:12 has an interesting situation in which the process noted above is reversed. The text had a two-consonant word which was definitely out of place, but the consonants could not be removed. To indicate the desired omission the vowel "i," which would normally complete the word, was omitted (Fig. 9—within the circle), and a note in the margin explained that the two consonants were "written, but not read." All the translations in English agree with this omission.

It should be clear from these examples that the Masoretic Hebrew text is more than just one standard text: it is a combination of texts. Therefore, when a translation claims to have been made from the Masoretic Hebrew the reader should realize that there was some freedom in choosing the text to be translated. It is instructive to note that whereas the King James Version *generally* follows the Qere (marginal readings), most of the twentieth-century versions are inclined to return to the Kethib (consonantal text), feeling that many times the Masoretic changes are not really improvements of the text.

But whether right or wrong the Masoretes made the attempt to discover the most accurate, meaningful Hebrew text possible. For this we must give them credit.

Recent Textual Changes

Modern textual scholars have endeavored in the same manner as their Masoretic predecessors to improve the consonantal text. A good illustration is Isa. 33:8 which was discussed in Chapter 1. The King James, American Standard, and Berkeley Versions follow the Masoretic text by translating "he hath despised (despises) cities." The American Translation realized that "cities" (Hebrew *'arim*) was dubious and changed the Hebrew text to read *'edim* "witnesses." This textual change was confirmed by the Dead Sea Isaiah Scroll and so the Revised Standard Version incorporated the variant reading into its text.

The Berkeley Version had the evidence from the Isaiah Scroll, but kept the Masoretic "cities" in the text while observing in a footnote, "*The Dead Sea Scrolls* read: 'despises witnesses.'"

Vowel Changes

Another means which textual scholars have for discovering the intent of the original writings is to supply to the consonantal Hebrew text different vowels from those which the Masoretes added. Isa. 49:17 begins, according to the Masoretic vowel pointing, "Your sons (children) make haste," and both the King James and American Standard Versions translate accordingly.

But by changing the first vowel of *banayik* "your sons," the form becomes *bonayik* "your builders." Moffatt made this change in translating, "Men are making haste to build you." The American Translation, Revised Standard Version, and Berkeley Version have "builders," though none of them has a footnote to inform the reader. The preface of the Revised Standard Version explains this lack as follows:

> The vowel-signs, which were added by the Masoretes, are accepted also in the main, but where a more probable and convincing reading can be obtained by assuming different vowels, this has been done. No notes are given in such cases, because the vowel points are less ancient and reliable than the consonants.

The Revised Standard and Berkeley Versions have the textual support of בוניך *bonayik* in the Isaiah Scroll. Although the Scroll does not have vowel "pointings," the letter ו (representing the vowel "o") is proof that the Scroll intended "your builders."

In Ps. 84:6 the American Standard Version reads, "Yea, the early rain covereth it with blessings." The American Translation and the Berkeley Version also translate "blessings," following the Masoretic text *beracoth*. On the other hand, the King James Version has, "the rain also filleth the pools," and the Revised Standard Version reads, "the early rain also covers it with pools." In both cases the translation "pools" *berecoth* was made possible by a single vowel change.

Another illustration of vowel change in the King James Version is found in Isa. 21:8. Where the Masoretic text has *'adonay* "Lord," the King James Version reads, "My lord," the equivalent of Hebrew *'adoniy*. But this form does not occur in the Hebrew manuscripts or in the ancient versions. Therefore, whether intentional or not, the translation "My lord" is equivalent to a shift in vowels. While the American

Standard, Revised Standard, and Berkeley Versions follow the Masoretic text, Moffatt, quite unexpectedly, agrees with the King James Version by rendering "my lord."

These examples of vowel change, only a small portion of those which could be noted, will illustrate what all modern translations have resorted to at one time or another.

Readings from Ancient Translations

A third means of improving the Hebrew text is to select valuable readings from the ancient translations into Greek, Aramaic, Syriac, and Latin. These were made before the Masoretic editions of the Hebrew and in some instances reflect earlier Hebrew readings. The oldest, and by far the most valuable, source for variant readings is the Septuagint, the Greek Old Testament.

It has some evidence to offer in Ps. 145:13. The psalm is in the form of an acrostic; that is, a poem in which the first letter of each verse (or a series of verses, as in Ps. 119), when taken together in order, make up the alphabet. It would appear that any person who went to the pains of composing such a psalm would know his alphabet and use all of its letters. Nevertheless, the Masoretic text has no verse for *nun*, the fourteenth letter of the Hebrew alphabet.

The Septuagint, to the contrary, has a verse for this fourteenth letter, yet some translators and textual scholars have rejected the reading on the grounds that the Septuagint translators simply composed the verse in Greek in order to remedy the Hebrew deficiency. This, of course, is a possibility, but do the facts justify such skepticism? Before we can answer this question we must consider the pertinent evidence concerning the textual value of the Septuagint.

Textual Value of the Septuagint

By the third century B.C. Greek had replaced Hebrew as the "mother tongue" of the Jews in Egypt, so there was an increasing demand for the Old Testament in Greek. At the start the *Torah* "Law" (Genesis through Deuteronomy) was translated, and at various intervals during the next century the rest of the Old Testament was completed. This Jewish translation, known as the Septuagint (LXX) was held in very high esteem. It was even preferred to the Hebrew by such Jewish scholars as Philo and Josephus. In fact, the Septuagint became the Old Testament for the Dispersion (that is, the Jews scattered throughout the Greek world). Furthermore, because it was in Greek the Gentiles were able to read it and learn of God's concern for them.

Many dispersed Jews, and Gentiles interested in Judaism, became converts to Christianity. It was quite natural that they would prefer to read the Septuagint. Most of the New Testament writers also seem to have preferred the Greek Old Testament over the Hebrew, a fact borne out by the books of the New Testament where quotations from Old Testament passages are from the Septuagint about 75 per cent of the time. To counteract the rise of Christianity and its extensive use of the Greek Old Testament Judaism rejected the Septuagint, declaring that the only authoritative source for the Old Testament was the Hebrew text. Their purpose was to undermine the authority for a number of the New Testament passages.

The tremendous feeling between the two groups led to some bitter disputes with charges of deliberate textual changes being made by both sides. Some copies of the Greek Old Testament read in Ps. 95:10 (96:10 in Hebrew and English), "Say among the nations, The Lord reigned from a tree." Justin Martyr defended the phrase "from a tree" as an obvious prophecy of Christ's death on the cross, but in spite of his good intentions the lack of the phrase in the best copies of the Septuagint, as well as the Hebrew, makes it certain that the addition resulted from some overzealous Christian scribe.

Deut. 21:23 reads in the Hebrew, "for he who is hanged is accursed by God," but Paul, in showing how Christ became a curse for all mankind, quoted the passage, "Cursed is everyone who hangs on a tree" (Gal. 3:13). Apparently he used the Septuagint, but he did not include the words "by God," and so many Christians, Jerome included, thought the Jews had inserted the phrase into the Hebrew text in order to insult all the followers of Christ. This view is unfounded, however, for the words "by God" are in the best manuscripts of the Septuagint.

Notwithstanding Jerome's doubt concerning the Hebrew text of Deut. 21:23, he came increasingly to feel that the Hebrew was superior to the Septuagint. This is not to say that he ignored the latter completely, but in preparation for translating the Old Testament of his Latin revision he went to Palestine to learn Hebrew and while there he based his translation primarily on the available Hebrew manuscripts, calling them the *Hebraica veritas* "Hebrew truth."

During the Reformation Period the Septuagint was used, but it had to compete with the Vulgate, the most important source at that time for remedying the Hebrew text. The many manuscript finds of the nineteenth century led to increased study of the Septuagint, but because it differed so widely at times from the Masoretic text it was considered a loose translation, and for this reason it was regarded as of little textual value. This low view of the Septuagint was held by many of the Old Testament scholars until recent years.

In 1941 Harry M. Orlinsky, one of the outstanding scholars in Septuagintal studies, wrote:

Of course there was at one time more than one text-tradition of the Hebrew Bible. The Hebrew manuscripts used by the several Septuagint translators of the various books in the Old Testament differ at times not in minor details alone, but, as is the case in such books as Jeremiah, Job, Esther, *recensionally* from the masoretic text-tradition. But these text-traditions have long perished.

Little did he realize that in a decade evidence of these text-traditions would be discovered.

While the scrolls of Cave 1 are very similar to the Masoretic text and bear witness to the remarkable accuracy with which the Masoretic text was copied and transmitted, yet strangely enough Cave 4 (at the edge of the plateau on which the Qumran ruins were found) contained portions of Exodus, Deuteronomy, and Samuel which agree more closely with the Septuagint than with the Masoretic text. Some scholars claim that these texts are translations of the Septuagint back into Hebrew, but while this is theoretically possible the few fragments in Greek which have been found near Qumran do not indicate that the people of this community valued the Septuagint or used it as a source. The most obvious interpretation of the evidence from Cave 4 is expressed by William F. Albright as follows:

We now know that in the fragments so far described from the Pentateuch and the Former Prophets (Joshua-Judges-Samuel-Kings) the Greek translators were almost slavish in their literalism. . . . When we find sections preserved in the LXX . . . that are missing in MT, as well as completely different forms of names, we may thus be reasonably certain that they are not inner Greek additions or corruptions, but go back to an older Hebrew recension which differed from MT.

The rise of varying types or recensions of Hebrew text must have been a very complex process for various parts of the Old Testament evidence different development. The beginnings of this process go back as early as the fateful year 597 B.C., the time of the first great exile to Babylonia. Those who were taken captive most certainly carried with them copies of the Old Testament books which had been completed by that time. Jeremiah and his scribe, Baruch, were permitted to stay on in Jerusalem, but soon after the final destruction of the Temple and Jerusalem in 586 B.C. they were taken forcibly into Egypt along with the Jews who fled there (Jer. 43:4–7). It is highly probable that they also took copies of Old Testament books with them, so from this time on there were at least two main areas where the text of the Old Testament was being copied and preserved.

Some scholars feel that after the Jews returned with Zerubbabel (last half of the sixth century B.C.) and with Ezra and Nehemiah (fifth century B.C.) a Palestinian type of text developed. At the same time another recension of the Hebrew text was forming among the Jews who remained in Babylonia. Apparently this text-type found its way to Palestine by the second century B.C. and later became the basis for the Masoretic text. Just how and when the Egyptian text found its way into Palestine is not known, but its presence at Qumran is certain. Some would explain the similarity between the Septuagint and Qumran scrolls as an indication that the Egyptian Hebrew text was an offshoot of the fifth-century Palestinian recension.

Psalm 145:13

In the light of this new evidence, difficult though it may be to explain, we may be "reasonably certain" that the Septuagint reading for the fourteenth letter of Ps. 145 stems from an early Hebrew text. This is confirmed further in that the Septuagint reading when translated back into Hebrew begins with the Hebrew letter *nun,* the missing letter in the Masoretic text of the Psalm. It is not possible to furnish absolute proof that this verse represents the original text which came from the psalmist, but in any case it can hardly be more erroneous than the complete omission in the Masoretic text and in the King James and American Standard Versions.

Moffatt includes the Septuagint reading in his text even though there is no footnote to inform the reader. The Revised Standard Version adds as part of verse 13, "The LORD is faithful in all his words, and gracious in all his deeds," and explains in the footnotes, "These two lines are supplied by one Hebrew Ms [Manuscript], Gk and Syr." The Berkeley Version ignores the Septuagint reading, but the heading of the psalm has a footnote which states, "This is an acrostic psalm but with the letter *nun* [n] missing."

1 Samuel 1:24–25

Another passage in which the Septuagint comes to the aid of the translator is 1 Sam. 1:24–25 where the King James Version reads:

24 And when she had weaned him she took him up with her, with three bullocks, and one ephah of flour, and a bottle of wine, and brought him unto the house of the LORD in Shiloh: and the child *was* young.

25 And they slew a bullock, and brought the child to Eli.

In verse 25 the American Standard has, with the Masoretic text, "the bullock," indicating that there was just one bullock or bull. The King James Version "a bullock" is seemingly an attempt to make sense of the "three bullocks" in verse 24. This textual difficulty in the Masoretic Hebrew is solved by the Septuagint which reads "three-year-old bull(ock)" instead of "three bull(ock)s." The Moffatt, American Translation, Revised Standard, and Berkeley Versions follow the Greek, but only the Revised Standard Version indicates the textual change with a footnote.

Exodus 8:23

A clear-cut mistake in the Masoretic text is found in Exod. 8:23 where it reads, "And I will put redemption between my people and your people." The Septuagint and Latin Vulgate have "put a division," the reading which appears in the text of the King James Version without a footnote. The American Standard, Moffatt, American Translation, Revised Standard, and Berkeley Versions also follow the Greek and Latin, and again only the Revised Standard Version includes a footnote giving the source of the reading.

1 Samuel 6:18

Part of 1 Sam. 6:18 in the King James Version reads, "even unto the great *stone of* Abel, whereon they set down the ark of the LORD," while the American Standard has, "even unto the great stone, whereon they set down the ark of Jehovah." A footnote on "stone" reads, "So the Sept. The Hebrew text has, *Abel*, (that is, *a meadow*)." It should be noted that this is one of the few instances in which the American Standard made use of the Septuagint. The English Revised Version (1885) made frequent use of the translations in an attempt to discover the best readings, but there was a decided return to the Masoretic text by the American scholars who made the revision of 1901. In the instance of 1 Sam. 6:18 the American revisers decided that *'abel* "meadow" was a scribal mistake for *'eben* "stone" (confusion of "n" for "l"). The Masoretic text is so obviously wrong the other twentieth-century translations follow the Greek without any footnote of explanation.

The King James Version, it should be noted, is misleading on two counts: (1) "Abel" has nothing to do with the Biblical character in Gen. 4, and (2) the King James translators have combined both the Septuagint and Masoretic texts. Although the Greek reading is put into italics (to show it is not in the Hebrew), the reader has no way of knowing the source.

Psalm 24:6

There are also instances of Septuagint readings in the marginal notes of the King James Version, but the reader is once again at a loss to detect it. In Ps. 24:6 the text, following the Masoretic Hebrew, reads, "This *is* the generation of them that seek him, that seek thy face, O Jacob." For the words "O Jacob" the translators had the marginal note, "Or, O God of Jacob." The "Or" would imply that this was another way of translating the same Hebrew, but in reality this alternate reading is based on the Greek.

Readings from the Latin Vulgate

Not only did the King James translators follow the Septuagint readings in a number of cases. Sometimes they used the Latin Vulgate as the source of their translations. One example is Job 37:7 where the Masoretic text reads, "He seals up the hand of every man, that all men whom he has made may know it." The American Standard follows this reading, but the King James, American Translation, Revised Standard, and Berkeley Versions follow the Latin in the last part of this verse by translating "that all men may know his work" or something similar. Only the Revised Standard Version informs the reader of this shift.

These examples, only a few of the many which could be given, are sufficient to show how all the versions have consulted various translations in an attempt to remedy passages where the Masoretic text appears to be mistaken. The King James translators showed no hesitancy in departing from the Hebrew (in the Old Testament) and Greek (in the New Testament) when the reading was difficult and a more convincing translation could be derived from the versions. The title page of the first King James Bible (see Fig. 11) stated quite frankly, "Newly Translated out of the Originall tongues & with the former Translations diligently compared and revised." This statement has appeared, with the exception of "Newly," in most editions of the King James Version down to the present time. The reference to "the former Translations" is made explicit in the preface, "The Translators to the Reader," where it states, "Neither did we think much [here "think much" is an old idiom meaning "hesitate"] to consult the translators or commentators, Chaldee [Aramaic], Hebrew, Syrian, Greek, or Latin; no, nor the Spanish, French, Italian, or Dutch." This readiness of the King James translators to consult any of the translations, even those almost contemporary with them, is evidenced in their work.

B. F. Westcott, after a detailed study of Isa. 53, concluded that of the variations of the King James Version from the Hebrew text "about seven-eighths are due to the Genevan version, either alone or in agreement with one or both of the Latin Versions." Many other passages confirm this observation that the Geneva Bible of 1560, along with the Latin versions, had a decided influence on the King James translators.

Revision of the Consonantal Hebrew Text

The fourth, and last, means of improving the Masoretic Hebrew is to revise the consonantal text. Of course this is resorted to only when the three previously noted methods do not produce the correct reading. The Revised Standard Version explains in its preface:

> Sometimes it is evident that the text has suffered in transmission, but none of the versions provides a satisfactory restoration. Here we can only follow the best judgment of competent scholars as to the most probable reconstruction of the original text. Such corrections are indicated in the footnotes by the abbreviation *Cn,* and a translation of the Masoretic Text is added.

The technical designation for this type of revision or restoration is "conjectural emendation," and as a general rule it is made on the strength of hints derived from the ancient translations and from the context of the passage in question. In other words, the conjecture is an *informed* guess as to what the original text must have read.

1 Samuel 13:1

One of the clearest examples of a faulty reading in the Masoretic text is 1 Sam. 13:1 where it reads, word for word, "Son of a year Saul when he reigned, and two years he reigned over Israel." The King James Version, trying to make the Hebrew intelligible, translates, "Saul reigned one year; and when he had reigned two years over Israel, Saul chose him three thousand *men* of Israel . . . ." Similarly, the Berkeley Version has, "By this time Saul had reigned for one year. When Saul had been king over Israel two years, he selected three thousand men of Israel . . . ." But in either translation the first part of the verse is pointless.

The Hebrew idiom for expressing the age of a person is "son of _____ years," and on the strength of this fact the American Standard Version translates, "Saul was [*forty*] years old when he began to reign; and when he had reigned two years over Israel, Saul chose him three thousand men of Israel . . . ." A footnote on *"forty"* reads, "The number is lacking in the Heb. text, and is supplied conjecturally."

Moffatt and the American Translation read, without footnotes, "Saul was . . . years old when he began to reign, and he reigned for . . . years over Israel." The Revised Standard Version has, "Saul was . . . years old when he began to reign; and he reigned . . . and two years over Israel." A footnote on the first blank reads, "The number is lacking in Heb," and another footnote on "two" informs the reader, "*Two* is not the entire number. Something has dropped out." Although the Berkeley Version tried to smooth out the difficult Hebrew text, a footnote acknowledges, "The Heb. has here: 'Saul was . . . years old when he began to reign, and he reigned . . . and two years over Israel!'" This, of course, is the identical reading found in the text of the Revised Standard Version. Thus, these four versions recognize, along with the American Standard Version, that the number indicating Saul's age at the beginning of his reign has been lost from the text.

The second blank in the text of Moffatt, American Translation, and Revised Standard Versions is inserted in the belief that verse 1 is a statistical summary of the type commonly found in the historical books. In 2 Kings 8:17, for example, it says of Jehoram, king of Judah, "He was thirty two years old when he became king, and he reigned eight years in Jerusalem."

While the King James and Berkeley Versions attempt to be true to the Masoretic text, their translations actually represent a revised or corrected consonantal text, and furthermore, unlike the other translations, their conjecture neither alleviates the difficulty, nor enlightens the reader.

2 Samuel 13:39

Another troublesome passage is 2 Sam. 13:39 where the Masoretic text begins, "And David the king longed to go forth to Absalom." The Septuagint reads, "And the spirit of the king grew weary to go out after Absalom." Hebrew דּוִד "David" and רוּחַ *ruah* "spirit" are similar enough, remembering the constant confusion of "d" and "r," to explain the reading in the Septuagint. The textual situation, therefore, has three possibilities: (1) the Masoretic text represents the original reading, (2) the Septuagint is the original form, or (3) the original text had "spirit of David" from which the Masoretic text lost the first part and the Septuagint the second.

While the Revised Standard Version follows the second possibility, giving Greek the credit in a footnote, the King James, English Revised, and American Standard Versions follow the third by reading, "And *the soul of* king David longed to go forth unto Absalom." This may well be the original reading, but in essence it requires a reconstruction of the

Masoretic text. In this instance the italics are equivalent to a *Cn* foot-note which the Revised Standard Version would have employed had it adopted this reconstruction. The Berkeley Version also accepts the third possibility by translating, "Then King David's heart longed for Absalom," but neither italics nor a footnote indicates the textual situation.

2 Samuel 23:8 and 1 Chronicles 11:11

A common textual difficulty in the Masoretic Hebrew is the differ-ence between parallel passages. A very striking illustration is 2 Sam. 23:8 and its parallel in 1 Chron. 11:11 which read in the American Standard Version:

2 *Sam.* 23:8   These are the names of the mighty men
1 *Chron.* 11:11 And this is the number of the mighty men

whom David had: Jo-sheb-bas-she-beth a Tah-che-mo-nite,
whom David had: Ja-sho-be-am, the son of a Hach-mo-nite,

chief of the captains; the same was Ad-i-no the Ez-nite,
the chief of the thirty; he lifted up his spear

against eight hundred slain at one time.
against three hundred and slew them at one time.

A glance should convince the reader that something has happened to the Masoretic text in either, or both, of these passages. The King James Version solution to this problem in Samuel is as follows:

These *be* the names of the mighty men whom David had: The Tach'mo-nite that sat in the seat, chief among the captains; the same was Ad'i-no the Ez'nite: *he lifted up his spear* against eight hundred, whom he slew at one time.

Instead of listing the name of "the Tachmonite" the King James Ver-sion translates it as "that sat in the seat." Furthermore, while retaining the enigmatic "Adino the Eznite," the translators add in italics the equivalent expression, "he lifted up his spear," from the parallel in 1 Chronicles. This also constitutes a revision of the consonantal Hebrew text.

For 2 Sam. 23:8 the Revised Standard Version translates:

These are the names of the mighty men whom David had: Josheb-basshe'-

beth a Tah-che'monite; he was chief of the three (*or* captains); he wielded his spear against eight hundred whom he slew at one time.

This follows the Masoretic text except for "Adino the Eznite" which has been displaced by "he wielded his spear," the parallel expression in I Chronicles. The Berkeley Version, on the other hand, has:

These are the names of David's mighty men: Josheb-basshebeth, a man of Tachemon, known also as Adino of Ezen, chief of the military leaders He stood up against eight hundred, whom he laid low at one time.

Thus, Berkeley follows the Masoretic text throughout, but in order to make complete sense it adds "He stood up." This, however, amounts to reconstructing the Hebrew text, so it becomes clear that no English translation can avoid reconstruction of the consonantal text if it is to make tolerable sense of 2 Sam. 23:8.

Joshua 21:13–14 and I Chronicles 6:57

The American Standard Version, following the Masoretic text closely, points up another variation between similar passages:

Josh. 21:13–14 And unto the children of Aaron the
I Chron. 6:57 And   to the   sons   of Aaron

priest they gave Hebron with its suburbs, the city of
   they gave   the cities of

refuge for the manslayer, and Libnah with its suburbs,
refuge, Hebron;   Libnah also with its suburbs,

14 and Jattir with its suburbs, and Eshtemoa with its suburbs.
   and Jattir,   and Eshtemoa with its suburbs.

Josh. 20:7–8 lists the six cities of refuge: Bezer, Ramoth, and Golan to the east of the Jordan River, and Kedesh, Shechem, and Hebron to the west. Libnah, Jattir, and Eshtemoa were *not* cities of refuge, therefore, I Chron. 6:57 should have "city of refuge" (referring to Hebron) as in Josh. 21:13. The mistake came about through an early scribal interchange of letters, the original text having עִיר "city of" as in Josh. 21:13 while the Hebrew manuscripts came to have עָרֵי "cities of."

The Old Testament translation published in 1917 by the Jewish Publication Society of America (reprinted in 1955) was made "according to the Masoretic Text," yet the translators rendered "city" in I Chron. 6:57 (verse 42 in Hebrew) with the footnote, "Heb. *cities*." Moffatt also accepts the singular form by translating "town of."

1. Codex Sinaiticus before Binding.

This vellum manuscript of the Bible in Greek, dating from about A.D. 350, was found by Konstantine Tischendorf in 1844 at the Monastery of St. Catherine near Mt. Sinai, whence its name. (See page 15.)

2. First Page of the Gospel according to John in Codex Sinaiticus

Each page has four columns of forty-eight lines, the words being written without separation. Note the title over the first column on the left. (See page 15.)

3. A Page in Codex Ephraemi Rescriptus

Originally this manuscript, dating from about A.D. 450, was a copy of the Bible in Greek, but because of the scarcity of writing material in the 12th century as much as possible of the original text (in one column, appearing right side up) was scraped off of the vellum and then the discourses of Ephraem of Syria copied in two columns (appearing upside down in the photograph). (See pages 16 and 19.)

4. A Page in the Chester Beatty Papyri of Paul's Letters

These papyri, dating from about A.D. 200, were discovered in Egypt about 1930. The fibers of the papyrus are clearly visible. (See page 16.)

5. Dead Sea (Qumran) Isaiah Scroll "A"

The complete Isaiah scroll, twenty-four feet in length, was found in 1947 in a cave overlooking the Dead Sea. It consists of seventeen sheets of leather sewn together with linen thread. Two seams are visible, one on the roll to the right, and the other to the left of the complete column of text. (See page 34.) The right-hand column is shown in detail in Fig. 7.

6. Siloam Inscription

This six-line inscription, carved in stone in old Hebrew script, was found in 1880 in the rock wall of the Siloam tunnel near its lower limits south of the temple area in Jerusalem. The text relates how the two crews of quarrymen (working from opposite ends) finally met and completed the tunnel. The inscription dates from the reign of Hezekiah (715-687 B.C.), confirming the accounts in 2 Kings 20:20 and 2 Chron. 32:30 which tell of Hezekiah closing up the waters of Gihon and bringing the water into Jerusalem through a conduit. (See page 35.)

7. Column 32 of the Isaiah Scroll

The circle, brackets, and parentheses identify examples of common scribal mistakes described in detail on page 38. The last line of the column is the beginning of Chapter 40.

וַתֹּאמֶר אֵלֶיהָ כֹּל אֲשֶׁר־תֹּאמְרִי אֵלַי אֶעֱשֶׂה: 16וַתֵּרֶד הַגֹּרֶן וַתַּעַשׂ
כְּכֹל אֲשֶׁר־צִוַּתָּה חֲמוֹתָהּ: 17וַיֹּאכַל בֹּעַז וַיֵּשְׁתְּ וַיִּיטַב לִבּוֹ וַיָּבֹא

8. Hebrew Text of Ruth 3:5

Desiring to add another word in Ruth 3:5 the scribes inserted into the text two vowels
(circled) by themselves, while the appropriate consonants were put in the margin to the
right with the note "Read, but not written." (See pages 40 and 41.)

אֲשֶׂה־לָּךְ כִּי יוֹדֵעַ כָּל־שַׁעַר עַמִּי כִּי אֵשֶׁת חַיִל אָתְּ: 12וְעַתָּה כִּי
אָמְנָם כִּי אם גֹאֵל אָנֹכִי וְגַם יֵשׁ גֹּאֵל קָרוֹב מִמֶּנִּי: 13לִינִי הַלַּיְלָה

9. Hebrew Text of Ruth 3:12

In contrast to Ruth 3:5 (top) the scribes desired to omit a word in 3:12. The two consonants (circled) were retained, but no vowel was added. In the margin to the left the
consonants were repeated with the note "Written, but not read." (See pages 40 and 41.)

10. Beginning of the Gospel according to John in the Lindisfarne Gospels

This Latin translation of the Gospels dates from about A.D. 700. Because many priests of
England spoke and read only English they needed interlinear translations to help them
conduct worship. The Old English (Anglo-Saxon) translation, added between the lines
about A.D. 950, indicates how greatly English has changed since that time. (See page 67.)

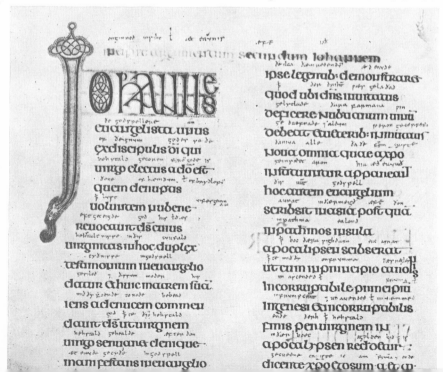

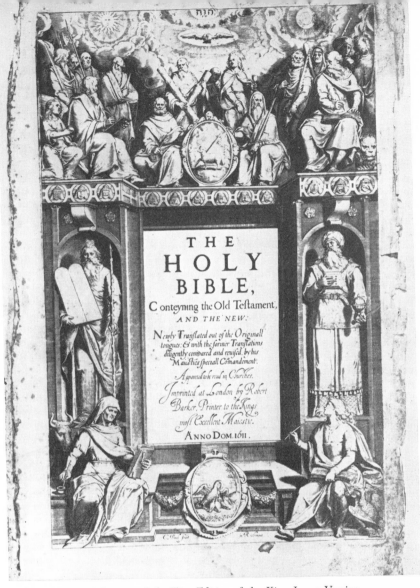

THE HOLY BIBLE,

Conteyning the Old Testament, AND THE NEW:

Newly Tranflated out of the Originall tongues: & with the former Tranflations diligently compared and reuifed, by his Maiesties speciall Comandement.

Appointed to be read in Churches.

Imprinted at London by Robert Barker, Printer to the Kings moft Excellent Maiestie.

ANNO DOM. 1611.

11. Title Page of the First Edition of the King James Version

The autograph "C. Boel fecit in Richmont," at the bottom of the page, identifies the engraver, Cornelius Boel of Antwerp, who was working at the time in Richmond, England, producing portraits of the Queen, Princess Elizabeth, and Prince Henry. At the top appears the personal name for God in Hebrew with a dove beneath it. In the upper panel Peter and James sit holding an oval frame with a depiction of the victorious "Lamb of God." Seated and writing are the Evangelists Matthew and Mark, while other Apostles look on. In the niches to the side of the title stand Moses and Aaron, and beneath them are seated Luke and John, the two other Gospel writers. The oval frame at the bottom pictures a pelican feeding her young. (See page 48.)

14. But by an equalitie: that now at this time your abundance may be a supply **for their want, that their abundance also may be** a supply **for your want, that there may be equalitie.**

12. 2 Corinthians 8:14 in a 1611 Edition of the King James Version
Words not found in the Greek text, but needed to smooth out the translation, appeared in small roman type in contrast to the large letters of the main text. (See page 113.)

14 But by an equalitie: that now at this time your abundance may bee *a supply* for their want, that their abundance also may bee *a supply* for your want, that there may be equalitie,

13. 2 Corinthians 8:14 in a 1612 Edition of the King James Version
After 1611, roman type was used for the text and italics for any additional words. The translators' and original editors' designation of these words was incomplete, however, and editors of editions from 1629 through 1769 had to italicize many more words—for example, the first "that" and the first "may be" of verse 14. (See pages 113 and 114.)

14. Column 10 of the Habakkuk Commentary
In this commentary on the Old Testament prophecy of Habakkuk, found with the Isaiah scroll at Qumran, the personal name for God, *Yahweh*, is written in old Hebrew script (circled) to distinguish it from the regular text in common square script. (See page 156.)

Strange to say, however, the English Revised, American Standard, American Translation, and Revised Standard Versions all follow the Masoretic text in reading "cities."

The Berkeley Version has, "Thus Aaron's descendants received of the cities of refuge, Hebron; also Libnah. . . ." This translation informs the reader that "Hebron" was one "of the cities of refuge." This, of course, is true, but it is not what the Hebrew of 1 Chron. 6:57 says. To get this translation the Hebrew word אֵת had to be changed to מִן. Obviously, this shift involves revision or reconstruction of the consonantal text, yet there is no footnote to indicate it.

The most extensive attempt at revision of 1 Chron. 6:57 is found in the King James Version. Present editions read, "And to the sons of Aaron they gave the cities of Judah, *namely*, Hebron, *the city* of refuge, and Libnah with her suburbs, and Jattir, and Eshtemoa, with their suburbs." Because the four cities mentioned in the verse were in Judah the translators inserted the word "Judah" and added "namely" before the listing. Then from Josh. 21:13 they inserted the words "the city of." This reconstruction makes good sense out of the verse, but, untrue to its principle of indicating all words not found in the Hebrew, the original edition in 1611 had none of the inserted words in italics. Later editors tried to correct this oversight by putting some words in italics, but they failed to do a complete job, and their failure persists to the present time. The middle of the verse should read, "the cities of *Judah, namely,* Hebron, *the city of* refuge," otherwise the reader would not know that the Hebrew has only "the cities of refuge Hebron."

Textual Revision and the Modern Versions

If this survey of the method for revising the consonantal text has been fairly difficult to follow, then the reader will begin to appreciate the complexity of the problem which faces every translator of the Old Testament. But difficult or not, there is no alternative if one is to have the most meaningful translation. This is made very clear in that all the translations, ancient and modern, have revised, at one time or another, the consonantal Hebrew text. The King James Version italics, where they are accurate, give the clue to the reader who understands what he sees. In the American Standard Version the italics and the rare notes acknowledging conjecture (as in 1 Sam. 13:1, noted above) also inform the reader. Moffatt and the American Translation do not employ italics (to indicate words not found in the Hebrew) or footnotes, therefore the reader has no means of knowing how they handled the Hebrew text. The Berkeley Version, likewise, has no italics, and although it has footnotes, these seldom deal with the matter of the Hebrew text, so in general the reader is unaware of the changes.

On the other hand, the Revised Standard Version, which does not employ italics, usually alerts the reader by means of the *Cn* footnotes. In such situations the reader is not forced to follow the text. He may always exercise his right to read the translation of the Masoretic text which is in the footnotes. At least the alternative is there, something which cannot be said of the other versions.

Considering the size of the Old Testament and the many centuries of its transmission by hand one marvels that there are so few mistakes in our present Hebrew manuscripts. As with the "Received Text" of the Greek New Testament, so with the Masoretic Hebrew of the Old Testament, we can be assured of its essential accuracy and trustworthiness. Yet if this "good" text is to be made "better," the best efforts of Biblical scholars, using all the available means (variant readings of Hebrew manuscripts, and ancient translations, change of vowels, and revision of the consonantal Hebrew text), are none too good.

4

Languages Change

The incomparable invitation which Jesus gives in Matt. 11:28–30 appears in one English version as follows:

alle ye that traueilen & ben chargid come to me & I schal fulfille you. take ye my yok on you & lerne ye of me for I am mylde and meke in herte: and ye schulen finde rest to youre soulis/ for my yok is softe & my charge liyt.

This translation is from John Wyclif's Version (about A.D. 1382), the oldest translation of the Bible into English. The same passage in the final edition of William Tyndale's New Testament (1534) reads as follows:

Come unto me all ye that laboure and are laden/ and I wyll ease you. Take my yoke on you and lerne of me/ for I am meke and lowly in herte: and ye shall fynd rest unto youre soules. For my yoke is easy/ and my burden is light.

The first (1611) edition of the King James Version has:

28 Come unto me all yee that labour, and are heauy laden, and I will give you rest.
29 Take my yoke upon you, and learne of me, for I am meeke and lowly in heart: and yee shall find rest unto your soules.
30 For my yoke is easie, and my burden is light.

Present-day editions of the King James Version read the same, except that most of them have modernized the old spelling, the most notable feature being the interchange of "u" and "v." This change in spelling and the other ways these versions differ from each other illustrate the universal fact that languages change.

Most people do not recognize language development because the change takes place so gradually, but it is going on all the time, discernible or not. For this reason the type of English used is (as one factor or element of a translation) equally as important as having accurate Greek and Hebrew sources.

Obsolete Words

Because of the change in the English language hundreds of words and phrases in the King James Version which were understood by the people in 1611 have become obscure, and pose, therefore, a real problem for modern readers.

Gen. 43:25 in the King James Version reads, "And they made ready the present against Joseph came at noon." The idiomatic expression "against Joseph came," although retained in the English Revised Version of 1885, is meaningless to most readers since it is a relic of the past. The American Standard Version makes tolerable sense by translating "against Joseph's coming," but the Revised Standard Version clears up the passage by having "for Joseph's coming." Moffatt and the Berkeley Version have "for Joseph's arrival," while the American Translation reads, "in anticipation of Joseph's arrival."

An obsolete word occurs in the King James and English Revised translations of Nah. 3:19: "all that hear the bruit of thee shall clap the hands over thee." The term "bruit," not in common use in America, was changed to "report" in the American Standard and Berkeley Versions and "news" in the American Translation and Revised Standard Version.

Tyndale was the first to incorporate "trow," in the sense of "think, suppose," in Luke 17:9 and it was retained in the King James: "Doth he thank that servant because he did the things that were commanded him? I trow not." In Wyclif the answer to the question reads (with modernized spelling), "No, I guess." The best Greek manuscripts do not have the answer to the question, accordingly most of the modern versions do not include it. Phillips, the one exception, reads clearly, "I don't think so."

Another usage originating with Tyndale was "do you to wit" meaning "want you to know." The King James Version in 2 Cor. 8:1, following Tyndale, has, "Moreover, brethren, we do you to wit of the grace of God bestowed on the churches of Macedonia." Wyclif translated "we make known to you," a translation much closer in idiom to "we want you to know," the reading found in the Revised Standard Version. The other modern versions translate similarly.

Ambiguous Words

Obsolete words such as "bruit," "trow," and "to wit" cause difficulty, but a more troublesome category of words (from the standpoint of the reader) is that in which terms still in use have acquired additional meanings and thus, capable of various interpretations, are ambiguous.

As a general rule the word "furniture" means "furnishings of a house or office, etc.," therefore the modern reader is puzzled when he reads in Gen. 31:34 of the King James Version, "Now Rachel had taken the images, and put them in the camel's furniture, and sat upon them." The American Standard and subsequent versions make it clear that Rachel hid the images in the camel's "saddle."

The term "abroad," especially in the United States, has come to mean primarily "beyond the limits of one's country," and herein lies the ambiguity of Deut. 24:11 in the King James Version: "Thou shalt stand abroad, and the man to whom thou dost lend shall bring out the pledge abroad unto thee." The English Revised and American Standard Versions change "abroad" to "without," also an ambiguous word, but the other translations get to the point by translating "outside."

In 1 Sam. 16:16 the King James and English Revised Versions have one of Saul's servants suggesting a search for a "cunning player on the harp." The reader could interpret "cunning" in the sense of "crafty, sly, wily" with reference to the character of the person, and not his ability to play, but this would hardly fit the context. The American Standard and subsequent versions dispel all uncertainty by translating "skilful," the clear meaning of the Hebrew.

Another example of an ambiguous word is found in Num. 24:14 which concludes in the King James, English Revised, and American Standard Versions, "I will advertise thee what this people shall do to thy people in the latter days." The idiom "advertise thee" has been changed to "let you know" in the Revised Standard Version, "tell you" in Moffatt, and "advise you" in the American Translation and the Berkeley Version.

A very strange idiom for English is the King James Version usage of "That" at the beginning of a direct statement: 2 Sam. 1:4 "And he answered, That the people are fled from the battle . . . ;" Mark 6:14

"and he said, That John the Baptist was risen from the dead . . . ;" and Mark 6:15 "Others said, That it is Elias. And others said, That it is a prophet, or as one of the prophets." This usage, not found in Tyndale or any other Protestant translation, stems from the Roman Catholic Rheims (Douay) Version, a translation which the King James translators followed in a number of instances even though it was not on the list of translations which they were to consult. Actually, these translations in Rheims resulted from a word-for-word translation of the Greek, both Septuagint and the New Testament, in which the Greek term *hoti* occurs at the beginning of these direct quotations. Although the word normally means "that, because," before direct statements it serves the same function as our quotation marks and is not to be translated. The translations subsequent to the King James Version have wisely omitted the superfluous "That."

Due to the influence of Latin the word "translate" was used formerly as a synonym for "transfer," but currently the basic idea of "translate" ("carry over") is applied chiefly to the task of expressing one language in terms of another. For this reason 2 Sam. 3:10 in the King James and English Revised Versions ("To translate the kingdom from the house of Saul") is quite ambiguous. The American Standard and subsequent translations read explicitly, "To transfer the kingdom."

In Heb. 11:5 the American Standard joins the King James and English Revised Versions in rendering, "By faith Enoch was translated that he should not see death; and was not found, because God had translated him." Wyclif also has "translated" twice, but Tyndale, while having "translated" in the first sentence, has "taken him away" in the second. The modern versions clarify the meaning with such translations as "transferred," "taken up," "promoted," and "transplanted."

Two ambiguous words, "company" and "published," occur in the King James translation of Ps. 68:11: "The Lord gave the word: great *was* the company of those that published *it.*" The English Revised and American Standard Versions eliminate one of the ambiguities by translating, "The Lord giveth the word: The women that publish the tidings are a great host," but Moffatt improves still more by having, "the women who told it were a mighty host." The American Translation has, "The messengers were a great host," the Revised Standard Version reads, "great is the host of those who bore the tidings," and the Berkeley Version translates, "those who proclaimed the good news were a great host."

The word "liberal" has so many meanings and connotations in our time the average reader is at a loss to interpret with any degree of certainty the King James translation of Isa. 32:8: "But the liberal deviseth liberal things; and by liberal things shall he stand." The English Revised Version retains "liberal" in all three instances, but the American Standard and most of the subsequent versions make the meaning explicit by translating "noble" in each instance.

The final example of ambiguity to be discussed is found in 2 Cor. 9:15 where the King James Version translates, "Thanks *be* unto God for his unspeakable gift." Tyndale was the first to use the term "unspeakable." Wyclif had translated "that may not be told." Even such modern versions as English Revised, American Standard, Moffatt, Charles B. Williams, Kingsley Williams, and Verkuyl retain Tyndale's word "unspeakable." Weymouth improves by having "unspeakably precious," but better still are the translations "indescribable" in Goodspeed and Phillips, and "inexpressible" in the Revised Standard Version.

Misleading Words

Obsolete and ambiguous words or phrases give readers just cause for concern, but the most deceptive type of difficulty (from the standpoint of interpretation) is that in which words still in use have changed radically, sometimes meaning almost the exact opposite. "Suffer," for example, used to mean "let, permit, allow," so the King James translators have in Gen. 20:6, "therefore suffered I thee not to touch her." The archaic word was permitted to stand in the English Revised and American Standard Versions, but the American Translation and Berkeley Version have "I kept (restrained) you from," while the Revised Standard Version reads, "I did not let you."

The most notable New Testament example of this misleading word is Mark 10:14: "Suffer the little children to come unto me," the translation in the King James, English Revised, and American Standard Versions. The rest of the translations eliminate any doubt by reading "Let," "Allow," or "Permit."

Not only did "suffer" formerly mean "let, allow," but "let" originally meant "hinder." Accordingly, Isa. 43:13 in the King James and English Revised Versions reads, "I will work, and who shall let it?" The American Standard and Revised Standard Versions have "hinder," Moffatt and American Translation translate "reverse," and the Berkeley Version reads "undo."

The best New Testament illustration of "let" is Rom. 1:13, the example noted in Chapter 1. Whereas the King James Version has "oftentimes I purposed to come unto you, (but was let hitherto)," the

English Revised and American Standard Versions have "hindered," Weymouth translates "disappointed," and all the rest read "prevented" in place of "let."

The word "prevent" also occurs in the King James Version, but it does not mean "hinder." Rather, the word originally derived its meaning from the Latin *praevenire* "come, go before." With this understanding the King James and English Revised Versions translate "I prevented the dawning of the morning" in Ps. 119:147. The American Standard Version clears up the misleading translation by reading "I anticipated the dawning of the morning." Moffatt "I am up before dawn," Berkeley Version "I was up before dawn," American Translation "I arise at dawn," and the Revised Standard Version "I rise before dawn" are attempts to translate the Hebrew more explicitly.

In 1 Thess. 4:15, also noted in Chapter 1, the King James Version translates "we which are alive *and* remain unto the coming of the Lord shall not prevent them which are asleep." Wyclif has "come before," while Tyndale reads "come yerre," an old expression similar in meaning. The word "prevent," found first in the Whittingham (Geneva) New Testament of 1557, becomes "precede" in the English Revised, American Standard, Revised Standard, and Phillips, "take precedence" in Moffatt and Verkuyl, "be there before" in Kingsley Williams, and "have no advantage (at all) over" in Goodspeed and Charles B. Williams.

Another very misleading translation in the King James Version is Phil. 3:20–21: "we look for the Saviour, the Lord Jesus Christ: who shall change our vile body, that it may be fashioned like unto his glorious body." In our time "vile" has the sense of "wicked, morally base, worthless," but for Tyndale, who was the first to use the word in this verse, the term meant, "low, poor." Wyclif read quite clearly "body of our meekness," and all modern translations rectify the misunderstanding by translating "body of our humiliation," or "our lowly (humiliated, poor) body."

Some of the misleading words give a comical twist to the Scriptures which was never intended originally. The King James and English Revised Versions inform us in 1 Kings 11:1 that "Solomon loved many strange women." Maybe some of them were "odd," but we find no justification for this view in the Hebrew. The word in this passage means "foreign," and this is the translation in the American Standard and subsequent versions.

In a similar vein Neh. 13:26 in the King James Version concludes, "nevertheless even him did outlandish women cause to sin." The term "outlandish" in its original, literal sense meant "foreign" (that is, "outside one's land") and this is the translation of the American Standard and following versions.

The King James Version refers in Exod. 28:8 to a "curious girdle," a translation which is puzzling to say the least. The American Standard and Revised Standard Versions translate "skilfully woven band," while the Berkeley Version has "artistic sash."

A singularly misleading translation in the King James Version is 1 Sam. 17:22: "And David left his carriage in the hand of the keeper of the carriage, and ran into the army." The English Revised Version and subsequent translations change the word "carriage" to read "baggage," "supplies," "stores," "things," or "pack."

The misleading translation in Job 31:35 of the King James Version stems from a literal translation of a specialized Hebrew idiom: "my desire is, *that* the Almighty would answer me, and *that* mine adversary had written a book." The American Translation has "scroll," but this too is misleading. The rest of the translations interpret the Hebrew word *sepher* "book, scroll" in accordance with the legal context of this passage in Job 31, therefore they translate "indictment."

Two expressions of time in the King James have changed so as to mean almost the opposite in modern English. Originally "anon" came from a combination of "in + one" with the meaning "in a moment, at once," but today it means "at another time." For this reason the average reader today is likely to misinterpret Matt. 13:20: "But he that received the seed into stony places, the same is he that heareth the word, and anon with joy receiveth it." The English Revised and ensuing versions have "straightway," "immediately," "at once," and "eagerly."

Similarly, the expression "by-and-by," which used to mean "right away, immediately," came to mean "a future time or occasion." Accordingly, Mark 6:25 loses the sense of urgency when one reads in the King James Version, "I will that thou give me by and by in a charger the head of John the Baptist." The modern versions remedy the situation by having "at once," "right away," "right now," "here and now," and "this (very) minute."

Thou and You in the Early English Versions

The foregoing examples of obsolete, ambiguous, and misleading words are a few indications of the change in the English language since Wyclif, Tyndale, and the King James Version. A satisfactory discussion of language change would be incomplete, however, without consideration of the archaic use of the personal pronouns "thou," "thee," and "thine" for the second person singular, and "ye," "you," and "your" for the second person plural. This was the common usage in the days of Wyclif and Tyndale and their translations employ all the forms. Some time after Tyndale, however, the word "you," the object form, began to displace "ye," the subject form, and eventually it made inroads on the singular forms "thou," the subject, and "thee," the object. At the same time "your," the plural possessive pronoun, was displacing "thine," the singular form.

This transition is clearly indicated in the works of William Shakespeare. Between 1589 and 1613 he wrote about thirty-eight plays, and from beginning to end there are numerous examples of "you" employed as the singular form. True, there is still much of "thou" and "thee" on the lips of certain characters, but as a general rule merchants, servants, nurses, common people, and independent thinkers use "you," some of them doing so consistently.

The King James Version itself has a few illustrations of the change from "ye" to "you." The Hebrew text of Job 19:3 (as found in all the texts from the Bomberg edition (1517) to the latest edition of Kittel's text) has three verb forms in the second person masculine plural. Modern editions of the King James Version read, "These ten times have ye reproached me: ye are not ashamed *that* ye make yourselves strange to me." The English Revised and American Standard Versions concur in having "ye" all three times. However, the original edition of the King James Version had "ye" the first time, but "you" the next two occurrences. There is no phonetic reason for the change, so it is highly probable that the two instances of "you" represent a momentary slip of the translators (or possibly the printers) into the common usage of their day, a slip which the original editors did not catch.

In Acts 17:23 the text of the King James Version has "your devotions," but a marginal note has the translation, "gods that you worship," another instance of "you" as the subject form for the plural. As an alternate reading for "because I have you in my heart" (Phil. 1:7) the King James Version has the marginal translation, "because you have me in your heart." The English Revised and American Standard Versions also have this marginal note, but they change "you" to read "ye." This attempt to make the King James Version consistent is further proof of the archaizing tendency of these two translations. They are closer to Tyndale in some respects than was the King James Version.

A third means of illustrating the shift in the use of pronouns is the dedication of the King James Version (Appendix D), some excerpts of which follow:

Great and manifold were the blessings, most dread Sovereign, which Almighty God, the Father of all mercies, bestowed upon us the people of England, when first he sent Your Majesty's Royal Person to rule and reign over us.

Then . . . to go forward with the confidence and resolution of a Man in maintaining the truth of Christ, and propagating it far and near, is that which hath so bound and firmly knit the hearts of all Your Majesty's loyal and religious people unto You, that Your very name is precious among them: their eye doth behold You with comfort, and they bless You in their hearts, as that sanctified Person, who, under God, is the immediate Author of their true happiness.

The Lord of heaven and earth bless Your Majesty with many and happy days, that, as his heavenly hand hath enriched Your Highness with many singular and extraordinary graces, so You may be the wonder of the world in this latter age for happiness and true felicity, to the honour of that great GOD, and the good of his Church, through Jesus Christ our Lord and only Saviour.

This dedication, unlike the translation which followed it, was written in a literary dialect of English current in 1611. Had the translators been consistent, and not under the restraint of the traditional language of Tyndale, they would have kept pace with the change in English by using "You" and "Your" for God and Jesus Christ. Already, however, this archaic English of Tyndale was becoming a religious or theological type of language distinct from the vernacular of the common man.

While "you," during the period of transition, was employed to address persons of honor and rank, the old singular forms "thou" and "thee" were used as familiar forms in addressing servants, children, and even pets. Thus, to people outside of religious circles (those unfamiliar with the religious overtones of Tyndale's language) the King James Version was speaking to God in familiar terms rather than honoring him.

At a later period even the familiar use of "thou" and "thee" passed out of existence in vernacular English, the pronoun "you" being used for both the familiar and polite forms of address in the singular and the plural. But this further development in English was also ignored by the Church. The language of Tyndale became more and more the "language of devotion," and it so thoroughly dominated the English-speaking Church that as recently as 1881 and 1901 (almost three hundred years after the King James Version) the English Revised and American Standard Versions were compelled (if they were to be accepted) to retain the archaic "thou" and "thee" throughout the entire Bible.

Thou and You in the Modern English Versions

In spite of the clear evidence warranting the use of "you" in our present translations some leaders in religious circles still contend for a return to Tyndale. They reason that since the Greek has separate forms for the singular and plural pronouns of the second person, English should conform by having the separate forms "thou" and "you." That the language of Tyndale happened to follow the Greek in this respect was a coincidence of linguistic development. In Hebrew most of the verb forms in the second and third persons, singular and plural, show whether the subject is masculine or feminine, but the Greek language has no separate forms to indicate gender in the verb. Yet no one has gone so far as to argue that Greek should be made to conform to Hebrew in this or any other respect. Accordingly, it is equally impossible to contend that English should conform to Greek usage.

The usage of "you" for both the singular and plural has the possibility of ambiguity, but as long as people continue to communicate satisfactorily there is little chance, in the foreseeable future, of any change in this idiomatic aspect of modern English.

The only place where this English deficiency need cause any concern is where the meaning of the Hebrew or Greek hinges on the distinction between the singular and the plural. A good example is Luke 22:31–32 which reads in the Revised Standard Version as follows:

"Simon, Simon, behold, Satan demanded to have you, that he might sift you like wheat, 32 but I have prayed for you that your faith may not fail; and when you have turned again, strengthen your brethren."

A footnote on both uses of "you" in verse 31 reads, "The Greek word for *you* here is plural; in verse 32 it is singular." Weymouth, Goodspeed, and Charles B. Williams indicate the plural by translating "all of you," the latter adding the footnote, "pl. of *you*; so *all of you*." Moffatt, Verkuyl, and Kingsley Williams translate "you all." The latter reading would be ambiguous in the southern part of the United States, however, because in some contexts "you all" is also a familiar expression for addressing one person.

The scarcity of such crucial passages as Luke 22:31 is proof that the distinction between singular and plural forms is not as important as some would imply. As a general rule the context makes it quite clear whether the "you" is singular or not. Therefore, from a linguistic standpoint the modern versions are perfectly justified in making the shift from "thou" to "you."

Most of the twentieth-century translations after the American Standard Version have employed "you" for addressing both men and Christ. Whereas the King James, English Revised, and American Standard Versions read in John 11:21-22:

Then said Martha unto Jesus, Lord, if thou hadst been here, my brother had not died. 22 But I know, that even now, whatsoever thou wilt ask of God, God will give it thee,

most of the translations from Weymouth on, including Verkuyl, have "you" for "thou" and "thee." Phillips, however, indicates the overtone of deity by employing "You" (initial capital letter) here, and elsewhere, for Christ.

In Matt. 16:16 the King James, English Revised, American Standard, and Verkuyl read, "Thou art the Christ, the Son of the living God," while most of the other modern versions have, "You are the Christ." The capital letter, due to its location at the beginning of Peter's reply, has no special meaning in the translations except, of course, in Phillips. The shift in usage by Verkuyl from "you" to "Thou" is explained in his preface:

For sake of reverence and of clarity we employ for such pronouns of Deity as He and Him, the initial capital; but where His disciples are still unaware of His deity, and certainly where His enemies accost Him, the use of initial capitals and of Thee and Thou would not reflect their attitude.

This attempt to alternate between "thou" and "you" appears to have merit, but the principle is impossible in practice. No translator or committee of translators has sufficient evidence to pass judgment in each case whether Jesus was addressed as deity or as a man. The overtone of deity is determined, after all, not from the pronoun used (whether it be "thou" or "you") but from the context. In fact, the pronouns used in the Greek text to address Christ have no theological overtones either. The same words were also used to address Satan, Judas, etc. The widespread claim that "thou" and "thee" are "the language of Christian devotion" is an argument from tradition and usage, not from the facts. When Jesus, in the King James Version, says, "Get thee behind me, Satan: thou art an offense unto me: for thou savorest not the things that be of God, but those that be of men" (Matt. 16:23), are the uses of "thee" and "thou" the language of devotion?

With the exception of Verkuyl and Phillips the major twentieth-century translations after the American Standard Version have employed "you" consistently, both for Christ and for men, leaving it to each reader to determine for himself when the context indicates recognition of deity. In Matt. 16:16, noted previously, when Jesus is called "the Christ, the Son of the living God," can any reader doubt that "you" is permeated with deity?

From the variety of theological backgrounds represented by the translations consulted in this chapter it should be evident that the use of "you" was in no way intended to deny or minimize the deity of Christ. Rather, in each instance it was a sincere attempt to make the New Testament a living, readable book capable of conveying God's message in the vernacular English of our time.

Thou and You in Worship

While the use of "you" for Christ has come into acceptance in some religious circles, no translation has attempted to employ "you" for God. The reason is obvious: the traditional language of prayer, both private and public, has addressed God as "thou." The time has not yet come when the majority of the English-speaking Protestant Church are mentally prepared to address God as "you," but aside from the traditional, psychological restrictions there is no reason for not doing so.

Many young Christians, most of whom were reared outside the tradition of the Church, are now addressing God in prayer as "you." Others are in a period of transition in which they use both "thou" and "you" intermittently in the same prayer. In spite of the fact that these petitions represent as much of the spirit of reverence and worship as do the prayers with only "thou" and "thee," some traditionalists are so offended they cannot even enter into the spirit of the prayers. God is wiser than men, however, for he accepts prayers on the basis of devotion and motive, not "shibboleths." Regardless of the form which Christians' religious acts may take God is never offended by those who *truly* worship and obey him. In other words, God permits each of us to determine his own "language of devotion." Inasmuch as many are choosing to follow current English usage in prayers the practice will most certainly spread. In fact, numbers of churches, representing all strata of society, are themselves in a period of transition in which part of the membership prays using "you" while the other part continues in the tradition of the Church. In some not too remote future translators will be able to employ "you" throughout the entire Bible for men, Christ, and even God.

Language Change in the History of the English Bible

The fact of language change and the necessity of keeping up with it should be evident from the discussion thus far, but an even stronger impression is gained from the history of the English Bible, a very important part being the ideas and convictions of translators down through the centuries.

The earliest forms of the English language were the Old English (Anglo-Saxon) dialects spoken by the common people of England during the period A.D. 450–1066. History tells us about the Venerable Bede (A.D. 673–735) who translated the Gospel of John into Old English, but unfortunately this early version has been lost. Some of the best examples of Old English available to us are the word-for-word translations found written over the Latin text in some old copies of the Psalter (book of Psalms) and the Gospels. Latin was the language of the schools and the Church, but often the priests were common people who spoke and read only English, and having had no chance for advanced schooling they needed these interlinear (between the lines) translations to aid them in conducting the worship services. From a glance at the interlinear glosses or additions in Fig. 10 the reader will see that Old English is removed so far from current English it is practically a foreign language.

Middle English

The invasion of England by the French-speaking Normans in A.D. 1066 was a crucial point in the history of the English language. French came to be the means of communication among the landed gentry and the social elite, thus sharing the prominence with Latin which continued as the language of the Church and schools. But in spite of the cultural supremacy of Latin and French the English language continued to thrive among the common people as the language of business and trade. Change and development were exceedingly rapid, and in time this new form of the language, known as Middle English, gradually gained ascendancy so that by the fourteenth century Geoffrey Chaucer (A.D. 1340–1400) used this type of English in his outstanding literary works *Troilus and Criseyde,* and *Canterbury Tales.*

A contemporary of Chaucer was John Wyclif (A.D. 1328–1384). It was Wyclif who made the first translation of the Bible into English, and in doing so he used the type of language common to his day. That he succeeded in putting the Bible into the mother tongue of the people is evidenced by one of his opponents who wrote, "Wyclif, by thus translating the Bible, made it the property of the masses and common to all . . . even to women who are able to read." This would not have been true had Wyclif translated into Old English.

William Tyndale

Good as Wyclif's translation was for the people of his day, the development of English by the sixteenth century necessitated another translation of the Scriptures. In telling the story (Appendix B) of his English New Testament of 1525–1526 William Tyndale wrote:

I had perceaved by experyence, how that it was impossible to stablysh the laye people in any truth, excepte the scripture were playnly layde before their eyes in their mother tonge, that they might se the processe, ordre and meaninge of the texte.

In his epilogue ("To the Reder") to the second (1526) edition of the New Testament, Tyndale wrote:

I had no man to counterfet, nether was holpe with englysshe of eny that had interpreted the same, or soche lyke thinge in the scripture before tyme.

Tyndale could write in this manner because he had made a fresh, new translation in the current English. On the other hand, although he had not consulted the Wyclif translation, some well-known passages from Wyclif had been preserved and passed on orally within Christian circles and they influenced Tyndale without his realizing it.

The Coverdale Bible (1535), Matthew Bible (1537) prepared by John Rogers a trusted friend of Tyndale, the Great (Cranmer) Bible (1539), and the Bishops' Bible (1568) relied heavily on the excellent translation by Tyndale. In fact, comparative studies indicate that about 70 per cent of the New Testament in the King James Version represents Tyndale's translation. Theoretically the King James translators championed the idea of translating in the language of the people, for they wrote in their preface:

So that to have the Scriptures in the mother tongue is not a quaint conceit lately taken up . . . , but hath been thought upon, and put in practice of old, even from the first times of the conversion of any nation; no doubt, because it was esteemed most profitable to cause faith to grow in men's hearts the sooner, and to make them to be able to say with the words of the Psalm, As we have heard, so we have seen.

From the standpoint of fact, however, they broadened the expression "mother tongue" so as to include the language of Tyndale.

The language of the preface and the dedication in the King James Version represents literary English current in 1611 and it differs substantially from the English of Tyndale's final revision in 1534, so much of which is found in the King James Bible. No other conclusion can be drawn but that the English-speaking segment of the Protestant Church was already failing to keep pace with the change in language. Tyndale had championed the idea of God's Word being in the language of the people and he had put his conviction into action by translating into English current in 1525. Yet with the success of the King James Version this conviction was lost sight of because Tyndale's own translation, to a large extent, was being perpetuated as the archaic, artificial language of the Church, deviating more and more each year from the English of the common man.

English and American Revised Versions
Nothing illustrates the tragic defeat of Tyndale's principle so forcibly as the first two principles (drawn up in 1870) for the guidance of the translators of the English Revised Version:

1. To introduce as few alterations as possible into the Text of the Authorised [King James] Version consistently with faithfulness.
2. To limit, as far as possible, the expression of such alterations to the language of the Authorised and earlier English versions.

In the preface to the English Revised New Testament (1881) the revisers state:

We have never removed any archaisms, whether in structure or in words, except where we were persuaded either that the meaning of the words was not generally understood, or that the nature of the expression led to some misconception of the true sense of the passage.

This deliberate retention of "archaisms" and expression of alterations in "the language of the Authorised and earlier English versions" was in reality a return to the days of Tyndale, a backward journey of three hundred and fifty years.

English in America was changing along different lines so the American Standard Version of 1901, based essentially on the English Revised Version, changed a number of words and expressions which were understood in England but not in America. Neither translation, however, was in the language of the common people. Furthermore, both of them were of such a wooden nature (almost word-for-word with the Hebrew and Greek) they did not read like good English. Due to publicity and a growing spirit of anticipation the initial sale of the English Revised Version was somewhat successful, but the revisers' fond hopes for continued success were shattered because the translation did not speak to the hearts and minds of the people, and as a result many returned to reading the King James Version. While the American Standard Version has had more success than the English Revised Version it too has failed to win its way.

Modern English Versions

It was noted in Chapter 1 that about five hundred translations of the Scriptures, ranging from full Bibles to portions of a book, were printed in English between 1611 and the present. While none of these had enough backing and sufficiently good qualities to displace the King James Version the repeated attempts at new translation indicated the continuing desire of Christians for God's Word in the "mother tongue," the language of thought and speech.

The failures of the English Revised and American Standard Versions heightened this desire even more, but inasmuch as no church-related agency seemed willing and financially able to sponsor another committee revision, individual translators took up the task of putting the Scriptures into modern English.

One of the earliest and best-known attempts was that of Richard Weymouth (1903). The title, *The New Testament in Modern Speech,* indicates the return to the principle of Wyclif and Tyndale. In his preface Weymouth writes, "But alas, the great majority of even 'new translations,' so called, are, in reality, only Tyndale's immortal work a little—often very little—modernized!" He declares further that in translating the New Testament into "English of the present day" he attempted to ascertain how "the inspired writer himself would have expressed his thoughts, had he been writing in our age and country."

The New Testament translation by James Moffatt appeared in 1913 and it, along with Weymouth's New Testament, served (in America as well as in Great Britain) to illuminate difficult passages in the King James, English Revised, and American Standard Versions.

However, the British background reflected in these translations did not suit them completely for the American scene. There was still a need for a truly American translation and in 1923 Edgar J. Goodspeed sought to meet this need with his own translation of the New Testament. In the preface he comments:

For American readers, especially, who have had to depend so long upon versions made in Great Britain, there is room for a New Testament free from expressions which, however familiar in England or Scotland, are strange to American ears.

Goodspeed's New Testament was incorporated in 1927 as the New Testament section of *An American Translation*.

Another United States translation, *The New Testament in the Language of the People*, made its appearance in 1937. The translator, Charles B. Williams, in answering the question of why another translation, writes in the foreword, "A distinguished Bible scholar answers, 'Language is a fluid thing. It does not remain fixed for a day. There is therefore constant need of retranslation.' " Williams explains further:

Our aim in publishing this new translation is that of Tyndale, "to cause the plowboy to know the Scriptures." Our aim is to make this greatest book in the world readable and understandable by the plain people. Only three books in the New Testament are written in anything like good literary Greek—Luke, the Acts, and Hebrews. In our translation of these books we have tried to use good, smooth English. Elsewhere we use simple everyday English which reproduces the everyday Greek which the writers used. In accord with this aim we have used practical everyday words to replace many technical religious and theological terms. In other words, we have tried to use the words and phrases that are understandable by the farmer and the fisherman, by the carpenter and the cowboy, by the cobbler and cab-driver, by the merchant and the miner, by the milkmaid and the housemistress, by the woodcutter and the trucker. If these can understand it, it is certain that the scholar, the teacher, the minister, the lawyer, the doctor, and all others can.

The preface of Gerrit Verkuyl's *Berkeley Version of the New Testament*, published in 1945, states:

The language, therefore, that must serve to bring us God's thoughts and ways toward us needs to be the language in which we think and live rather than that of our ancestors who expressed themselves differently.

The New Testament of the Revised Standard Version, the first major committee translation in English since the English Revised and American Standard Versions, appeared in 1946. The preface observes, "Let it be said here simply that all of the reasons which led to the demand for revision of the King James Version one hundred years ago are still valid, and are even more cogent now than then." With respect to language the preface notes:

The Bible carries its full message . . . to those who read it that they may discern and understand God's Word to men. . . . That Word must not be disguised in phrases that are no longer clear, or hidden under words that have changed or lost their meaning. It must stand forth in language that is direct and plain and meaningful to people today.

Necessity of Periodic Translations

The preceding survey of the motivation behind the important English translations should underline the danger of ignoring the universal law of language change. To do so is to perpetuate an artificial "Church language" which becomes increasingly ineffective as the common language continues its diverse development. C. S. Lewis, in the Introduction to *Letters to Young Churches* by J. B. Phillips (1947), writes very pointedly:

> The truth is that if we are to have translation at all we must have periodical re-translation. There is no such thing as translating a book into another language once and for all, for a language is a changing thing. If your son is to have clothes it is no good buying him a suit once and for all: he will grow out of it and have to be re-clothed.

If the Church is to remain *in* the world and communicate its message with power it *must* keep pace with language development by periodic translations.

In October, 1947, the first International Conference of Bible Translators, held in "Woudschoten," Zeist, Holland, went on record as favoring a new translation every fifty years, and this recommendation has been adopted as a working principle by the United Bible Societies, an international organization representing the major Bible Societies of the world.

A new translation will invariably be followed by a transitional period of uneasiness for those who have memorized portions of the old translation, but this difficulty will more than be offset by the increased effectiveness which God's Word will have among the common people, especially those reared outside of Church influence. While, as a general rule, the older generation will continue to use and cherish the familiar version this should not prevent the younger generation from reading, memorizing, and living by the new.

5

Artistic Style and the Truth

While the type of English used in a translation is an issue of crucial importance, the decision to translate into Modern English does not adequately handle the problem of language. There is still the matter of *style*. Languages have layers or strata which at any given time or period of development may be equally up-to-date and yet quite different. In our own culture, for example, there is, on the one hand, the direct style of the good news reporter, and, on the other hand, the flowing style of the first-rate novelist. For this reason good translators always give consideration to the question, "What style of English is best suited to communicate God's Word?"

Literary Style in the Original Writings
Literary styles vary considerably in the books of the Old Testament. There is the grandeur of Isaiah, the talented prophet who, reared in an environment providing the best his age could afford, had access to the court of the king and the homes of the elite. In contrast there is the direct, forceful style of Micah, Isaiah's contemporary, the unsophisticated country preacher who pointed up the terrible oppressions and injustices perpetrated by the urban rich against the poor peasants whom he counted as his fellows. In addition to these varying contemporary styles must be considered the evident changes in style which occur over the centuries between the earliest and latest writings of the Old

Testament. Notwithstanding these variations, however, the Hebrew Old Testament is written essentially in an active, forthright style employing many verbs and few adjectives. Where the language paints word pictures the result is more like a color movie than oils on a canvas.

As indicated previously the New Testament writings are, with few exceptions, in the common (*Koine*) Greek of the first century A.D. J. B. Phillips remarks in his preface to *The Gospels*:

> Yet, though we may not like it, there is in fact very little sublime simplicity or simple grandeur in the original Greek of the four Gospels. We face a queer paradox—that the earliest and most reliable accounts of the life of the very Son of God Himself were written in a debased language which had lost its classical beauty.

Literary Style and the Early English Versions

This being the case, then, how is it we have come to think of the Bible in terms of literary excellence? Wyclif and Tyndale are not responsible for this concept because in general they followed the example of the New Testament writers, translating with directness and clarity into the language of the common man. We must look to the King James Version as the primary reason for the emphasis on literary excellence. How it acquired this superiority is indicated by Charles C. Butterworth in his excellent book *The Literary Lineage of the King James Bible*. He illustrates this development by means of word-for-word studies of various passages (chosen for their *literary* value) from representative English translations ranging all the way from Wyclif in 1382 (in some cases from the Psalter of Richard Rolle in 1340) down through the King James Version in 1611.

One of the important insights derived from Butterworth's book is the extent to which the King James Bible incorporated various features of the early English versions. In discussing the contributions of previous translators and translations he writes:

> The chief place of honor is undoubtedly Tyndale's. It was he who gave to our biblical speech its organic features, shaping it out of the language of his time. . . . To Tyndale we owe the tone of simple earnestness, the plainness of speech, and the economy of words, that characterize so much of our Bible. He set the general standard to which the later versions adhered. Had he lived longer, no doubt we should have owed him more, for he left his work unfinished.

Of Miles Coverdale who made his own translation (1535) and then edited the Great (Cranmer) Bible of 1539 Butterworth comments:

> The work of Miles Coverdale is hard to estimate with fairness. It is much or little, according to one's sense of values. . . . If we judge Coverdale by his finished product in the Cranmer Bibles, rather than by his first venture or by the makeshift Testaments of 1538, then we must acknowledge that his contribution was great; for he had the requisite sense of humility to discern where Tyndale's work was better than his own and to prefer it, and he had the vital sense of harmony that could adjust and conjoin the various elements of the Coverdale and Matthew Bibles and bring forth a product better than either. . . . It was no small achievement to have improved on the work of Tyndale.

From a literary point of view, Coverdale's share in our Authorized Version is marked by its smoothness, its even-flowing tempo, its ease and naturalness and harmony. He seems to have been more concerned with being a good man than a great man. There is a sweetness in his work that has greatly enriched our Bible.

In regard to the Geneva Bible of 1560 Butterworth observes:

> The Geneva Bible holds an important place, next to that of Tyndale, in preparing the way for the King James translators. Time and again we find the wording in this Bible to be identical with our Authorized Version. . . . There is also a difference in the mood. The Geneva Bible is above all anxious to be accurate; it is clean-cut, honest, and straightforward; it is both scholarly and pious. It resolved many obscurities in the English text, especially in the Old Testament, and added strength and vigor to the translation. It sought to preserve the force and the idiom of the original tongues, and thus imparted fresh vitality to the lineage of the Authorized Version.

According to Butterworth the Bishops' Bible (1568) "was helpful only in parts . . . . Insofar as it can be said to have had any general effect as a version, it contributed a note of elegance and propriety to the final result."

We have already drawn attention to the fact that the King James translators went beyond the bounds of their instructions by consulting the Rheims (Douay) Roman Catholic Version. Butterworth comments further:

> The Rheims-Douay version, most noticeably in the Epistles of the New Testament, affected the King James Bible in two ways. First, it recalled the thought of the translators to the Latin structure of the sentences, which

they sometimes preferred to the Greek for clarity's sake, thus reverting to the pattern of Wycliffe or of the Coverdale Latin-English Testaments and forsaking the foundation laid by Tyndale. Second, it infused a new assortment of words, thus extending and enriching the vocabulary that was available to the King James companies.

Literary Style and the King James Version

What of the King James translators themselves? Did they make any real contribution to this developing literary tradition? On this point Butterworth declares:

Much every way, but most in poetry and beauty—in fitness of word, fineness of shading, variety of rhythm, and grace of cadence. It imparted a literary finish that was incomplete before. It enhanced the Scriptures' loveliness.

Lest it be inferred from our enthusiastic tone that the literary tact of the King James translators was infallible, we ought to say plainly that it was not. But it is rare to catch them in a fault. Nearly everything they altered was improved.

Butterworth's word-for-word comparison of Ps. 90:10, one of the examples cited, appears as follows:

The Psalter of 1530	The dayes of owre yeares	are
Coverdale of 1535	The dayes of oure age	are
Geneva Bible of 1560	The time of our life	is
Bishops' Bible of 1568	The dayes of our yeres	be in all
King James of 1611	The dayes of our yeres	*are*

thre score & tenne: and yf we be sumwhat strong
iij. score yeares & ten: & though men be so stronge that
threscore yeres & ten, and if they be of strength
threescore yeres and tenne, and yf through strength [of nature]
threescore yeeres and ten, and if by reason of strength

they are fower score/ and the best of them are
they come to iiij. score yeares, yet is their strength
foure score yeres: yet their strength
men come to foure score yeres: yet is their iolitie
they *be* fourescore yeeres, yet is their strength

passed in sinne and hevenes [i.e., *heaviness*]:
then but laboure and sorowe: so soone passeth it
is but labour and sorowe: for it is cut of
but labour and care, yea moreouer it passeth in
labour and sorrow: for it is soone cut

swiftly	we muste flee awaye.
awaye,	& we are gone.
quickely,	and we flee away.
haste from us,	and we flee from it.
off,	and we flie away.

In regard to this study of Ps. 90:10 Butterworth writes:

To observe in this instance how the King James workers took hold of the materials left to them by the earlier versions and built of them this little masterpiece, is to gain a valuable bit of instruction in the contrivance and management of artistic prose. Not one clause is left as it was, yet all the materials are derived from previous translators, with Coverdale supplying the pattern.

In listing further examples of the skillful touch of the King James Version, Butterworth remarks, "there is perhaps no place where the translators' intuitive sense of what is right shows forth to better advantage than in the thirty-fifth chapter of Isaiah." Miles Coverdale's rendering of this chapter begins:

But the deserte & wildernesse shal reioyse, ye waist grounde shal be glad, and florish as the lilly. She shal florish pleasauntly, and ioyful, and euer be geuynge of thankes more and more.

The Geneva Version changes to read:

The desert and the wildernes shal reioyce: and the waste grounde shalbe glad and florish as the rose. It shal florish abundantly & shal greatly reioyce also and ioy: . . .

Concerning these translations Butterworth comments:

Now these are not poor specimens by any means. Had we known no better, they might well have contented us. But to recognize the great skill in rhythm and the perfection of touch of the King James Version, one need only carefully use his ears:

The wildernesse and the solitarie place shall be glad for them: and the desert shall reioyce and blossome as the rose. It shall blossome abundantly, and reioyce euen with ioy and singing: . . .

The means are not elaborate: "solitarie place," "blossome," "singing,"—these are conspicuous, but they do not account for the transformation by themselves. There has been a sense of rapture (shall we call it?) imparted to the words which makes them sing and glow.

This keen sense of the King James translators is also evidenced in the way different contexts influenced, probably unconsciously, their translations of passages which are identical in the original language. Their translation of Isa. 35:9–10 is as follows:

9 No lion shall be there, nor *any* ravenous beast shall go up thereon, it shall not be found there; but the redeemed shall walk *there:*

10 And the ransomed of the LORD shall return, and come to Zion with songs and everlasting joy upon their heads: they shall obtain joy and gladness, and sorrow and sighing shall flee away.

But in Isa. 51:10–11 we find:

10 *Art* thou not it which hath dried the sea, the waters of the great deep; that hath made the depths of the sea a way for the ransomed to pass over?

11 Therefore the redeemed of the LORD shall return, and come with singing unto Zion; and everlasting joy *shall be* upon their head: they shall obtain gladness and joy; *and* sorrow and mourning shall flee away.

The Hebrew of Isa. 35:10 and 51:11 is virtually identical, so there is no textual or linguistic reason for varying the translations of the two verses. The justification for the difference lies in the preceding verses. Because Isa. 35:9 speaks of "the way of holiness," the translators considered "redeemed" as the proper word for the Hebrew ge'ulim. Isa. 51:10, however, deals with those "who pass over the sea" so the identical word ge'ulim was translated "ransomed." This freedom of expression is explained by the translators in their preface:

Another thing we think good to admonish thee of, gentle Reader, that we have not tied ourselves to an uniformity of phrasing, or to an identity of words, as some peradventure would wish that we had done, because they observe, that some learned men somewhere have been as exact as they could that way. Truly, that we might not vary from the sense of that which we had translated, before, if the word signified the same thing, (for there be some words that be not of the same sense everywhere) we were especially careful, and made a conscience, according to our duty. But that we should express the same notion in the same particular word; as for example, if we translate the Hebrew or Greek word once by 'purpose', never to call it 'intent'; if one where 'journeying', never 'travelling'; if one where 'think', never 'suppose'; if one where 'pain', never 'ache'; if one where 'joy', never 'gladness', &c. thus to mince the matter, we thought to savour more of curiosity than wisdom, and that rather it would breed scorn in the atheist, than bring profit to the godly reader. For is the kingdom of God become words or syllables? Why should we be in bondage to them, if we may be free? use one precisely, when we may use another no less fit as commodiously?

Because "ransomed" in Isa. 51:10 was more "commodious" or suitable to the context and just as "fit" as "redeemed" in 35:9 the translators made the change. This resulted in further changes for the Hebrew word *peduye*, a synonym of *ge'ulim*, occurs in 35:10 and 51:11. Inasmuch as "redeemed" was employed in 35:9 it would have savored "more of curiosity than wisdom" to use the same word in 35:10, therefore they translated "ransomed." The reverse was true in chapter 51 because the use of "ransomed" in verse 10 necessitated the change to "redeemed" in verse 11. From this evidence Butterworth concludes:

All of which goes to prove that the translators of the King James Bible were men of sensitive ears. They had a regard for the melody and the tempo of what they wrote. They could hear what was lovely in nearly every passage, and they were not going to be bound while they might be free.

In general Butterworth's conclusions regarding the King James Version are unassailable. However, his observation concerning varying literary tastes, noted in connection with Coverdale's contribution, needs some elaboration. The Revised Standard Version translated the Psalms in a literary style which it considered consistent with the Hebrew. Yet, at the appearance of the Old Testament in 1952 some critics ridiculed the Psalms as "poor literary quality," "barbarisms" which made "shambles of what was poetry in the King James Version," and still others passed the Psalms off as "prose in poetic format." Evidently most of these comments were made in light of the assumed excellence of the Psalms in the King James Version.

On the contrary, F. H. A. Scrivener in *The Authorized Edition of the English Bible* (1611), published in 1884, wrote with respect to the King James Version:

A more legitimate subject of complaint is the prosaic tone of its translation of the Psalms, which, however exact and elaborate, is so spiritless as to be willingly used by few that are familiar with the version in the Book of Common Prayer; a recension which, though derived immediately from the Great Bible, is in substance the work of that consummate master of rhythmical prose, Bishop Miles Coverdale.

Seemingly, "the old is better" (Luke 5:39), even in the realm of translations.

The feeling of charm which "the old" has for many people in every generation springs, more often than not, from qualities which are quaint and distinctive. One such feature in the King James Version is the tendency to invert the word order of a sentence. In a normal English sentence the subject comes first, then the verb or predicate, and finally the object. Whereas we invert the subject and predicate for emphasis or for asking questions, the King James Version does so as a variation of the normal sentence: for example, 2 Sam. 8:14, "And he put garrisons in Edom; throughout all Edom put he garrisons." This practice stems from Tyndale and is in some cases due to a literal translation of the Greek word order. In John 17:1 the King James Version translates, "These words spake Jesus . . . ," and in verse 13 it has, "And now come I to thee . . . ." Acts 11:16 reads, "Then remembered I the word . . . ," and 1 Cor. 5:16 has, "Wherefore henceforth know we no man . . . ."

While these inversions have an appeal akin to the delight evoked by certain features of current English dialects, they have no inherent literary excellence. There is no literary merit in praying "Our Father which art in heaven," but many people cling to the old wording, some in the conviction that "which" is the special form of the relative pronoun setting God apart from man. What they do not realize is that in 1611 "which" was equal to our "who" and so the King James translators were simply expressing themselves then as we would now by saying, "Our Father who art in heaven."

In Matt. 16:13 Jesus is made to ask, "Whom do men say that I, the Son of man, am?" Admittedly this translation of the King James Version flows more freely than "Who do men say that I, the Son of man, am?" but the charm of the distinctive "Whom" is hardly sufficient reason for perpetuating the bad grammar.

Artistic Style and the Truth

On the basis of literary merit (actual and assumed) many, Christian and non-Christian alike, believe that the King James Version should remain for all time the standard Bible for the English-speaking peoples. It is erroneous, so they reason, to return to the style of the New Testament, a style representative of the Silver Age of the Greek language. Some consider it the Providence of God that the Scriptures were translated during the Golden Age of the English language. But one could argue just as cogently that the scribal additions to the Greek text which were made a part of the King James Version are due to Providence and, accordingly, not to be removed. In fact, some Protestants believe this, not realizing that such a view is playing into the hands of the Roman Catholic Church. The Catholics deny that revelation ceased with the New Testament writers. For them the teachings of the Church Fathers and even the decrees of the Pope are revelation from God. No theologically alert Protestant, however, subscribes to this view, for it undermines the authority of the sixty-six books which comprise our Bible.

Furthermore, this stress on the King James Version as God's *supreme revelation* to the English-speaking world blinds people to the historical fact that the most successful translations, as far as communication of truth is concerned, have been those which have spoken to the reader in his own language. As J. B. Phillips observes:

Most people refuse to believe that the majesty and dignified simplicity of the Authorised Version, however lovely in themselves, are no more a part of the original message than the scarlet and blue and gold illumination [decoration] on a medieval manuscript.

No amount of trying to "turn back the clock" will help. The stern truth is that we live in the "here and now." If we could return, the "back-to-King-James" campaign would hardly satisfy those who prefer a "back-to-Coverdale" or even a "back-to-Tyndale" movement.

One of the other assumptions of those who cherish the King James Version is that man, having capacity for feeling, understands best what he understands with feeling. In other words, the element of rapture conveyed by the King James Version is considered essential to a vital understanding of its message. But invariably those who speak in such terms are persons highly sensitive to the beautiful, aesthetic features of life. Their delight is a sonnet, a sunset, a symphony, and a song. To them there can be no exalted worship of God and reading of his Word except in this exquisite form.

On the other hand, many Christians view the Bible more as God's revelation than as a piece of literature. For them the primary question is whether all this aesthetic, literary excellence has been for the betterment and growth of Christianity. That it has influenced English literature in innumerable ways no one will question, but this is not to say that its message has always carried over into the lives of those who cherished it. Furthermore, when it is evident that the majority of people today have neither the taste nor the training to appreciate the literary qualities of the King James Version are we still to insist that it be read, even though it has no appeal and its message does not come alive in the heart and imagination of the reader?

C. S. Lewis discusses (in Phillips' *Letters to Young Churches*) this whole matter of style, etc. in a very forthright way. He writes:

Dozens of sincerely pious people in the sixteenth century shuddered at the idea of turning the time-honoured Latin of the Vulgate into our common and (as they thought) "barbarous" English. A sacred truth seemed to them to have lost its sanctity when it was stripped of the polysyllabic Latin long heard at Mass and at Hours, and put into "language such as men do use" —language steeped in all the commonplace associations of the nursery, the inn, the stable, and the street. The answer then was the same as the answer now. The only kind of sanctity which scripture can lose (or, at least New Testament scripture) by being modernised is an accidental kind which it never had for its writers or its earliest readers.

After noting the type of language in which the New Testament was written, Lewis adds:

Does this shock us? It ought not to, except as the Incarnation itself ought to shock us. The same divine humility which decreed that God should become a baby at a peasant-woman's breast, and later an arrested field-preacher in the hands of the Roman police, decreed also that He should be preached in a vulgar, prosaic and unliterary language. If you can stomach the one, you can stomach the other. The Incarnation is in that sense an irreverent doctrine: Christianity, in that sense, an incurably irreverent religion. When we expect that it should have come before the World in all the beauty that we now feel in the Authorised Version we are as wide of the mark as the Jews were in expecting that the Messiah would come as a great earthly King. The real sanctity, the real beauty and sublimity of the New Testament (as of Christ's life) are of a different sort: miles deeper or *further in*.

In giving his concluding reason for new translations, Lewis comes to the crux of the problem—the "beauty" of the King James Version. He states:

And finally, though it may seem a sour paradox—we must sometimes get away from the Authorised Version, if for no other reason, simply *because* it is so beautiful and so solemn. Beauty exalts, but beauty also lulls. Early associations endear but they also confuse. Through that beautiful solemnity the transporting or horrifying realities of which the Book tells may come to us blunted and disarmed and we may only sigh with tranquil veneration when we ought to be burning with shame or struck dumb with terror or carried out of ourselves by ravishing hopes and adorations. Does the word "scourged" really come home to us like "flogged"? Does "mocked him" sting like "jeered at him"?

"Charity" or "Love"

We cannot, on the other hand, draw the conclusion that those who react against the King James Version are, therefore, unalterably opposed to literary qualities in a translation. The translators of the Revised Standard Version claim that they also gave care "to rhythm, euphony, and cadences," and the same can be said for some other modern translators. The elements of literary excellence and clarity are not always necessarily contradictory (for example, the quotations from C. S. Lewis), but there are times when a choice must be made between artistic style and the truth.

An excellent example is 1 Cor. 13 where Paul uses the Greek word *agape* nine times (according to the Greek text used by the King James and earlier versions). The problem is how to translate this word into English—should it be "charity" or "love"? Wyclif, working from the Latin (which had *caritas* "esteem, affection" as the translation for *agape*), employed "charity" throughout the chapter. Tyndale, working from the Greek, translated *agape* as "love" throughout.

In 1530 Thomas Lupset, apparently a man of some training, wrote in one of his letters, "For I note that in the last englysh translation of the gospels out of laten, the translatour alway for *Charitas* wryteth Loue: wherein I canne not consent with hym." This objection was most certainly referring to Tyndale's translation of 1525–1526. The contrast between "charity" and "love" Lupset likened to that between a "pen" and a "quill." All pens are quills, but not all quills pens; that is, all charity is love, but not all love is charity. In other words, Lupset felt that "love" was too broad a term for the context of 1 Cor. 13. But this argument was far from convincing and it seemed to die out.

The term "love" was employed in all the translations up through the first edition of the Bishops' Bible (1568), so the issue appeared to be settled. In the edition of 1572, however, "love" gave way, apparently for euphonic reasons, to the prettier word "charity." It enhanced the rhythm of the passage and so the King James translators retained it, in spite of the fact that since the time of Wyclif "charity" had also acquired the meaning "alms, alms-giving" and that by 1611 this meaning was becoming the dominant one. The inconsistency of the King James translators is made quite obvious by the following evidence: the Greek verb *agapao* occurs about 142 times in the New Testament and they translate it invariably "love" or "beloved = the loved one," and the related noun *agape* (occurring about 116 times) is translated "charity" only 29 times, 9 of these being in 1 Cor. 13. Even in such vital passages as 1 John 4:8 (where the Latin has *Deus caritas est*) the King James translators have "God is love."

When John claims that God is *agape*, and Paul insists with equal emphasis that God's true sons must partake of *agape*, what right has any translator or committee of translators to change 1 Cor. 13 so that the reader fails to associate the two passages? Nothing is more destructive to practical Christianity than the failure to realize that God expects those in the Church to share and express his love in an effective, personal way.

Most of the translations from the English Revised Version down to the present correct this inconsistency by returning to Tyndale's translation "love." In spite of all this evidence, however, as recently as the appearance of the Revised Standard Version New Testament in 1946 some people still took exception to the change of "charity" to "love," and they expressed their disapproval by accusing the translators of "tampering with the King James Bible."

Literary Style and the Modern English Versions

With few exceptions the primary purpose of modern translators has been to express the message of God's Word in clear, piercing language. It is this quality which often contributes to the superiority of the twentieth-century translations. In Prov. 4:18, for example, the ambiguous expression "perfect day" (found in the King James and American Standard Versions) has generally been interpreted to mean "the day of the LORD" or "the day of the Lord's return." Observe how the modern translations bring out the true meaning of the verse.

King James Version	But the path of the just	*is* as
American Standard	But the path of the righteous	is as
Moffatt	the course of good men,	like
American Translation	But the path of the righteous	is like
Revised Standard	But the path of the righteous	is like
Berkeley Version	But the path of the righteous	is like

the shining light,	that shineth more and more
the dawning light,	That shineth more and more
a ray of dawn,	shines on and on
the light of the dawn,	That shines ever more brightly
the light of dawn,	which shines brighter and brighter
the dawning light	shining brighter, brighter

unto the perfect day.
unto the perfect day.
 to the full light of day.
till the day is full.
until full day.
until the full-orbed day.

An example of superiority in the modern versions, even from the standpoint of beauty and rhythm, is Judg. 14:14:

King James Version	Out of the eater came forth meat,
American Standard	Out of the eater came forth food,
Moffatt	From the eater came something to eat,
American Translation	Out of the eater came something to eat,
Revised Standard	Out of the eater came something to eat.
Berkeley Version	Out of the eater came something to eat,

and out of the strong came forth sweetness.
And out of the strong came forth sweetness.
   from   the strong came something sweet.
And out of the strong came something sweet.
   Out of the strong came something sweet.
and out of the strong came something sweet.

Notice how the American Translation, Revised Standard, and Berkeley Versions combine the best features of the King James Version and Moffatt.

The Hebrew text of 2 Chron. 4:10 is quite idiomatic and when it is translated almost word-for-word (as in the King James Version) the reader is usually confused. Note again how the modern translations clarify the meaning.

King James Version	And he set the sea on the right
American Standard	And he set the sea on the right
Moffatt	The tank was placed on the right
American Translation	He put the sea on the right
Revised Standard	and he set the sea at the
Berkeley Version	He put the reservoir on the right

side of the east end, over against the south.
side *of the house* eastward, toward the south.
of the temple, facing southeast.
side of the house facing the southeast.
southeast corner of the house.
side of the temple, facing southeast.

The King James Version translation of Isa. 59:4 is another passage in which the original meaning eludes the average reader. Observe the manner in which most of the recent versions bring the "courtroom" scene vividly to mind.

King James Version	None calleth for justice, nor *any*
American Standard	None sueth in righteousness, and none

Moffatt   in court no one sues honestly, no
American Translation   There is none who sues honestly, None who
Revised Standard   No one enters suit justly, no one
Berkeley Version   No one demanded justice nor did anyone

     pleadeth   for truth: they trust in vanity, etc.
     pleadeth   in truth: they trust in vanity
     plea is   just; pretence you rely on
     pleads his case truthfully; But each one trusts in vanity
     goes to law   honestly; they rely on empty pleas
     plead   for honesty; they trusted in confusion

One of the most devastating criticisms God ever leveled at his willful people is found in Jer. 2:23–24. The translation in the King James Version does not have the sting which the Hebrew conveys. The whorelike shamelessness with which the people of Israel went after the pagan gods is made ever so clear in the modern versions.

King James Version   *thou art* a swift dromedary traversing
American Standard   *thou art* a swift dromedary traversing
Moffatt   you are a swift young camel, that doubles on
American Translation   You are a light young camel, doubling on
Revised Standard   a restive   camel interlacing
Berkeley Version   You are as a swift, young she-camel entangling

     her ways; 24 a wild ass used to the wilderness, *that*
     her ways;   a wild ass used to the wilderness, that
     her tracks;   a heifer running wild in the wold.
     her tracks,   A wild ass trained to the desert,
     her tracks,   a wild ass used to the wilderness,
     her walk; like a wild donkey accustomed to the wilderness,

                snuffeth up the wind at her pleasure; in her occasion
                snuffeth up the wind in her   desire; in her occasion
     heated with passion, snuffing the breeze, in the rutting season
               snuffing the wind in her passion—
        in her heat sniffing the wind!
     in the heat of her passion snuffing up the wind, in the time of her

            who can   turn her away? all that seek her will not
            who can   turn her away? all that seek her will not
            who can   control   her? No male need trouble to search
            Who can restrain her lust? None that seek her need
            Who can restrain her lust? None who seek her need
     mating, who can turn her lust away? All those pursuing her will not

weary themselves; in her month they shall find her.
weary themselves; in her month they shall find her.
     for her; all can find her at mating-time.
weary themselves; In her month they shall find her.
weary themselves; in her month they will find her.
be disappointed, because in her month they shall find her.

These illustrations are only a small sampling of the extensive improvements in the modern translations of the Old Testament. It should be evident, however, that any lack of beauty, rhythm, and cadence in the modern versions (and this lack is not as great as some have made out) is more than compensated for by the clear-cut manner in which they communicate (especially from Moffatt on) the meaning of the Hebrew text.

In the New Testament the modern translations exhibit marked improvement in the extremely important section Romans through Jude. This unit, the Pauline and General Epistles, was translated by the sixth company of the King James translators, a seven-man committee, concerning most of whom we know virtually nothing. The renowned Greek scholars of that time were assigned to the fourth company (entrusted with the Apocrypha) and the fifth company (entrusted with the Gospels, Acts, and Revelation). Apparently the section Romans through Jude was assigned to the younger scholars on the assumption that it contained the least difficulties of the whole Bible. Whatever the reasons for the assignment the decision was a most unhappy one for this crucial portion of the New Testament is done with the least skill of all the King James Version. It was this company which, as Butterworth observed, also made such extensive use of the Rheims (Douay) Version.

The meaning of 2 Cor. 6:12-13, half buried in the King James Version, comes clearly into view in the recent versions.

King James Version Ye are not straitened in us, but ye are straitened in your own bowels. 13 Now for a recompense in the same, (I speak as unto *my* children,) be ye also enlarged.

American Standard Ye are not straitened in us, but ye are straitened in your own affections. 13 Now for a recompense in like kind (I speak as unto *my* children), be ye also enlarged.

Weymouth There is no narrowness in our love to you; the narrowness is in your own feelings. 13 And in just requital—I speak as to my children—let your hearts expand also.

Moffatt 'Restraint'?—that lies with you, not me. 13 A fair exchange now, as the children say! Open your hearts wide to me.

Goodspeed It is not that I am cramping you, it is your own affections. 13 To pay me back, I tell you, my children, you must open your hearts too.

Charles B. Williams You are not squeezed into a tiny corner in my heart, but you are in your own affections. 13 To pay me back, I tell you, my children, you too must stretch your hearts with love for me.

Verkuyl You are not hedged in by us; but you are cramped in your own affections. 13 So, a fair return, as children say, you also open wide your hearts.

Phillips Any stiffness between us must be on your side, for we assure you there is none on ours. 13 Do regard me (I talk to you as though you were my own children) with the same complete candour!

Kingsley Williams If you feel narrowly shut in, the fault is not in us, but in your own narrow hearts. 13 As a fair exchange (I am speaking to my children), be large-hearted too.

Revised Standard You are not restricted by us, but you are restricted in your own affections. 13 In return—I speak as to children—widen your hearts also.

The reader is urged to compare on his own such chapters as 1 Cor. 7; 2 Cor. 6 and 8; Phil. 2; 1 Thess. 4; and Titus 1. In the interest of accuracy it needs to be pointed out that in the illustrations, as well as these suggested passages, there are other factors which help produce the heightened effect of the modern versions, but at least one of these is that quality, often quite intangible, which we call style.

Literary Style and Public Worship

Another aspect of translation style which deserves consideration is that of suitability for public reading. Inasmuch as the recent versions have eliminated the misleading, inappropriate expressions found in the King James Version—for example, "refresh my bowels in the Lord" (Philem. 20), and "my bowels were moved for him" (Song of Sol. 5:4) —ministers have read publicly from various of the translations, often with telling results. At times, however, even some of the modern versions (especially those intended for private reading and study) lack the dignity which the average congregation demands.

The Revised Standard Version, under instructions from the International Council of Religious Education, was "designed for use in public and private worship, and to be in the direction of the simple, classic English style of the King James Version." This was an indirect reference to the laborious, unnatural style of the American Standard Version. On the other hand, notwithstanding the claims of the Revised Standard translators, some critics of the version maintain that they find little of the "classic English style of the King James Version" in it. Obviously, there is a difference of opinion as to what constitutes "classic English style." The translators of the Revised Standard Version, among whom were James Moffatt and Edgar J. Goodspeed, shared the conviction that the true beauty of the King James Version lay not in its archaisms, artistic style, and inaccurate translations, but rather in its crisp, concise basic structure, a style which derived from Tyndale. In accordance with this interpretation of their instructions they produced a translation with fewer words, simpler sentences, and greater directness than either the King James or the American Standard Version. Luke 9:17 is illustrative of this point.

King James Version	And they did eat, and were all filled:
American Standard	And they ate, and were all filled:
Revised Standard	And all ate and were satisfied.

and there was taken up of fragments that remained to them
and there was taken up that which remained over to them
And they   took up what was left over,

twelve baskets.
of broken pieces, twelve baskets.
twelve baskets of broken pieces.

This lucid style results in a clarity which is especially appropriate for public reading.

As further consideration for public worship the Revised Standard Version tended to retain the most familiar passages of the Bible with as little change from the King James Version as possible, the more modern phrasings being placed in the footnotes.

The ultimate in Bible translating is a combination of clarity and artistic style. But where these are incompatible and a choice must be made, the wise translator will always give precedence to clarity and the truth.

6

New Meanings for Biblical Words

In 1 Cor. 7:36–38 Paul instructs his readers how a man should act toward "his virgin." The Greek text does not specify, unfortunately, what relationship (daughter, spiritual bride, or fiancée) this "virgin" has to the man, so the only way of determining this is to check the context. The King James Version translates the unit as follows:

36 But if any man think that he behaveth himself uncomely toward his virgin, if she pass the flower of *her* age, and need so require, let him do what he will he sinneth not: let them marry.

37 Nevertheless he that standeth steadfast in his heart, having no necessity, but hath power over his own will, and hath so decreed in his heart that he will keep his virgin, doeth well.

38 So then he that giveth *her* in marriage doeth well; but he that giveth *her* not in marriage doeth better.

The key word of this passage, *gamizo* (occurring twice in verse 38), was known to have the meaning "give in marriage," and so the King James Version translated accordingly. It is implicit or understood that "virgin" in verse 36 refers to a daughter for no normal person would (as in verse 38) give his engaged "virgin" in marriage to some other man. The American Standard Version makes this interpretation explicit by translating "virgin *daughter*" in verse 36. Weymouth accomplished the same purpose by translating "unmarried daughter."

However, the statement "let them marry" (verse 36) gives difficulty to this interpretation because it implies another man, the husband-to-be, who has not been mentioned previously. Furthermore, would a father's decision concerning his daughter's marriage involve the inner struggle which is evident in verses 36–37?

Subsequent to the King James and American Standard Versions it was learned (from Greek papyri) that in New Testament times *gamizo* also meant "to marry." This too was the meaning for the verb *gameo* which occurs in verse 36 and is translated "let them marry." On discovering that *gamizo* and *gameo* were essentially synonymous translators were able to interpret "virgin" as the man's fiancée or as his spiritual bride (that is, a young woman under his protection, in some instances living with him, but always under vows of celibacy). Those versions interpreting "virgin" to mean "fiancée" translate verse 36 as follows:

Goodspeed But if a man thinks he is not acting properly toward the girl to whom he is engaged, if his passions are too strong, and that is what ought to be done, let him do as he pleases; it is no sin; let them be married.

Phillips But if any man feels he is not behaving honourably towards the woman he loves, especially as she is beginning to lose her first youth and the emotional strain is considerable, let him do what his heart tells him to do—let them be married, there is no sin in that.

Revised Standard If any one thinks that he is not behaving properly toward his betrothed, if his passions are strong, and it has to be, let him do as he wishes: let them marry—it is no sin.

The translations which interpret "virgin" to mean "spiritual bride" read as follows in verse 36:

Moffat At the same time if any man considers that he is not behaving properly to the maid who is his spiritual bride, if his passions are strong and if it must be so, then let him do what he wants—let them be married; it is no sin for him.

Kingsley Williams But if a man thinks that he is not treating his companion in chastity properly, if she is of full age, and if it is better that he should do so, let him do what he wishes to do; he is not sinning; let them marry.

Verkuyl translates ambiguously "his virgin," but a footnote observes, "Either one's daughter, or one's fiancée; probably the latter." Charles B. Williams passes over the possibility afforded by the new linguistic evidence and reverts to the traditional interpretation by translating "his single daughter" in verse 36. Accordingly, he expands the statement "let them marry" to read "Let the daughter and her suitor marry."

1 Kings 10:28–29

A notable Old Testament example of new meanings producing a radically revised translation is 1 Kings 10:28–29. The King James and American Standard Versions translate verse 28 as follows:

King James Version	And	Solomon had horses
American Standard	And the horses which Solomon had were

brought out of Egypt, and linen yarn: the king's merchants
brought out of Egypt; and the king's merchants received them

received the linen yarn at a price.
in droves, each drove at a price.

The translations "linen yarn" and "droves" were attempts to show the meaning of the Hebrew word *miqweh* (occurring twice in verse 28). This was ill-advised, however, for the earliest translations had indicated that the form was a place name. The Septuagint read "from Tekoa," interpreting the strange Hebrew word as an erroneous form of the name Tekoa (the home town and district of Amos the prophet). In his Latin Vulgate, Jerome translated "from Coa," although it is doubtful that he knew the location of Coa.

The inscriptions of Shalmaneser III (858–824 B.C.), one of the great Assyrian kings, give an itemized list of the coalition of Syrian kings which was defeated by Shalmaneser's army at Karkar. The list reads in part, "2,000 chariots, 10,000 foot soldiers of Ahab, the Israelite, 500 soldiers from Que, 1,000 soldiers from Muṣri." The Old Testament makes no reference to Ahab engaging in any such battle, but there is no reason to doubt the historicity of this event. Yet the significance of this inscription for 1 Kings 10:28 lies in the mention of Que and Muṣri, both of which were in Asia Minor.

On the basis of this evidence Moffatt, American Translation, Revised Standard, and Berkeley Versions give different "pointing" to the Hebrew word *miqweh* so as to read *miqqueh* "from Que" (*min* "from" + *queh* "Que or Kue"). Moffatt goes further in treating the Hebrew word *miṣraim* "Egypt" as a mistake for Muṣri or Muzri, the province bordering on Que. The Berkeley Version takes the most drastic action of all by deliberately dropping "Egypt and" from the text. A footnote explains, "The Hebrew has 'from Egypt and Cilicia,' but the former was not a producer of horses." The available archaeological and inscriptional evidence points in this direction. Maybe the Berkeley Version is correct in dropping out part of the Hebrew text (considering it as *dittography* "double writing"), but in all likelihood Moffatt has given the solution to verse 28 by translating "from Muzri and from Kue." He is probably mistaken, however; in changing "Egypt" to "Muzri" in verse 29.

Other inscriptions in which Que is mentioned indicate beyond question that the name was an ancient designation for the territory known in later times as Cilicia. In using this place name the Berkeley Version has improved on all the versions because the average reader of the Bible (knowing that Paul's home town, Tarsus, was in Cilicia) gains a clearer picture of the geographical setting.

1 Kings 10:28–29 appears as follows in the more recent versions:

Moffatt	Solomon's horses were imported from
American Translation	Solomon's transport of horses was between
Revised Standard	And Solomon's import of horses was from
Berkeley Version	Solomon's horses came from

Muzri and from Kue; the royal dealers used to bring a troop of
Egypt   and   Kue; the king's traders   received
Egypt   and   Kue, and the king's traders   received
          Cilicia; the royal merchants   brought

horses from Kue, paying cash for them; 29 a chariot could be
 them from Kue   at a price, 29 and a chariot could be
 them from Kue   at a price. 29 A chariot could be
[them] from Cilicia at the prevailing price—29 an

imported from Muzri for seventy-five pounds in silver, and a horse
imported from Egypt for six hundred shekels of silver, and a horse
imported from Egypt for six hundred shekels of silver, and a horse
Egyptian chariot for 400 dollars in silver and a [Cilician]   horse

for about twenty pounds in silver (the dealers supplied all the
for a hundred and fifty. Even so through their means they carried on
for a hundred and fifty; and so through the king's traders they were
for 100 dollars—and so at that price they delivered them by their

kings of the Hittites and the Arameans at the same rate).
trade with all the kings of the Hittites and the kings of the Arameans.
exported to all the kings of the Hittites and the kings of Syria.
hand to all   the Hittite and Syrian kings.

The puzzling "linen yarn" and "droves" of the earlier translations have been eliminated, thanks to our new information, but, as noted above, the Hebrew text still presents some difficulties. Yet, enough is known to get a fairly clear picture of the situation. Solomon's huge building operations made it necessary to raise new revenue. Egypt seemed to have the craftsmen and materials to produce first-rate chariots, while Asia Minor knew how to breed the best horses. Each needed the product of the other, and other countries needed both. Apparently, Solomon, recognizing this situation, had his official merchants act as middle men in an extensive import-export trade of horses and chariots, making a profit, of course, on all the two-way transactions. Archaeological findings indicate that he also kept some of the horses and chariots for his own empire.

Proverbs 26:23

The King James Version in Prov. 26:23 reads, "Burning lips and a wicked heart *are like* a potsherd covered with silver dross." Moffatt translates "silvery dross," American Translation has "silver slag," and the American Standard and Berkeley Versions retain "silver dross." A footnote in the Berkeley Version reads, "Gives the appearance of genuine solid silver."

The Hebrew of this expression is *kesep* "silver" followed by *sigim* "dross," but the normal Hebrew idiom would demand *sigim kesep* "dross of silver." Furthermore, no examples of pottery covered with silver slag or dross have been found even though archaeologists have excavated tremendous masses of pottery and potsherds (broken pieces of pottery) all over the Near East.

A possible solution to the difficulty has been found in the Ugaritic texts which were discovered in 1929 at Ras Shamra along the Mediterranean coast of Syria. The language of these inscriptions (written in an alphabetical script formerly unknown) was related to Hebrew and in one of the texts scholars discovered the word *kesapsigim* where the meaning seems to be "like whiteness" or "like white glaze." On the basis of this new evidence the Revised Standard Version translates, "Like the glaze covering an earthen vessel are smooth lips with an evil heart." The word "smooth" (from the Septuagint) was preferred to the Hebrew word "burning" because it was more in keeping with the translation "glaze." A footnote on "glaze" reads, "Cn: Heb *silver of dross.*" The correction (Cn) of the Hebrew was very slight, however, because it consisted solely in putting the two words *kesep* and *sigim* together, not in changing any of the consonants.

John 3:16

The well-beloved verse John 3:16 is another New Testament example of translation change resulting from linguistic evidence. Bible lovers, accustomed to reading "only begotten Son," have been surprised (and some even incensed) at many of the new versions because they translate "only Son" without any explanatory footnote. *Monogenes*, the Greek word in question, occurs nine times in the New Testament and the King James Version passages (translating the word "only" sometimes and "only begotten" at other times) appear as follows:

Luke 7:12 Now when he came nigh to the gate of the city, behold, there was a dead man carried out, the only son of his mother, and she was a widow: and much people of the city was with her.

Luke 8:42 For he had one only daughter, about twelve years of age, and she lay a dying. But as he went the people thronged him.

Luke 9:38 And, behold, a man of the company cried out, saying, Master, I beseech thee, look upon my son; for he is mine only child.

John 1:14 And the Word was made flesh, and dwelt among us, (and we beheld his glory, the glory as of the only begotten of the Father,) full of grace and truth.

John 1:18 No man hath seen God at any time; the only begotten Son, which is in the bosom of the Father, he has declared *him*.

John 3:16 For God so loved the world, that he gave his only begotten Son, that whosoever believeth in him should not perish, but have everlasting life.

John 3:18 He that believeth on him is not condemned: but he that believeth not is condemned already, because he hath not believed in the name of the only begotten Son of God.

Heb. 11:17 By faith Abraham, when he was tried, offered up Isaac: and he that had received the promises offered up his only begotten *son*.

1 John 4:9 In this was manifested the love of God toward us, because that God sent his only begotten Son into the world, that we might live through him.

All English translations prior to the King James Version have essentially the same, except the Whittingham (Geneva) New Testament of 1557 inserts "begotten" in Luke 7:12, while Tyndale, quite unexpectedly for his time, *omits* "begotten" in John 3:16 and 18.

This general pattern of translating *monogenes* stems from the Latin Vulgate of Jerome. For the three occurrences in Luke he translated *unicus* "only, only one," while the remaining six cases he translated *unigenitus* "only begotten one." Previous Latin translations had employed *unicus* throughout, but Jerome, strongly influenced by the Nicene Creed (A.D. 325), felt compelled to indicate that the Son, the second person of the Trinity, was begotten (not made or created) by the Father. Isaac, the miraculous child of Sarah's old age, was considered as a type of Christ (Heb. 11:17) and so Jerome translated *unigenitus* "only begotten," even though he knew that Abraham had "begotten" Ishmael earlier. The American Standard Version holds to this same pattern of translation, thereby perpetuating the precedent and thinking of Jerome.

It is now clearly established that *monogenes* (composed of *monos* "alone, only" + *genos* "race, stock, kind") means "the only one of its kind." The Septuagint uses *monogenes* many times for the Hebrew word *yaḥid* "only"; for example, in Judg. 11:34 where Jephthah's daughter is described as "his only child; beside her he had neither son nor daughter." Furthermore, "only begotten" is impossible in Luke 7:12, as all translations (except the Geneva New Testament) recognize, because the widow of Nain did not "beget" her son. Biological science and even Matt. 1:1–16 define *begetting* as strictly a male function—the female "bears, gives birth to."

The Old Testament makes it clear that Abraham "begat" Ishmael thirteen years prior to Isaac, so it is quite unnecessary (even contrary to fact) to insist on reading "only begotten" in Heb. 11:17. The translation "only son" is far better because Isaac, as the "son of promise," was indeed Abraham's "only son" of this kind.

The English translation of the Apostles' Creed begins, "I believe in God the Father Almighty, Maker of heaven and earth: and in Jesus Christ His only [*monogenes*] Son our Lord." Yet there has never been any significant opposition or theological discussion concerning the translation of *monogenes*.

In the light of all these considerations Weymouth, Moffatt, Goodspeed, Charles B. Williams, Phillips, Kingsley Williams, and Revised Standard Version *omit* "begotten" in each instance of *monogenes*. Notwithstanding the omission in John 3:16 Charles B. Williams adds the footnote, "*Only begotten* in Grk." If he actually believed this one wonders why he did not put it into the text of John 3:16 and elsewhere with reference to Christ.

Verkuyl tends to retain the traditional English wording, but a note on John 3:16 reads, "Unique and not as we are His children; His a never begun relationship." His omission of "begotten" in Heb. 11:17 and the translation "such glory as an only son receives from his father" (John 1:14) are intended to distinguish the Incarnation of the Son of God from any human birth, Isaac included.

That there is a qualitative difference between the uniqueness of Jesus and the uniqueness of Jairus' daughter (Luke 8:42), for example, is granted by all, but this assurance is gained from the Biblical context, not the word *monogenes*. For this reason the omission of "begotten" in the modern versions cannot be interpreted as being due to theological bias. The omission stems solely from the linguistic evidence and the resultant desire to eliminate the specific interpretation which Jerome read into the text.

Leviticus 26:30

Sometimes the linguistic information which archaeology contributes is derived from inscribed objects, not from documents. In Chapter 1 we noted how the discovery of little weights (inscribed *pim* or *payim*) helped clarify the meaning of 1 Sam. 13:19-21. Another Hebrew word which formerly caused difficulty is *hamman*, a term which occurs eight times in the Old Testament (Lev. 26:30; 2 Chron. 14:5; 34:4 & 7; Isa. 17:8; 27:9; and Ezek. 6:4 & 6), always in the plural. The King James Version translates the word "images" throughout (except "idols" in 2 Chron. 34:7). The American Standard Version tends to translate "sun-images," while Moffatt prefers "sun-pillars." The American Translation alternates between "sun-images" and "sun-pillars," with the notable exception of Lev. 26:30 where it reads "incense altars." The wisdom of this latter translation (by Theophile J. Meek who did Leviticus) was confirmed when an altar of incense was found in Palmyra of Syria on which was inscribed the word *hamman*. Accordingly, the Revised Standard Version translates "incense altars" throughout (except "altars of incense" in Isa. 17:8).

The Berkeley Version, in very unscholarly fashion, translates "incense altars" in Lev. 26:30; 2 Chron. 14:5; and Ezek. 6:4; "incense stands" in 2 Chron. 34:4 & 7; "sun-images" in Isa. 17:8 and Ezek. 6:6; and "sun-pillars" in Isa. 27:9. In other words, even within Isaiah and Ezekiel the translators were not consistent, let alone all the Old Testament occurrences.

There are still a number of passages in the Hebrew and Greek where the text is clear but the key word (or words) occurs so infrequently in the Bible (in some cases only once) translators are unable to determine with any degree of certainty what the word really means. Due to the lack of enough qualified scholars, many of the inscriptions discovered during the last seventy-five years have not been studied carefully, and some have yet to be read. From these inscriptions (many in languages related to Biblical Hebrew and Greek) and from the linguistic discoveries which will certainly be made in the future will come new meanings for Biblical words, meanings which will reduce the number of difficult passages and give us even more accurate translations.

In the meantime, however, we are ever in debt to the twentieth-century Biblical scholars who have, with few exceptions, provided more accurate, understandable translations of God's Word than our parents or grandparents possessed.

7

Alternative Translations

The text of Matt. 27:65 in the King James Version reads, "Pilate said unto them, Ye have a watch: go your way, make *it* [the sepulchre] as sure as ye can." The text of the American Standard, Weymouth, and Revised Standard Versions, and the footnote of Kingsley Williams translate similarly, "You have a guard," but the text of Kingsley Williams and the footnotes of American Standard, Weymouth, and Revised Standard Versions translate, "Take (Have) a guard." This uncertainty of translation stems from the Greek word *echete* which can mean either the indicative mood (the statement of fact "You have") or the imperative mood (the command "Take" or "Have"). Although American Standard, Weymouth, Revised Standard, and Kingsley Williams did not agree on the interpretation of the Greek word they considered the alternative possibility as having sufficient significance to be given in a footnote.

Validity of Alternative Translations
Some Bible readers feel, however, that alternative translations in the footnotes or margins tend to confuse and to detract from the authority of Scripture. "God has spoken," so they say, "and His word is clear." But this point of view assumes that everywhere the *meaning* of the Hebrew and Greek text is absolutely certain. As much as we wish this were so our study thus far has shown the fallacy of such an assumption.

Over and above ambiguous verb forms such as *echete* are instances in which the Hebrew or Greek text is clear and the meaning of the individual words is certain, but the arrangement or relationship of the various words (known as syntax) is such that translators disagree as to the correct meaning of the text. Because the decision hinges on the interpretation of the translator it is certainly valid to inform the reader of such doubtful passages by giving the alternative possibility in the footnotes.

This procedure is in accord with Protestant tradition where the Scriptures, not the interpreter (whether he is Pope or translator), are considered authoritative. There have always been some Protestants, however, who have opposed the principle of indicating alternative translations. A number of these lived in 1611 and the King James translators, anticipating their objections, defended the use of marginal translations as follows:

> Some peradventure would have no variety of senses to be set in the margin, lest the authority of the Scriptures for deciding of controversies by that show of uncertainty should somewhat be shaken. But we hold their judgment not to be so sound in this point . . . . For as it is a fault of incredulity, to doubt of those things that are evident; so to determine of such things as the Spirit of God hath left (even in the judgment of the judicious) questionable, can be no less than presumption. Therefore as St Augustine saith, that variety of translations is profitable for the finding out of the sense of the Scriptures: so diversity of signification and sense in the margin, where the text is not so clear, must needs do good: yea, is necessary, as we are persuaded.

Unfortunately for the Protestant Church the preface, "The Translators to the Reader" (Appendix C) has been eliminated from most editions of the King James Version printed, especially in the United States, during the last one hundred and fifty years. As a result most readers have been deprived of the wise counsel and instruction concerning alternative translations and other problems, information which the King James translators intended their readers should have.

The hundreds of marginal notes in the 1611 and later editions of the King James Version were also for the instruction and guidance of the readers, but alas, these too have been greatly reduced or entirely omitted in the nineteenth- and twentieth-century editions.

Habakkuk 2:4

An Old Testament illustration of alternative notes is Hab. 2:4. With this verse begins a vision, God's answer to the prophet Habakkuk who in 1:2 complained, "O LORD, how long shall I cry for help, and thou wilt not hear?" The gist of the vision is that the proud, arrogant person (presumably a reference to the Chaldeans = Babylonians) will not be able to continue for long. His soul is not straight or upright, therefore his days are numbered. Verse 2:4 concludes, on the other hand, "the righteous shall live by his faithfulness." The Hebrew word in question, 'emunah, means "faithfulness, steadfastness" for it comes from the verb 'amen "to be steady, firm, trustworthy." The meanings "trust, belief, faith" are implicit because no one is faithful to a cause or person in this life without first having faith and trust. While the King James, American Standard, and Revised Standard Versions have "faith" in the text, the latter two have "faithfulness" in the footnotes.

Moffatt translates, "the good man lasts and lives as he is faithful," while the American Translation reads, "But the righteous lives by reason of his faithfulness." The Berkeley Version, however, returns to the traditional translation, "But the righteous shall live by his faith." A footnote reads, "Some prefer 'faithfulness' to 'faith,' but Paul [Rom. 1:17 and Gal. 3:11] quotes 'faith'; so Heb. 10:38, where only 'faith' would serve."

Regardless of the translation, however, the *primary* emphasis in the passage is on *living a life* characterized by faithfulness (and implicitly by faith) if one is to withstand the persecution and pressures of this earthly journey.

Hebrews 10:38

The author of Hebrews touches on the *same theme* in 10:36: "For you have need of endurance, so that you may do the will of God and receive what is promised." Accordingly, as an illustration of his point he quotes Hab. 2:4 in verse 38 as follows: "But my righteous one shall live by faith." The variation from the Hebrew text of Hab. 2:4 is due to the Septuagint, the source for all the quotations of the Old Testament found in the book of Hebrews. Furthermore, the Berkeley Version to the contrary, the idea of "faithfulness" has as much place (if not more) here than does "faith."

Romans 1:17

In Rom. 1:17 and Gal. 3:11 Paul also quotes (with the exception of the possessive pronoun or adjective "my") the Septuagint of Hab. 2:4, but with a *decidedly different emphasis* from either the prophet Habakkuk or the author of Hebrews. Here Paul is not primarily concerned with the idea of "living by faith(fulness)," but rather with "being made righteous by faith." The King James, American Standard, Weymouth, Moffatt, Verkuyl, and Phillips read in the traditional manner, "The just (righteous) shall live by faith."

On the other hand, in line with Paul's clear teaching, Goodspeed translates the Greek, "The upright will have life because of his faith." Kingsley Williams has, "He that is righteous by faith shall live," while the Revised Standard Version translates similarly, "He who through faith is righteous shall live." The Revised Standard Version also gives the traditional translation in the footnotes, thereby being the only version to indicate an alternative.

John 5:39

Similar to the case of *echete* in Matt. 27:65 is *ereunate* in John 5:39. The word itself can be interpreted with equal justification as the indicative or the imperative. The texts of Weymouth, American Standard, Revised Standard, and Kingsley Williams translate the indicative, "You search the scriptures," while the imperative, "Search the scriptures," is found in the text of the King James Version and the footnotes of the American Standard Version, Weymouth, and Kingsley Williams. Apparently, the King James translators felt sure that the imperative was the correct interpretation of the passage because they inserted no alternative in the margin. Conversely, the Revised Standard Version felt with equal certainty that the indicative form was correct so it listed no footnote.

Matthew 27:54

The passage in Matt. 27:54 is another example where the translations vary in determining whether sufficient doubt exists to warrant a footnote. The King James Version translates:

> Now when the centurion, and they that were with him, watching Jesus, saw the earthquake, and those things that were done, they feared greatly, saying, Truly this was the Son of God.

The text of the American Standard Version also reads, "the Son of God," and Weymouth has the equivalent translation, "God's Son."

But the Greek text has no definite article, therefore the texts of Kingsley Williams and the Revised Standard Version as well as the footnote of the American Standard Version translate, "a son of God." It was Tyndale who first translated using "the," but his text read, "the son of God." The use of "Son" (initial capital) appears first in the

Whittingham (Geneva) New Testament of 1557. The King James translators accepted this translation without question, therefore they did not indicate the alternative in the margin. Note that only the English Revised and American Standard Versions include both interpretations of this passage.

Presumably the translators who supplied the definite article "the" did so in the conviction that the centurion and his soldiers were consciously acknowledging Jesus as the promised Messiah of the God of Israel. While most of the translators who have preferred "a son of God" (following the literal Greek text) would doubt that the Roman soldiers understood the true significance of the drama unfolding before their eyes, they would, on the other hand, readily grant that the centurion and his guard recognized supernatural aspects in the actions of Jesus and in the circumstances surrounding his death.

It is easy to see why some Christians are inclined to believe that the soldiers confessed, "Truly this was the Son of God"—it is what they would have said had they been present at that awesome scene. However, there is no evidence that these soldiers had a personal faith in any way comparable to that which we have in the risen Christ. When we permit the centurion and his guard to speak for themselves in their own terms their testimony is not weakened as some would contend. Rather, their confession ("Truly this was a son of God!") becomes all the more convincing proof of the deity of Christ.

Alternative Translations and the Modern Versions

The foregoing illustrations show the desirability of indicating alternative translations where doubt exists. But in spite of its validity not all the modern English versions have made use of this principle. The American Translation (Goodspeed in the New Testament) has no footnotes at all. With the exception of a few historical notes in an appendix, Phillips also eliminates all notes. Evidently this was done because the translations were intended primarily for private, uninterrupted reading. Moffatt has a few alternative translations, but most of his notes deal with the Hebrew or Greek text. While the Berkeley Version (Verkuyl in the New Testament) has many notes, most of them are commentary on the text. This principle of interpreting for the reader is one which made the Geneva Bible of 1560 and the Scofield Bible of our time so popular, but it runs counter to the principle and practice of traditional Protestantism which has preferred Scriptures without theological notes or comments. Charles B. Williams has numerous footnotes giving a word-for-word translation of the Greek where the English in the text has been expanded or changed, but these are seldom genuine alternative translations.

Only the King James, English Revised, American Standard, Weymouth, Kingsley Williams, and Revised Standard Versions make a practice of indicating alternative translations. Therefore, the careful Bible student will choose one or more of these translations for standard reference.

8

One Word Corresponds to Many

The final consideration of this study, and in some ways the most important, is the matter of equivalence between the meaning of the Hebrew or Greek text and the meaning of the English translation. The primary purpose of every translation should be to convey to the modern reader the same ideas which the author intended his original readers to have. Few would disagree with this statement of purpose, but the problem lies in accomplishing it. What is the surest way of achieving this equivalence of expression?

Word-for-word Translation

According to some scholars the best way to obtain equivalence is a word-for-word or literal translation of the Hebrew and Greek text. This is not a new idea. In fact, the most outstanding example of this type of translation is that made by Aquila around A.D. 125. Aquila, a Greek proselyte (convert) to the Jewish religion, studied under Rabbi Aqiba, the Jewish scholar who attempted to standardize the consonantal Hebrew text. Aquila's earnest desire to produce the most exact Greek translation of the Old Testament (with the intent of supplanting the Septuagint) led him to translate every detail of the Hebrew text, even words or particles which could never be put into Greek in any intelligible form.

Aquila must have prepared a kind of dictionary in which every

Hebrew word had a corresponding Greek word, otherwise it would be difficult to account for the consistent manner in which he always translated the same Hebrew words with the same Greek words. This element of correspondence was carried even to the length of the words, a long Hebrew word having a similarly lengthy Greek word, and if possible the same number of letters. While Aquila's ingenuity demands our respect, it most certainly did not produce an accurate translation. The result was such outrageous Greek no Greek-speaking person could read it with any ease, comprehension, or appreciation.

The most notable examples of word-for-word translation into English are the English Revised Version of 1881 and 1885, and the American Standard Version of 1901. Although the revisers did not go to the extremes of Aquila, they translated with a view to reproducing in English, as far as possible, the word order, idioms, and feeling of the Greek and Hebrew. Their sincerity is expressed by Philip Schaff, an American scholar, who while still working with the Anglo-American Committee which prepared the translations wrote optimistically:

> This providential juncture, the remarkable harmony of the Revisers in the prosecution of their work, and the growing desire of the churches for a timely improvement and rejuvenation of our venerable English Version, justify the expectation of a speedy and general adoption of the New Revision in Great Britain and America.

But his fond hopes of "general adoption" were never realized here or in Great Britain. Charles Spurgeon, the world-famous English preacher, aptly pointed out the reason for this lack of success when he remarked, "Strong in Greek, weak in English." An article in the *Edinburgh Review* of July, 1881, discussed the English Revised Version (favorably in many instances), but concluded, "The revisers were not appointed to prepare an interlinear translation for incompetent school-boys." Yet this very feature explains much of the popularity which the English Revised and American Standard Versions have among beginning students of Hebrew and Greek. This same characteristic has also made these translations valuable for those who (not knowing Hebrew or Greek) wish to do detailed, careful study of the Bible in English.

Genesis 12:14

Following is a word-for-word study of the various translations as contrasted with the exact units and word order of the Hebrew text in Gen. 12:14:

Masoretic text	And it was	as to go Abram
King James	And it came to pass, that, when	Abram was come
American Standard	And it came to pass, that, when	Abram was come
Moffatt		When Abram entered
American Translation		When Abram arrived
Revised Standard		When Abram entered
Berkeley Version		As soon as Abram entered

to Egypt and saw the Egyptians	the woman for	
into Egypt,	the Egyptians beheld the woman that	
into Egypt,	the Egyptians beheld the woman that	
Egypt,	the Egyptians did notice that the woman	
in Egypt,	the Egyptians saw that the woman	
Egypt,	the Egyptians saw that the woman	
Egypt,	the Egyptians noticed how rarely beautiful	

beautiful she very.
she *was* very fair.
she was very fair.
was very handsome.
was very beautiful.
was very beautiful.
a woman she was.

It should be clear that so-called accuracy or exactness of translation is at best a relative matter, for even the King James and American Standard Versions deviate considerably from the exact Hebrew order.

There are four major problems of equivalence in this short verse. The first is the idiom "And it was," commonly translated "And it came to pass" in the older English versions. English, however, does not have this idiom. It is unnecessary to say, "And it came to pass when I went to the store I bought some groceries." We say in a direct manner, "When I went to the store I bought some groceries." Accordingly, Moffatt, American Translation, Revised Standard, and Berkeley Versions omit the Hebrew expression in their translations where it is pointless in our English idiom. The King James and American Standard Versions preserve some of the Hebrew flavor by retaining the idiomatic expression, but it certainly is not required by any principle of language equivalence.

The second expression, "as to go Abram," involves two idioms. The normal word order in Hebrew has the subject after the verb form, but all the English translations put "Abram" before the verb. Furthermore,

English does not use "as" with the infinitive, so this very common Hebrew idiom must be put into its English equivalent, normally an adverbial clause beginning with "when" or "while." The third expression, "saw the Egyptians," is another example of the verb preceding the subject.

The fourth problem of equivalence is the expression "beautiful she very." Hebrew prefers to put the adverb last. Moreover, a very common practice in Hebrew was the omission of the verb "to be," but in English idiom the sentence is incomplete without saying "she was very beautiful." When the reader came to this Hebrew idiom it can be said that he supplied the verb mentally, so actually it is a part of the Hebrew even though it is not written in the text. The King James Version, in its attempt to show the words which were not written in Hebrew, put "was" in italic letters, but observe that the American Standard Version did not do so, even though it generally employed italics.

Thus, this short verse illustrates how even the most literal translations have had to rearrange the idiomatic units into their nearest English equivalents.

Luke 12:20

An excellent New Testament example for comparative study is Luke 12:20.

Greek text	Said but to him the God,	Fool,
King James	But God said unto him,	*Thou* fool,
American Standard	But God said unto him,	Thou foolish one,
Weymouth	But God said to him,	Foolish man,
Moffatt	But God said to him,	Foolish man,
Goodspeed	But God said to him,	You fool!
Charles Williams	But God said to him,	You fool!
Verkuyl	But God said to him,	Simpleton,
Revised Standard	But God said to him,	Fool!
Kingsley Williams	But God said to him,	Fool,
Phillips	But God said to him,	You fool,

this the night the soul of you	they require from you.
this night thy soul	shall be required of thee.
this night is thy soul	required of thee.
this night your life	is demanded from you.
this very night your soul	is required from you.
This very night your soul	will be demanded of you.
This very night your soul	is to be demanded of you.

this	night your soul	will be demanded of you.
This	night your soul	is required of you.
this very night your soul		will be demanded of you.
this very night		you will be asked for your soul!

The word order of this passage is quite normal for the Greek language, but it varies so from the English order the only plausible method of translating is to work with equivalent units.

In the first unit, "Said but to him the God," there are three major idioms: (1) the Greek word translated "but" cannot appear at the beginning of a sentence or clause, so it has to come into the sentence as the second or third word; (2) the subject of the sentence appears after the object; and (3) "God" has the definite article in Greek. All these are changed into normal English idiom by translating, "But God said to him."

In the second unit, "this the night the soul of you," there are two more idioms: (1) Greek uses the definite article with a noun when it is modified by "this"; and (2) Greek also tends to show possession with such expressions as "of you," whereas we would employ the possessive pronoun "your."

The final idiom of this passage, "they require from you," employs the indefinite subject "they." There is nothing in the preceding verse or verses to tell the reader who "they" are. This idiom is similar to the French *on dit* "one says," where there is no attempt to explain who "one" is. In English, however, we tend to use the passive voice, so for the French idiom we translate "it is said," and in Luke 12:20 the Greek idiom becomes "your soul is (will be) required of you."

Job 17:3

In addition to grammatical idioms there are many customs mentioned in the Bible which need to be put into equivalent terms if the reader is to get the true meaning of the passage. An excellent example is Job 17:3 which the King James Version translates, "Lay down now, put me in a surety with thee; who *is* he *that* will strike hands with me?"

Job's friends have refused to accept his pleas of innocency, so Job turns to God and requests that a bond or guarantee be posted with God himself until Job proves his case. Then Job, realizing the presumption of such a request, inquires, "Who will strike hands with me?" The expression "striking hands" referred to the ancient custom in which a person interceded in behalf of another by providing bail until a trial could be arranged. But this idea is discernible neither in the King James Version, nor the American Standard Version. Moffatt translates the last part of the verse, "who else would undertake my cause against thee," while the Berkeley Version retains "who will strike hands with me?" The Revised Standard Version translates concisely, "Lay down a pledge for me with thyself; who is there that will give surety for me?"

Luke 7:36–37

The problem of equivalence is well illustrated in Luke 7:36–37 which the King James Version translates as follows:

36 And one of the Pharisees desired him that he would eat with him. And he went into the Pharisee's house, and sat down to meat.

37 And, behold, a woman in the city, which was a sinner, when she knew that *Jesus* sat at meat in the Pharisee's house, brought an alabaster box of ointment.

Back of the expression "sat down to meat" (verse 36) is the Greek verb *kataklino* and back of "sat at meat" (verse 37) is the verb *katakeimai*. Both of these verbs have the basic meaning "to recline, lie down." They were used in this passage because the common manner for eating a meal was to recline on a couch or mat, resting on one elbow. But this is not done normally in our culture, so how is it to be expressed in equivalent English terms?

The basic elements of any custom and practice are *form* and *function*. The form of this old custom was "reclining on a couch," but the function was "eating." When we perform the function of "eating" we are not in the "reclining" position or form. An elementary principle in translation is to select the closest *functional* equivalent where the form is different. In this case, because we do not "recline" while eating we should translate according to the form or position we take while "eating," that is, "sitting down at the table," or "taking our place at the table."

The King James and American Standard Versions translate "sat down" in verse 36, although they keep the archaic expression "to meat." Strangely enough, Weymouth, Moffatt, and Verkuyl translate, "reclined at (the dinner) table." While this preserves some of the Greek flavor it also has the disadvantage of suggesting (to readers who do not understand ancient customs) that Jesus was slouching on the dinner table like some modern boy who is too tired to eat his meal. Goodspeed, Charles B. Williams, Kingsley Williams, and Phillips translate wisely, "took his place at (the) table," while the Revised Standard Version reads similarly, "sat at table."

Matthew 23: 27

Another aspect of determining equivalence in meaning is illustrated by Matt. 23:27. The King James Version reads:

27 Woe unto you, scribes and Pharisees, hypocrites! for ye are like unto whited sepulchres, which indeed appear beautiful outward, but are within full of dead *men's* bones, and of all uncleanness.

Jesus' comment about "whited sepulchres" was a reference to the Jewish practice of brightening up the front of the burial places just before Passover. This was done to prevent anyone from accidentally coming close enough to be defiled or made unclean, thereby disqualifying him from participation in the very important Feast of Passover.

A secondary result of this custom was the improved appearance of these burial places, and it was this feature which permitted Jesus to liken the scribes and Pharisees to them. The form or manner of this brightening-up process was "whitewashing." Although we do not use "whitewash" with the function or purpose of warning people to stay away from burial places, we can understand the manner or form of the custom because most of us have seen a whitewashed fence or milkshed "down on the farm." For this reason practically all the versions from Weymouth on have translated "whitewashed" in place of the archaic "whited."

The other part of the problem has to do with "sepulchres." The normal burial place in Jesus' day was a chamber or vault. Some were cut into the side of a hill or mound, while others were underground, but generally they were entered through a doorway. On the other hand, the normal burial in our time consists of interment in a grave which has been dug vertically into the ground. If we had the custom in our culture of warning people away from burial places it would be wise to translate "whitewashed graves," as is done in Kingsley Williams, but this is not the case.

The best solution, therefore, is to supply a modern word for the archaic word "sepulchre," thereby giving the reader the idea of the ancient type of burial place. In other words, because the function of the ancient custom is lacking today we attempt to retain the form of the object Jesus was discussing. Most everyone has seen a vault or tomb in a mausoleum, and many have visited or seen pictures of "The Tomb of the Unknown Soldier" (known now as "Tomb of the Unknowns") in Arlington Cemetery, Washington, D.C. Therefore, the most appropriate modern English equivalent is "tomb," the reading found in the majority of the modern versions.

Although these illustrations point up some of the complexity in trying to find the nearest equivalent English expression, it should be apparent that there is no other way of producing a good, readable, translation which communicates the meaning of the original writings.

Origin of the Use of Italics

A very important matter closely related to problems of equivalence is the use of italics by the King James, English Revised, and American Standard Versions to indicate those words (missing in the Hebrew or Greek text) which have been added to make the translation conform to English idiom.

In modern English usage, however, italics indicate emphasis. With respect to the old prophet of Bethel, 1 Kings 13:27 states, according to the King James Version, "And he spake to his sons, saying, Saddle me the ass. And they saddled *him.*" Public reading with stress on "him" would certainly result in a convulsion of laughter. Notwithstanding this ambiguous use of italics, however, there are many who feel deeply that italics should be a part of every translation. Accordingly, the modern versions have come in for some severe criticism in certain circles within the Protestant Church.

The deep feeling with which some people contend for the use of italics gives the impression that the idea originated with the New Testament writers or some early Church Father, but this is far from the truth. Much of what we find in the Gospels was given first in Aramaic, so the original Gospels (written in Greek) were largely translation, yet there is no evidence whatsoever that the New Testament writers were concerned to indicate which Greek words came from the literal Aramaic source and which did not.

The idea of indicating in some special way words which were not in the original languages is *relatively new.* The man whom we have to thank for all of this is Sebastian Munster. In his Latin version of the Old Testament, published in 1534, the inserted words were put in small roman type in contrast to the large black letters of the words which were based on the Hebrew. This novel idea was adopted by the Great Bible of 1539, but it was modified so as to point out only those words which had been added on the basis of the Latin: for example, Matt. 25:1 where "and the bride" was added at the end of the verse in small letters to show that it came from the Latin, not the Greek.

Theodore Beza's Latin New Testament of 1556 and Whittingham's English New Testament of 1557 returned to Munster's original idea of indicating in small letters all the English words not based on some

Hebrew or Greek words in the manuscripts of that time. This practice was taken up by the Geneva Bible of 1560 and the Bishops' Bible of 1568, and eventually it appeared in the 1611 editions of the King James Version (Fig. 12). In the 1612 edition of the King James Version, however, the regular text was put into roman type instead of the large black letters so common to all the earlier editions of the English Bible. Because this new type was fairly close in appearance to the inserted words in the previous editions it was decided to put these additional words in italics (letters sloping up toward the right—see Fig. 13), thereby setting them off more clearly from the regular text. So it was that Munster's original idea came, after seventy-eight years, to be known as the "use of italics."

Impracticality of Using Italics

While the theory of italics sounds very plausible, it is impossible to carry it out in a consistent, enlightening manner. The King James translators attempted to do so, but the two editions of 1611 have hundreds of examples of faulty and inconsistent italics. For example, Lev. 11:20 has the expression "upon all four," but the identical Hebrew expression in verses 21, 27, and 42 is translated, "upon *all* four." This inconsistency within the same chapter was corrected in many cases by the Cambridge editions of the King James Version which were printed in 1629 and 1638. Yet, in spite of their good motives, the editors introduced almost as many inconsistencies as they eliminated. In Deut. 2:4 the 1629 edition was revised to read, "Ye *are* to pass," but it failed to change "Thou art to pass" in verse 2:18 where "art" should be in italics. The 1638 edition changed Deut. 2:23 to read, "*even* unto Azzah," but in verse 22 (just two lines above) it left "even unto this day" unchanged although "even" is not in the Hebrew in either verse.

Italics and the Paris Edition

From the standpoint of italics the next important edition of the King James Version was the two-volume Cambridge edition of 1762. The anonymous editor of these volumes was Dr. Thomas Paris, a Fellow of Trinity College, Cambridge University. He did a great amount of work and improved the general accuracy of the italics, but besides overlooking some errors already in the text, he too made a few errors.

A tricky example is found in Eccles. 7:1 where the Masoretic text reads literally, "Good name from oil good." The meaning of the Hebrew idiom is seen more clearly by rephrasing it to read, "A name is good from good oil," supplying the verb "is." The King James translators rendered the idiomatic expression "good from" as "better than," and translated "good oil" as "precious ointment." Therefore, at this stage the translation read, "A name *is* better than precious ointment." But this was not true of a "bad" name, so the finished translation in the 1611 editions was, "A *good* name *is* better than precious ointment." Dr. Paris, in an unguarded moment, changed "good" from italic letters to regular type, thus originating an error which persists in practically all of the King James editions today. The American Standard Version reads correctly, "A *good* name is better than precious oil."

Italics and the Blayney Edition

In 1769 another edition of the King James Version appeared, this one published by the Clarendon Press of Oxford University. The editor, Dr. Benjamin Blayney, in a letter to his superiors, mentions the many corrections in italics made by Dr. Paris, but adds, "there still remained many necessary alterations, which escaped the Doctor's notice." However, the day of perfection did not arrive with Blayney either. He missed the grave mistake of Paris in Eccles. 7:1 and made (or possibly some of his assistants) some changes which resulted in further inconsistencies. In Luke 17:29 he revised the text to read, "*them* all," but the same Greek word, just two verses earlier, appears as "them all," an inconsistency which exists in most of the King James editions today.

In spite of all the tremendous effort to be supremely accurate in the matter of italics there are still a number of examples of erroneous italics, or lack of them, which were present in the 1611 editions and still remain today. Heb. 3:3 reads "this *man*," but the same Greek word in Heb. 8:3 is rendered "this man." In Ezek. 20:41 the King James Version reads, "I will accept you with your sweet savor," but while "your" is an addition not found in any Hebrew manuscript it has never been in italics in any of the standard editions of the King James Version. The American Standard Version reads, "As a sweet savor will I accept you," and the Revised Standard Version has, "As a pleasing odor I will accept you."

Validity of Using Italics

The only possible conclusion from this evidence is that expressed by F. H. A. Scrivener:

The changes introduced from time to time have been too unsystematic, too much the work of the moment, executed by too many hands, and on too unsettled principles, to hold out against hostile, or even against friendly criticism.

But beyond the question of the inaccurate use of italics in the King James Version must be considered their validity—do they actually achieve the purpose for which they were originally intended? There are undoubtedly passages of theological importance where the reader should be informed that the translation involves words not in the Hebrew or Greek, but these are relatively few. Earlier in the chapter attention was called to the very common Hebrew idiom in which the verb "to be" is understood, but not written. These implied forms the King James Version puts in italics, and as a result there is hardly a page without one or more examples of italics used in this way. These plus all the other uses of italics for words which must be supplied to translate the Hebrew idioms adequately mean that from 75 per cent to 90 per cent of the italics in the King James Version are worthless. With such a large proportion of irrelevant italics it is little wonder that the reader cannot determine when they point out difficult passages in which theological issues are at stake.

Italics and the American Standard Version

While the American Standard Version eliminates a great many unnecessary italics, it too has a number of inconsistencies which are quite misleading for the reader. In 2 Chron. 2:3 it reads with the King James Version, "As thou didst deal with David my father, and didst send him cedars to build him a house to dwell therein, *even so deal with me.*" The words in italics are not in the Masoretic text, but they must be supplied to complete the meaning of the Hebrew, so there is no point in putting them in italics. This picayunish attention to the letter of the text is contrary to the spirit and meaning of the Hebrew passage. Furthermore, it often causes the reader to draw wrong inferences from the evidence.

Exod. 19:12 has a good example of misleading italics which fail to convey the whole truth to the reader. The King James Version translates:

12 And thou shalt set bounds unto the people round about, saying, Take heed to yourselves, *that ye go not* up into the mount, or touch the border of it: whosoever toucheth the mount shall be surely put to death.

In the middle of the verse the Masoretic text reads, "Take heed to yourselves to go up into the mountain," but with the impending threat of death it is impossible to interpret the Hebrew as a command to "go up into the mountain." If this Hebrew idiom were expressed in the nearest English equivalent it would read, "Beware of going into the mountain." But another means of expressing this idea would be to translate, "Take care (heed) not to go into the mountain." Thus, in English idiom "Beware of" (while lacking the word "not") is equivalent to "Take care not." In like fashion the negative "not" is just as much a part of the Hebrew idiom as if it were written out in the text. Therefore, to put the additional English words in italics is to confuse and mislead the reader. The American Standard Version wisely omitted the use of italics in this verse.

Italics and the Modern Versions

In the process of rendering the Hebrew or Greek into the nearest English equivalent there are occasions when it is necessary to inform the reader of inserted words. A case in point is Prov. 9:9 where the Masoretic text (in poetic, abbreviated form) reads, "Give to wise and he shall be wise still." But give what? The Hebrew does not answer this question, so the translator must make an intelligent guess from the context. The King James Version translates, "Give *instruction* to a wise *man*, and he will be yet wiser." The American Standard Version concurred in this interpretation, but it made one change in italics. Because "man" was implied in the Hebrew idiom, just as in English we imply "ones" or "people" when we speak of "the wise," the italics were removed.

The Revised Standard Version translates this verse, "Give instruction to a wise man, and he will be still wiser." A footnote on "instruction" reads, "Heb lacks *instruction*." This is one of many such notes in the Revised Standard Version which achieve, in a different way, the same result as that accomplished by italics in the older versions. For this reason there can be no valid objection to the lack of italics in the Revised Standard Version.

The Berkeley Version translates, "Inform a wise man and he will become yet wiser," but while "Inform" is equivalent to "Give instruction" there is no footnote to show the addition. In the case of the modern versions which have neither italics nor footnotes there are, obviously, no means of discerning difficult passages where the translation has elements of uncertainty, and so the reader must rely solely on the judgment and interpretation of the translator.

Equivalence and Public Worship

In Chapter 5 consideration was given to the important role which

English style plays in a readable translation. Closely related to the element of style is this extremely vital matter of the nearest English equivalent. If the ideas of the Hebrew and Greek text are put into corresponding words in English a direct, forceful style will be inevitable. While this factor of clarity is always desirable, it is absolutely indispensable for effective reading in public worship. On this point, Walter R. Bowie, one of the New Testament Committee of the Revised Standard Version, wrote:

If a person is sitting down with the Bible in his hand, able to look again at any phrase which does not convey its meaning at the first glance, able indeed to take as much time as he chooses whenever he chooses, then he can be fairly sure to get the meaning of a passage even if its style is not that to which he is instinctively accustomed. But when the Scriptures are read aloud in Church, there is no such chance for men and women in the congregation to stop the reading in order to consider it again. They must catch the sense of it the first time, or miss it altogether. Therefore, in this translation, it has been a constant purpose to make every word and sentence clear, to avoid involved constructions, and to make the current of the central thought flow in such a straight, sure channel that the minds of listeners will be carried forward unmistakably and not dropped into verbal whirlpools by the way.

This same concern for clarity and understandability was shared by the King James translators, for from the outset of their labors they knew that their translation was to replace the Bishops' Bible as the pulpit Bible in the cathedrals and churches of England. Miles Smith, speaking for the translators, wrote in the preface:

Translation it is that openeth the window, to let in the light; that breaketh the shell, that we may eat the kernel; that putteth aside the curtain, that we may look into the most holy place; that removeth the cover of the well, that we may come by the water; even as Jacob rolled away the stone from the mouth of the well, by which means the flocks of Laban were watered.

The translators endeavored to achieve this ideal, but they recognized, nevertheless, deficiencies in their work, and so they considered themselves "greater in other men's eyes than in their own." Yet, these humble men showed rare wisdom and common sense, consulting all the means at their disposal in order that they might make "out of many good" translations "one principal good one." There are many today who admire and even venerate the King James Version and yet, in spite of all the advantages which three and a half centuries have afforded us, do not comprehend with as much insight and clearness of vision as the King James translators did the basic essentials of a good translation. Generally speaking, modern translators, learning from the experience of their predecessors, have done essentially what the King James translators themselves would have done had they been alive and commissioned anew to make a translation for the English-speaking Protestant Church.

Translation and Evangelical Zeal

The increasing number of modern versions has been considered by some to be divisive and detrimental to the total impact and witness of the Church. On the contrary, this multiplicity of translations is a healthy sign which should be welcomed by all. The study of Church History reveals a definite correlation between Bible translating and the spiritual vigor of the Church. When the Church is awake to its mission and actively engaged in this task, at home and abroad, there is a great deal of translation going on. So in our time the variety of translations indicates an increased interest in the Written Word. While some versions seem to have greater appeal, the others have their following as well. In fact, God has been pleased to use all of the translations, both old and new, for his glory.

For this reason it is unwise, indeed impossible, to dictate which version a person should read. The King James Version with all of its defects is essentially a good translation, and, for those who understand it, it still speaks as the Word of God. This is equally true for those who are used to the American Standard Version with its artificial style and archaic language. But for the vast majority of English-speaking people only a modern version will convey the truth as it ought to be.

While a number of these twentieth-century translations are suitable for private reading (where the chief purpose is to meditate and to let the Bible speak for itself), most readers will want to choose one good, all-purpose version for close study and reference. This translation, if it is to be the best, should be one which by means of a direct, simple style of current English reproduces in the nearest equivalent terms the message of the best Hebrew and Greek texts. It should utilize the latest linguistic and philological evidence, and also indicate by footnotes those difficult passages which have either a corrected reading or an alternative translation.

That we can have translations of this caliber is possible only because we are debtors to the past. Many "others have labored" faithfully (copying, collecting, correcting, and translating the Hebrew and Greek texts), and we "have entered into their labors." While knowledge of how we got our Bible should bring forth expressions of thankfulness to God for his care and good providence in seeing that the torch of truth has been passed on from generation to generation, it should also humble us with the realization that from him "to whom much is given, much will be required."

Paul, the greatest of the New Testament apostles, said of the Old Testament, "whatever was written in former days was written for our instruction, that by steadfastness and by the encouragement of the scriptures we might have hope." This, we affirm, is all the more true of the New Testament. Therefore, in this day of disillusionment and crumbling of false foundations we should ever be grateful to those who have put God's Word in a form which speaks forth with such self-authenticating authority. For now the spiritually hungry and thirsty, "having no hope and without God in the world," may also come to rejoice "in hope of eternal life."

A Chronology of Representative English Translations from Wyclif to the Present

Date	Translation
1382	Wyclif Bible
1525	Tyndale New Testament
1531	Tyndale Pentateuch and Jonah
1535	Coverdale Bible
1537	Matthew Bible
1539	Great (Cranmer) Bible
1557	Whittingham New Testament
1560	Geneva Bible (Whittingham as New Testament)
1568	Bishops' Bible
1582	Rheims New Testament
1609	Douay Bible (Rheims as New Testament)
1611	King James Version
1755	John Wesley New Testament
1881	English Revised Version New Testament
1885	English Revised Version Old Testament
1901	American Standard Version
1901	The Twentieth Century New Testament
1903	Richard Weymouth New Testament
1913	James Moffatt New Testament
1917	Jewish Publication Society Old Testament
1923	Edgar Goodspeed New Testament
1924	James Moffatt Old Testament
1924	Helen Montgomery (Centenary) New Testament
1927	An American Translation (Goodspeed as New Testament)
1935	Westminster New Testament
1937	Charles B. Williams New Testament
1941	Confraternity New Testament
1944	Ronald Knox New Testament
1945	Gerrit Verkuyl (Berkeley) New Testament
1946	Revised Standard Version New Testament
1947	J. B. Phillips: Letters to Young Churches (Romans through Jude)

1948   Ronald Knox Old Testament: Volume 1 (Genesis through Esther)
1949   C. Kingsley Williams New Testament
1950   Ronald Knox Old Testament: Volume 2 (Job through Maccabees)
1952   E. V. Rieu: The Gospels
1952   J. B. Phillips: The Gospels
1952   Confraternity Old Testament: Volume 1 (Genesis through Ruth)
1952   Revised Standard Version Old Testament
1954   James Kleist: The Gospels
         Joseph Lilly: Acts of the Apostles, Epistles, and Apocalypse
1955   Confraternity Old Testament: Volume 3 (Job through Sirach)
1955   J. B. Phillips: Acts of the Apostles
1956   Kenneth S. Wuest: Expanded Translation, Volume 1, The Gospels
1957   J. B. Phillips: Revelation
1958   Frances E. Siewert: Amplified New Testament
1958   Kenneth S. Wuest: Expanded Translation, Volume 2, Acts through Ephesians
1959   Berkeley Version (Verkuyl as New Testament)
1960   Kenneth S. Wuest: Expanded Translation, Volume 3, Philippians through Revelation

1960   New American Standard Gospel of John
1961   Confraternity Old Testament: Volume 4 (Isaiah through Malachi)
1961   The New English Bible New Testament
1961   The Twentieth Century New Testament (reprint of 1904 edition)
1961   New World Translation of the Bible (revised edition)
1962   New American Standard Gospels (Matthew through John)
1962   Amplified Old Testament: Part 2 (Job through Malachi)
1963   New Jewish Publication Society Old Testament: First Section— The Torah: The Five Books of Moses
1963   J. Wash Watts: A Distinctive Translation of Genesis
1963   J. B. Phillips: Four Prophets (Amos Hosea, Isaiah, and Micah)
1963   C. Kingsley Williams. The New Testament in Plain English (reprint)
1963   New American Standard Bible — New Testament
1964   Amplified Old Testament: Part 1 (Genesis through Esther)

"W. T. To the Reader"
Tyndale's Story of His Translation

(the preface to Tyndale's translation of Genesis in his Pentateuch printed in 1530)

When I had translated the newe testament, I added a pistle vnto the latter ende, In which I desyred them that were learned to amend [it] if ought were founde amysse. But oure malicious and wylye hyprocrytes which are so stubburne and hard herted in their weked abhominacions that it is not possible for them to amend any thinge at all (as we see by dayly experience when their both lyvinges and doinges are rebuked with the trouth) saye, some of them that it is impossible to translate the scripture in to English, some that it is not lawfull for the laye people to have it in their mother tonge, some that it wold make them all heretykes, as it wold no doute from many thinges which they of longe tyme haue falsely taught, and that is the whole cause wherfore they forbyd it, though they other clokes pretende. And some or rather every one, saye that it wold make them ryse ageynst the kinge, whom they them selves (vnto their damnatyon) never yet obeyed. And leste the temporall rulars shuld see their falsehod, if the scripture cam to light, causeth them so to lye.

And as for my translation in which they afferme vnto the laye people (as I haue hearde saye) to be I wotte not how many thousande heresyes, so that it can not be mended or correcte, they haue yet taken so greate payne to examyne it, and to compare it vnto that they wold fayne haue it and to their awne imaginations and iugglinge termes, and to haue some what to rayle at, and vnder that cloke to blaspheme the treuth, that they myght with as little laboure (as I suppose) haue translated the moste parte of the bible. For they which in tymes paste were wont to loke on no more scripture then they founde in their duns [the commentaries of Duns Scotus] or soch like develysh doctryne, haue yet now so narowlye loked on my translatyon, that there is not so much as one I therin if it lacke a tytle over his hed, but they haue noted it, and nombre it vnto the ignorant people for an heresy. Fynallye in this they be all agreed, to dryve you from the knowledge of the scripture, and that ye shall not haue the texte therof in the mother tonge, and to kepe the world styll in darkenesse, to thentent they might sitt in the consciences of the people, thorow vayne superstition and false doctrine, to satisfye their fylthy lustes their proude ambition, and vnsatiable couetuousnes, and to exalte their awne honoure aboue kinge & emperoure, yee and aboue god him silfe.

A thousand bokes had they lever to be put forth agenste their abhominable doynges and doctrine, then that the scripture shulde come to light. For as longe as they may kepe that doune, they will so darken the ryght way with the miste of their sophistrye, and so tangle them that ether rebuke or despyse their abhominations with argumentes of philosophye and with wordly [i.e worldly] symylitudes and apparent reasons of naturall wisdom. And with wrestinge the scripture vnto their awne purpose clene contrarye vnto the processe, order and meaninge of the texte, and so delude them in descantynge vppon it with alligoryes, and amase them expoundinge it in manye senses before the vnlerned laye people (when it hath but one symple litterall sense whose light the owles can not abyde) that though thou feale in thyne harte and arte sure how that all is false that they saye, yet coudeste thou not solve their sotle rydles.

Which thinge onlye moved me to translate the new testament. Because I had perceaved by experyence, how that it was impossible to stablysh the laye people in any truth, except the scripture were playnly layde before their eyes in their mother tonge, that they might se the processe, ordre and meaninge of the texte: for els what so ever truth is taught them, these ennymyes of all truth qwench it ageyne, partly with the smoke of their bottomlesse pytte wherof thou readest apocalipsis ix. that is, with apparent reasons of sophistrye and traditions of their awne makynge, founded with out grounde of scripture, and partly in iugglinge with the texte, expoundinge it in soch a sense as is impossible to gether of the texte, if thou see the processe ordre and meaninge thereof.

And even in the bisshope of londons house I entended to have done it. For when I was so turmoyled in the contre where I was that I coude no lenger there dwell (the processe wherof were to longe here to reherce) I this wyse thought in my silfe, this I suffre because the prestes of the contre be vnlerned, as god it knoweth there are a full ignorant sorte which haue sene no more latyn then that they read in their portesses [breviaries or prayers for the canonical hours] and missales which yet many of them can scacely read (except it be Albertus [i.e. Albertus Magnus] de secretis mulierum in which yet, though they be neuer so soryly lerned, they pore day and night and make notes therin and all to teach the mydwyves as they say, and linwood [William Lyndewode's *Prouinciale,* a digest of English canon law written in 1433] a boke of constitutions to gether tithes, mortuaryes [customary gifts claimed from the heirs of dead parishioners], offeringes, customs, and other pillage, which they calle, not theirs, but godes parte and the deuty of holye chirch, to discharge their consciences with all: for they are bound that they shall not dimynysh, but encreace all thinge vnto the vttmost of their powers) and therfore (because they are thus vnlerned thought I) when they come to gedder to the alehouse, which is their preachinge place, they afferme that my sainges are heresy. And besydes that they adde to of thir awne heddes which I never spake, as the maner is to prolonge the tale to shorte the tyme with all, and accuse me secretly to the chauncelare [i.e. the Bishop's Chancellor of the diocese] and other bishopes officers, And in deade when I cam before the chauncelare, he thretened me grevously, and revyled me and rated me as though I had bene a dogge, and layd to my charge wherof there coude be none accuser brought forth (as their maner is not to bringe forth the accuser) and yet all the prestes of the contre were that same day there. As I this thought the bishope of London came to my remembrance whome Erasmus (whose tonge maketh of litle gnattes greate elephantes and lifteth vpp above the starres whosoever geveth him a little exhibition) prayseth excedingly amonge other in his annotatyons on the new testament for his great learninge. Then thought I, if I might come to this mannes service, I were happye. And so I gate me to london, and thorow the accoyntaunce of my master came to sir harry gilford the kinges graces countroller, and brought him an oration of Isocrates which I had translated out of greke in to English, and desyred him to speake vnto my lorde of london for me, which he also did as he shewed me, and willed me to write a pistle to my lorde,

and to goo to him my silf which I also did, and delivered my pistle to
a servant of his awne, one Wyllyam hebilthwayte, a man of myne old
accoyntaunce. But god which knoweth what is within hypocrites, sawe
that I was begyled, and that that councell was not the nexte way
vnto my purpose. And therfore he gate me no favoure in my lordes
sight.

Wherevppon my lorde answered me, his house was full, he had mo
then he coude well finde, and advised me to seke in london, wher he
sayd I coude not lacke a service. And so in london I abode almoste an
yere, and marked the course of the worlde, and herde oure pratars, I
wold say oure preachers how they bosted them selves and their hye
authorite, and beheld the pompe of oure prelates and how besyed they
were as they yet are, to'set peace and vnite in the worlde (though it
be not possible for them that walke in darknesse to contue longe in
peace, for they can not but ether stomble or dash them selves at one
thinge or another that shall clene vnquyet all togedder) and sawe
thinges wherof I deferre to speak at this tyme, and vnderstode at the
laste not only that there was no rowme in my lorde of londons palace to
translate the new testament, but also that there was no place to do it
in all englonde, as experience doth now openly declare.

Vnder what maner therfore shuld I now sumbitte this boke to be
corrected and amended of them, which can suffer nothinge to be well?
Or what protestacyon shuld I make in soch a matter vnto oure prelates
those stubburne Nimrothes which so mightely fight agenste god and
resiste his holy spirite, enforceynge with all crafte and sotelte to
qwench the light of the everlastinge testament, promyses, and apoynte-
mente made betwene god and vs: and heapinge the firce wrath of
god vppon all princes and rulars, mockinge them with false fayned
names of hypocryse, and servinge their lustes at all poyntes, and dis-
pensinge with them even of the very lawes of god, of which Christe
him silf testifieth, Mathew v. that not so moch as one tittle therof maye
perish or be broken. And of which the prophete sayth Psalme cxviij.
Thou hast commaunded thy lawes to be kepte meod, that is in hebrew
excedingly, with all diligence, mighte and power, and haue made them
so mad with their iugglinge charmes and crafty persuasions that they
thinke it full satisfaction for all their weked lyvinge, to torment soch as
tell them trouth, and to borne the worde of their soules helth and sle
whosoever beleve theron.

Not withstondinge yet I submytte this boke and all other that I have
other made or translated, or shall in tyme to come (if it be goddes will

that I shall further laboure in his hervest) vnto all them that submytte themselues vnto the worde of god, to be corrected of them, yee and moreover to be disalowed & also burnte, if it seme worthy when they have examyned it wyth the hebrue, so that they first put forth of their awne translatinge a nother that is more correcte.

"The Translators to the Reader"
Preface to the King James Version

(the text, in more modernized spelling, from Cambridge
University Edition, 1950, with explanatory notes
in brackets added by the author of the book)

The best things have been calumniated
Zeal to promote the common good, whether it be by devising any
thing ourselves, or revising that which hath been laboured by others,
deserveth certainly much respect and esteem, but yet findeth but cold
entertainment in the world. It is welcomed with suspicion instead of
love, and with emulation instead of thanks: and if there be any hole
left for cavil to enter, (and cavil, if it do not find an hole, will make
one) it is sure to be misconstrued, and in danger to be condemned.
This will easily be granted by as many as know story [history], or have
any experience. For was there ever any thing projected, that savoured
any way of newness or renewing, but the same endured many a storm
of gainsaying or opposition? A man would think that civility, wholesome laws, learning and eloquence, synods, and Church-maintenance,
(that we speak of no more things of this kind) should be as safe as a
sanctuary, and out of shot, as they say, that no man would lift up the
heel, no, nor dog move his tongue against the motioners of them. For
by the first we are distinguished from brute beasts led with sensuality:
by the second we are bridled and restrained from outrageous behaviour,

and from doing of injuries, whether by fraud or by violence: by the third we are enabled to inform and reform others by the light and feeling that we have attained unto ourselves: briefly, by the fourth, being brought, together to a parley face to face, we sooner compose our differences, than by writings, which are endless: and lastly, that the Church be sufficiently provided for is so agreeable to good reason and conscience, that those mothers are holden to be less cruel, that kill their children as soon as they are born, than those nursing fathers and mothers (wheresoever they be) that withdraw from them who hang upon their breasts (and upon whose breasts again themselves do hang to receive the spiritual and sincere milk of the word) livelihood and support fit for their estates. Thus it is apparent, that these things which we speak of are of most necessary use, and therefore that none, either without absurdity can speak against them, or without note of wickedness can spurn against them.

Yet for all that, the learned know that certain worthy men have been brought to untimely death for none other fault, but for seeking to reduce their countrymen to good order and discipline: And that in some Commonweals it was made a capital crime, once to motion the making of a new law for the abrogating of an old, though the same were most pernicious: And that certain, which would be counted pillars of the State, and patterns of virtue and prudence, could not be brought for a long time to give way to good letters and refined speech; but bare themselves as averse from them, as from rocks or boxes of poison: And fourthly, that he was no babe, but a great Clerk, that gave forth, (and in writing to remain to posterity) in passion peradventure, but yet he gave forth, That he had not seen any profit to come by any synod or meeting of the Clergy, but rather the contrary: And lastly, against Church-maintenance and allowance, in such sort as the ambassadors and messengers of the great King of kings should be furnished, it is not unknown what a fiction or fable (so it is esteemed, and for no better by the reported himself, though superstitious) was devised: namely, That at such time as the professors and teachers of Christianity in the Church of Rome, then a true Church, were liberally endowed, a voice forsooth was heard from heaven, saying, Now is poison poured down into the Church, &c. Thus not only as oft as we speak, as one saith, but also as oft as we do any thing of note or consequence, we subject ourselves to every one's censure, and happy is he that is least tossed upon tongues; for utterly to escape the snatch of them it is impossible. If any man conceit that this is the lot and portion of the meaner sort only, and that princes are privileged by their high estate, he is deceived. As, The sword devoureth as well one as another, as it is in Samuel; nay, as the great commander charged his soldiers in a certain battle to strike at no part of the enemy, but at the face; and as the king of Syria commanded his chief captains, To fight neither with small nor great, save only against the king of Israel: so it is too true, that envy striketh most spitefully at the fairest, and at the chiefest. David was a worthy prince, and no man to be compared to him for his first deeds; and yet for as worthy an act as ever he did, even for bringing back the ark of God in solemnity, he was scorned and scoffed at by his own wife. Solomon was greater than David, though not in virtue, yet in power; and by his power and wisdom he built a temple to the Lord, such an one as was the glory of the land of Israel, and the wonder of the whole world. But was that his magnificence liked by all? We doubt of it. Otherwise why do they lay it in his son's dish, and call unto him for easing of the burden? Make, say they, the grievous servitude of thy father, and his sore yoke, lighter. Belike he had charged them with some levies, and troubled them with some carriages; hereupon they raise up a tragedy, and wish in their heart the temple had never been built. So hard a thing it is to please all, even when we please God best, and do seek to approve ourselves to every one's conscience.

The highest personages have been calumniated

If we will descend to later times, we shall find many the like examples of such kind, or rather unkind, acceptance. The first Roman Emperor did never do a more pleasing deed to the learned, nor more profitable to posterity, for conserving the record of times in true supputation [calculation], than when he corrected the Calendar, and ordered the year according to the course of the sun: and yet this was imputed to him for novelty and arrogancy, and procured to him great obloquy. So the first Christened Emperor, (at the leastwise, that openly professed the faith himself, and allowed others to do the like) for strengthening the empire at his great charges, and providing for the Church, as he did, got for his labour the name Pupillus, as who would say, a wasteful Prince, that had need of a guardian or overseer. So the best Christened Emperor, for the love that he bare unto peace, thereby to enrich both himself and his subjects, and because he did not seek war, but find it, was judged to be no man at arms, (though in deed he excelled in feats of chivalry, and shewed so much when he was provoked) and condemned for giving himself to his ease, and to his pleasure. To be short, the most learned Emperor of former times, (at the least, the greatest politician) what thanks had he for cutting off the superfluities of the laws, and digesting them into some order and method? This, that he hath been blotted by some to be an Epitomist, that is, one that extinguished worthy whole volumes, to bring his abridgments into request. This is the measure that hath been rendered to excellent Princes in former times, even, Cum bene facerent, male audire, For their good deeds to be evil spoken of. Neither is there any likelihood that envy and malignity died and were buried with the ancient. No, no, the reproof of Moses taketh hold of most ages, Ye are risen up in your fathers' stead, an increase of sinful men. What is that that hath been done? that which shall be done: and there is no new thing under the sun, saith the wise man. And St Stephen, As your fathers did, so do ye.

His Majesty's constancy, notwithstanding calumniation, for the survey of the English translations

This, and more to this purpose, his Majesty that now reigneth (and long and long may he reign, and his offspring for ever, Himself and children and children's children always!) knew full well, according to the singular wisdom given unto him by God, and the rare learning and experience that he hath attained unto; namely, That whosoever attempteth any thing for the publick, (especially if it appertain to religion, and to the opening and clearing of the word of God) the same setteth himself upon a stage to be glouted upon by every evil eye; yea, he casteth himself headlong upon pikes, to be gored by every sharp tongue. For he that meddleth with men's religion in any part meddleth with their custom, nay, with their freehold [an estate or office held for term of life]; and though they find no content in that which they have, yet they cannot abide to hear of altering. Notwithstanding his royal heart was not daunted or discouraged for this or that colour, but stood resolute, As a statue immoveable, and an anvil not easy to be beaten into plates, as one saith; he knew who had chosen him to be a soldier, or rather a captain; and being assured that the course which he intended made much for the glory of God, and the building up of his Church, he would not suffer it to be broken off for whatsoever speeches or practices. It doth certainly belong unto kings, yea, it doth specially belong unto them, to have care of religion, yea, to know it aright, yea, to profess it zealously, yea, to promote it to the uttermost of their power. This is their glory before all nations which mean well, and this will bring unto them a far most excellent weight of glory in the day of the Lord Jesus. For the Scripture saith not in vain, Them that honour me

I will honour: neither was it a vain word that Eusebius delivered long ago, That piety towards God was the weapon, and the only weapon, that both preserved Constantine's person, and avenged him of his enemies.

The praise of the Holy Scriptures

But now what piety without truth? What truth, what saving truth, without the word of God? What word of God, whereof we may be sure, without Scripture? The Scriptures we are commanded to search. John v.39. Isaiah viii.20. They are commended that searched and studied them. Acts xvii.11 and viii.28,29. They are reproved that were unskilful in them, or slow to believe them. Matth. xxii.29. Luke xxiv.25. They can make us wise unto salvation. 2 Tim. iii.15. If we be ignorant, they will instruct us; if out of the way, they will bring us home; if out of order, they will reform us; if in heaviness, comfort us; if dull, quicken us; if cold, inflame us. Tolle, lege; tolle, lege; Take up and read, take up and read the Scriptures, (for unto them was the direction) it was said unto St Augustine by a supernatural voice. Whatsoever is in the Scriptures, believe me, saith the same St Augustine, is high and divine; there is verily truth, and a doctrine most fit for the refreshing and renewing of men's minds, and truly so tempered, that every one may draw from thence that which is sufficient for him, if he come to draw with a devout and pious mind, as true religion requireth. Thus St Augustine. And St Hierome [Jerome], Ama Scripturas, et amabit te sapientia, &c. Love the Scriptures, and wisdom will love thee. And St Cyrill against Julian, Even boys that are bred up in the Scriptures, become most religious, &c. But what mention we three or four uses of the Scripture, whereas whatsoever is to be believed, or practised, or hoped for, is contained in them? or three or four sentences of the Fathers, since whosoever is worthy the name of a Father, from Christ's time downward, hath likewise written not only of the riches, but also of the perfection of the Scripture? I adore the fulness of the Scripture, saith Tertullian against Hermogenes. And again, to Appeles an heretick of the like stamp he saith, I do not admit that which thou bringest in (or concludest) of thine own (head or store, de tuo) without Scripture. So St Justin Martyr before him; We must know by all means (saith he) that it is not lawful (or possible) to learn (any thing) of God or of right piety, save only out of the Prophets, who teach us by divine inspiration. So St Basil after Tertullian, It is a manifest falling away from the faith, and a fault of presumption, either to reject any of those things that are written, or to bring in (upon the head of them, ἐπεισάγειν) any of those things that are not written. We omit to cite to the same effect St Cyrill, Bishop of Jerusalem in his 4. Cateches. St Hierome against Helvidius, St Augustine in his third book against the letters of Petilian, and in very many other places of his works. Also we forbear to descend to latter Fathers, because we will not weary the reader. The Scriptures then being acknowledged to be so full and so perfect, how can we excuse ourselves of negligence, if we do not study them? of curiosity, if we be not content with them? Men talk much of εἰρεσιώνη [an olive bow wrapped about with wool, whereupon did hang figs and bread and honey in a pot, and oil], how many sweet and goodly things it had hanging on it; of the Philosopher's stone, that it turneth copper into gold; of Cornucopia, that it had all things necessary for food in it; of Panaces the herb, that it was good for all diseases; of Catholicon the drug, that it is instead of all purges; of Vulcan's armour, that it was an armour of proof against all thrusts and all blows, &c. Well, that which they falsely or vainly attributed to these for bodily good, we may justly and with full measure ascribe unto the Scripture for spiritual. It is not only an armour, but also a whole armoury of weapons, both offensive and defensive; whereby we may save ourselves, and put the enemy to flight. It is not an herb, but a tree, or rather a whole paradise of trees of life, which bring forth fruit every month, and the fruit thereof is for meat, and the leaves for medicine. It is not a pot of Manna or a cruse of oil, which were for memory only, or for a meal's meat or two; but as it were a shower of heavenly bread sufficient for a whole host, be it never so great, and as it were a whole cellar full of oil vessels; whereby all our necessities may be provided for, and our debts discharged. In a word, it is a panary [storehouse, pantry] of wholesome food against fenowed traditions; a physician's shop (St Basil calleth it) of preservatives against poisoned heresies; a pandect [compendium, complete collection] of profitable laws against rebellious spirits; a treasury of most costly jewels against beggarly rudiments; finally, a fountain of most pure water springing up unto everlasting life. And what marvel? the original thereof being from heaven, not from earth; the author being God, not man; the inditer [one who prompts or dictates or composes], the Holy Spirit, not the wit of the Apostles or Prophets; the penmen, such as were sanctified from the womb, and endued with a principal portion of God's Spirit; the matter, verity, piety, purity, uprightness; the form, God's word, God's testimony, God's oracles, the word of truth, the word of Salvation, &c.; the effects, light of understanding, stableness of persuasion, repentance from dead works, newness of life, holiness, peace, joy in the Holy Ghost; lastly, the end and reward of the study thereof, fellowship with the saints, participation of the heavenly nature, fruition of an inheritance immortal, undefiled, and that never shall fade away: Happy is the man that delighteth in the Scripture, and thrice happy that meditateth in it day and night.

Translation necessary

But how shall men meditate in that which they cannot understand? How shall they understand that which is kept close in an unknown tongue? as it is written, Except I know the power of the voice, I shall be to him that speaketh a barbarian, and he that speaketh shall be a barbarian to me. The Apostle excepteth no tongue; not Hebrew the ancientest, not Greek the most copious, not Latin the finest. Nature taught a natural man to confess, that all of us in those tongues which we do not understand are plainly deaf; we may turn the deaf ear unto them. The Scythian counted the Athenian, whom he did not understand, barbarous: so the Roman did the Syrian and the Jew: (even St Hierome himself calleth the Hebrew tongue barbarous; belike, because it was strange to so many:) so the Emperor of Constantinople calleth the Latin tongue barbarous, though Pope Nicolas do storm at it: so the Jews long before Christ called all other nations Lognasim, which is little better than barbarous. Therefore as one complaineth that always in the Senate of Rome there was one or other that called for an interpreter; so, lest the Church be driven to the like exigent, it is necessary to have translations in a readiness. Translation it is that openeth the window, to let in the light; that breaketh the shell that we may eat the kernel; that putteth aside the curtain, that we may look into the most holy place; that removeth the cover of the well, that we may come by the water; even as Jacob rolled away the stone from the mouth of the well, by which means the flocks of Laban were watered. Indeed without translation into the vulgar [common] tongue, the unlearned are but like children at Jacob's well (which was deep) without a bucket or something to draw with: or as that person mentioned by Esay [Isaiah], to whom when a sealed book was delivered with this motion, Read this, I pray thee, he was fain to make this answer, I cannot, for it is sealed.

The translation of the Old Testament
out of the Hebrew into Greek

While God would be known only in Jacob, and have his name great in Israel, and in none other place; while the dew lay on Gideon's fleece only, and all the earth besides was dry; then for one and the same people, which spake all of them the language of Canaan, that is, Hebrew, one and the same original in Hebrew was sufficient. But when the fulness of time drew near, that the Sun of righteousness, the Son of God, should come into the world, whom God ordained to be a reconciliation through faith in his blood, not of the Jew only, but also of the Greek, yea, of all them that were scattered abroad; then, lo, it pleased the Lord to stir up the spirit of a Greek prince, (Greek for descent and language) even of Ptolemy Philadelph king of Egypt, to procure the translating of the book of God out of Hebrew into Greek. This is the translation of the Seventy interpreters [Septuagint], commonly so called, which prepared the way for our Saviour among the Gentiles by written preaching, as St John Baptist did among the Jews by vocal. For the Grecians, being desirous of learning, were not wont to suffer books of worth to lie moulding in kings' libraries, but had many of their servants, ready scribes, to copy them out, and so they were dispersed and made common. Again the Greek tongue was well known and made familiar to most inhabitants in Asia by reason of the conquests that there the Grecians had made, as also by the colonies which thither they had sent. For the same causes also it was well understood in many places of Europe, yea, and of Africk too. Therefore the word of God being set forth in Greek, becometh hereby like a candle set upon a candlestick, which giveth light to all that are in the house; or like a proclamation sounded forth in the market-place, which most men presently take knowledge of; and therefore that language was fittest to contain the Scriptures, both for the first preachers of the Gospel to appeal unto for witness, and for the learners also of those times to make search and trial by. It is certain, that that translation was not so sound and so perfect, but that it needed in many places correction; and who had been so sufficient for this work as the Apostles or apostolick men? Yet it seemed good to the Holy Ghost and to them to take that which they found, (the same being for the greatest part true and sufficient) rather than by making a new, in that new world and green age of the Church, to expose themselves to many exceptions and cavillations, as though they made a translation to serve their own turn, and therefore bearing witness to themselves, their witness not to be regarded. This may be supposed to be some cause, though it was commended generally, yet it did not fully content the learned, no not of the Jews. For not long after Christ, Aquila fell in hand with a new translation, and after him Theodotion, and after him Symmachus: yea, there was a fifth and a sixth edition, the authors whereof were not known. These with the Seventy made up the Hexapla, and were worthily and to great purpose compiled together by Origen. Howbeit the edition of the Seventy went away with the credit, and therefore not only was placed in the midst by Origen, (for the worth and excellency thereof above the rest, as Epiphanius gathereth) but also was used by the Greek Fathers for the ground and foundation of their commentaries. Yea, Epiphanius abovenamed doth attribute so much unto it, that he holdeth the authors thereof not only for interpreters, but also for prophets in some respect: and Justinian the Emperor, injoining the Jews his subjects to use especially the translation of the Seventy, rendereth this reason thereof, Because they were, as it were, enlightened with prophetical grace. Yet for all that, as the Egyptians are said of the Prophet to be men and not God, and their horses flesh and not spirit: so it is evident, (and St Hierome affirmeth as much) that the Seventy were interpreters, they were not prophets. They did many things well, as learned men; but yet as men they stumbled and fell, one while through oversight, another while through ignorance; yea, sometimes they may be noted to add to the original, and sometimes to take from it: which made the Apostles to leave them many times, when they left the Hebrew, and to deliver the sense thereof according to the truth of the word, as the Spirit gave them utterance. This may suffice touching the Greek translations of the Old Testament.

Translation out of Hebrew and Greek into Latin

There were also within a few hundred years after Christ translations many into the Latin tongue: for this tongue also was very fit to convey the law and the Gospel by, because in those times very many countries of the West, yea of the South, East, and North, spake or understood Latin, being made provinces to the Romans. But now the Latin translations were too many to be all good, for they were infinite; (Latini interpretes nullo modo numerari possunt, saith St Augustine.) Again, they were not out of the Hebrew fountain, (we speak of the Latin translations of the Old Testament) but out of the Greek stream; therefore the Greek being not altogether clear, the Latin derived from it must needs be muddy. This moved St Hierome, a most learned Father, and the best linguist without controversy of his age, or of any other that went before him, to undertake the translating of the Old Testament out of the very fountains themselves; which he performed with that evidence of great learning, judgment, industry, and faithfulness, that he hath for ever bound the Church unto him in a debt of special remembrance and thankfulness.

The translating of the Scripture into the vulgar tongues

Now though the Church were thus furnished with Greek and Latin translations, even before the faith of Christ was generally embraced in the Empire: (for the learned know that even in St Hierome's time the Consul of Rome and his wife were both Ethnicks, and about the same time the greatest part of the Senate also) yet for all that the godly learned were not content to have the Scriptures in the language which themselves understood, Greek and Latin, (as the good lepers were not content to fare well themselves, but acquainted their neighbours with the store that God had sent, that they also might provide for themselves) but also for the behoof and edifying of the unlearned which hungered and thirsted after righteousness, and had souls to be saved as well as they, they provided translations into the vulgar for their countrymen, insomuch that most nations under heaven did shortly after their conversion hear Christ speaking unto them in their mother tongue, not by the voice of their minister only, but also by the written word translated. If any doubt hereof, he may be satisfied by examples enough, if enough will serve the turn. First, St Hierome saith, Multarum gentium linguis Scriptura ante translata docet falsa esse quae addita sunt, &c. i.e. The Scripture being translated before in the language of many nations doth shew that those things that were added (by Lucian or Hesychius) are false. So St Hierome in that place. The same Hierome elsewhere affirmeth that he, the time was, had set forth the translation of the Seventy, Suae linguae hominibus; i.e. for his countrymen of Dalmatia. Which words not only Erasmus doth understand to purport, that St Hierome translated the Scripture into the Dalmatian tongue; but also Sixtus Senensis, and Alphonsus a Castro, (that we speak of no more) men not to be excepted against by them of Rome, do ingenuously confess as much. So St Chrysostome, that lived in St Hierome's time, giveth evidence with him: The doctrine of St John (saith he) did not in such sort (as the Philosophers' did) vanish away: but the Syrians, Egyptians, Indians, Persians, Ethiopians, and infinite other nations, being barbarous people, translated it into their (mother) tongue and have learned to be (true) Philosophers (he meaneth Christians). To this may be added Theodoret, as next unto him both for antiquity, and for learning. His words be these, Every country that is under the sun is full of these words, (of the Apostles and Prophets) and the Hebrew tongue (he meaneth the Scriptures in the Hebrew tongue) is turned not only into the language of the Grecians, but also of the Romans, and Egyptians, and Persians, and Indians, and Armenians, and Scythians, and Sauromatians, and, briefly, into all the languages that any nation useth. So he. In like manner Ulpilas is reported by Paulus Diaconus and Isidore, and before them by Sozomen, to have translated the Scriptures into the Gothick tongue: John Bishop of Sevil by Vasseus, to have turned them into Arabick about the Year of our Lord 717: Beda by Cistertiensis, to have turned a great part of them into Saxon: Efnard by Trithemius, to have abridged the French Psalter (as Beda had done the Hebrew) about the year 800; King Alured by the said Cistertiensis, to have turned the Psalter into Saxon: Methodius by Aventinus (printed at Ingolstad) to have turned the Scriptures into Sclavonian: Valdo Bishop of Frising by Beatus Rhenanus, to have caused about that time the Gospels to be translated into Dutch rhyme, yet extant in the library of Corbinian: Valdus by divers, to have turned them himself, or to have gotten them turned, into French about the year 1160: Charles the fifth of that name, surnamed The wise, to have caused them to be turned into French, about 200 years after Valdus his time; of which translation there be many copies yet extant, as witnesseth Beroaldus. Much about that time, even in our King Richard the second's days, John Trevisa translated them into English, and many English Bibles in written hand are yet to be seen with divers; translated, as it is very probable, in that age. So the Syrian translation of the New Testament is in most learned men's libraries, of Widminstadius his setting forth; and the Psalter in Arabick is with many, of Augustinus Nebiensis' setting forth. So Postel affirmeth, that in his travel he saw the Gospels in the Ethiopian tongue: and Ambrose Thesius allegeth the Psalter of the Indians, which he testifieth to have been set forth by Potken in Syrian characters. So that to have the Scriptures in the mother tongue is not a quaint conceit lately taken up, either by the Lord Cromwell in England, or by the Lord Radevile in Polony, or by the Lord Ungnadius in the Emperor's dominion, but hath been thought upon, and put in practice of old, even from the first times of the conversion of any nation; no doubt, because it was esteemed most profitable to cause faith to grow in men's hearts the sooner, and to make them to be able to say with the words of the Psalm, As we have heard, so we have seen.

The unwillingness of our chief adversaries that the Scriptures should be divulged in the mother tongue, &c.

Now the Church of Rome would seem at the length to bear a motherly affection towards her children, and to allow them the Scriptures in their mother tongue: but indeed it is a gift, not deserving to be called a gift, an unprofitable gift: they must first get a licence in writing before they may use them; and to get that, they must approve themselves to their Confessor, that is, to be such as are, if not frozen in the dregs, yet soured with the leaven of their superstition. Howbeit it seemed too much to Clement the eighth that there should be any licence granted to have them in the vulgar tongue, and therefore he overruleth and frustrateth the grant of Pius the fourth. So much are they afraid of the light of the Scripture, (Lucifugae Scripturarum, as Tertullian speaketh) that they will not trust the people with it, no not as it is set forth by their own sworn men, no not with the licence of their own Bishops and Inquisitors. Yea, so unwilling they are to communicate the Scriptures to the people's understanding in any sort, that they are not ashamed to confess that we forced them to translate it into English against their wills. This seemeth to argue a bad cause, or a bad conscience, or both. Sure we are, that it is not he that hath good gold, that is afraid to bring it to the touchstone, but he that hath the counterfeit; neither is it the true man that shunneth the light, but the malefactor, lest his deeds should be reproved; neither is it the plaindealing merchant that is unwilling to have the weights, or the meteyard, brought in place, but he that useth deceit. But we will let them alone for this fault, and return to translation.

The speeches and reasons, both of our brethren, and of our adversaries, against this work

Many men's mouths have been opened a good while (and yet are not stopped) with speeches about the translation so long in hand, or rather perusals of translations made before: and ask what may be the reason, what the necessity, of the employment. Hath the Church been deceived, say they, all this while? Hath her sweet bread been mingled with leaven, her silver with dross, her wine with water, her milk with lime? (Lacte gypsum male miscetur, saith St Irenee.) We hoped that we had been in the right way, that we had had the oracles of God delivered unto us, and that though all the world had cause to be offended, and to complain, yet that we had none. Hath the nurse holden out the breast, and nothing but wind in it? Hath the bread been delivered by the Fathers of the Church, and the same proved to be lapidosus [stony], as Seneca speaketh? What is it to handle the word of God deceitfully, if this be not? Thus certain brethren. Also the adversaries of Judah and Hierusalem, like Sanballat in Nehemiah, mock, as we hear, both at the work and the workmen, saying, What do these weak Jews, &c. will they make the stones whole again out of the heaps of dust which are burnt? Although they build, yet if a fox

go up, he shall even break down their stony wall. Was their translation
good before? Why do they now mend it? Was it not good? Why then
was it obtruded [presented] to the people? Yea, why did the Catholicks
(meaning Popish Romanists) always go in jeopardy for refusing to go
to hear it? Nay, if it must be translated into English, Catholicks are
fittest to do it. They have learning, and they know when a thing is
well, they can manum de tabula. We will answer them both briefly:
and the former, being brethren, thus with St Hierome, Damnamus
veteres? Minime, sed post priorum studia in domo Domini quod pos-
sumus laboramus. That is, Do we condemn the ancient? In no case:
but after the endeavours of them that were before us, we take the best
pains we can in the house of God. As if he said, Being provoked by
the example of the learned that lived before my time, I have thought
it my duty to assay whether my talent in the knowledge of the tongues
may be profitable in any measure to God's Church, lest I should seem
to have laboured in them in vain, and lest I should be thought to
glory in men (although ancient) above that which was in them. Thus
St Hierome may be thought to speak.

A satisfaction to our brethren

And to the same effect say we, that we are so far off from con-
demning any of their labours that travelled before us in this kind,
either in this land, or beyond sea, either in King Henry's time, or King
Edward's, (if there were any translation, or correction of a translation,
in his time) or Queen Elizabeth's of ever renowned memory, that we
acknowledge them to have been raised up of God for the building and
furnishing of his Church, and that they deserve to be had of us and
of posterity in everlasting remembrance. The judgment of Aristotle is
worthy and well known: If Timotheus had not been, we had not had
much sweet musick: But if Phrynis (Timotheus his master) had not
been, we had not had Timotheus. Therefore blessed be they, and most
honoured be their name, that break the ice, and give the onset upon
that which helpeth forward to the saving of souls. Now what can be
more available thereto, than to deliver God's book unto God's people
in a tongue which they understand? Since of an hidden treasure, and
of a fountain that is sealed, there is no profit, as Ptolemy Philadelph
wrote to the Rabbins or masters of the Jews, as witnesseth Epiphanius:
and as St Augustine saith, A man had rather be with his dog than
with a stranger (whose tongue is strange unto him.) Yet for all that,
as nothing is begun and perfected at the same time, and the latter
thoughts are thought to be the wiser: so, if we building upon their

foundation that went before us, and being holpen by their labours, do endeavour to make that better which they left so good; no man, we are sure, hath cause to mislike us; they, we persuade ourselves, if they were alive, would thank us. The vintage of Abiezer, that strake the stroke: yet the gleaning of grapes of Ephraim was not to be despised. See Judges viii.2. Joash the king of Israel did not satisfy himself till he had smitten the ground three times; and yet he offended the Prophet for giving over then. Aquila, of whom we spake before, translated the Bible as carefully and as skilfully as he could; and yet he thought good to go over it again, and then it got the credit with the Jews to be called κατ' ἀκρίβειαν, that is, accurately done, as St Hierome witnesseth. How many books of profane learning have been gone over again and again, by the same translators, by others? Of one and the same book of Aristotle's Ethics there are extant not so few as six or seven several translations. Now if this cost may be bestowed upon the gourd, which affordeth us a little shade, and which to day flourisheth, but to morrow is cut down; what may we bestow, nay, what ought we not to bestow, upon the vine, the fruit whereof maketh glad the con-science of man, and the stem whereof abideth for ever? And this is the word of God, which we translate. What is the chaff to the wheat? saith the Lord. Tanti vitreum, quanti verum margaritum! (saith Tertul-lian,) if a toy of glass be of that reckoning with us, how ought we to value the true pearl? Therefore let no man's eye be evil, because his Majesty's is good; neither let any be grieved, that we have a Prince that seeketh the increase of the spiritual wealth of Israel; (let San-ballats and Tobiahs do so, which therefore do bear their just reproof) but let us rather bless God from the ground of our heart for working this religious care in him to have the translations of the Bible maturely considered of and examined. For by this means it cometh to pass, that whatsoever is sound already, (and all is sound for substance in one or other of our editions, and the worst of ours far better than their authentick Vulgar) the same will shine as gold more brightly, being rubbed and polished; also, if any thing be halting, or superfluous, or not so agreeable to the original, the same may be corrected, and the truth set in place. And what can the King command to be done, that will bring him more true honour than this? And wherein could they that have been set at work approve their duty to the King, yea, their obedience to God, and love to his Saints, more, than by yielding their service, and all that is within them, for the furnishing of the work? But besides all this, they were the principal motives of it, and therefore ought least to quarrel it. For the very historical truth is, that upon the importunate petitions of the Puritans at his Majesty's coming to this crown, the conference at Hampton Court having been appointed for hearing their complaints, when by force of reason they were put from all other grounds, they had recourse at the last to this shift, that they could not with good conscience subscribe to the Communion book, since it maintained the Bible as it was there translated, which was, as they said, a most corrupted translation. And although this was judged to be but a very poor and empty shift, yet even hereupon did his Majesty begin to bethink himself of the good that might ensue by a new translation, and presently after gave order for this translation which is now presented unto thee. Thus much to satisfy our scrupulous brethren.

An answer to the imputations of our adversaries

Now to the latter we answer, That we do not deny, nay, we affirm and avow, that the very meanest translation of the Bible in English set forth by men of our profession (for we have seen none of theirs of the whole Bible as yet) containeth the word of God, nay, is the word of God: as the King's speech which he uttered in Parliament, being translated into French, Dutch, Italian, and Latin, is still the King's speech, though it be not interpreted by every translator with the like grace, nor peradventure so fitly for phrase, nor so expressly for sense, every where. For it is confessed that things are to take their denomination of the greater part; and a natural man could say, Verum ubi multa nitent in carmine, non ego paucis offendar maculis, &c. A man may be counted a virtuous man, though he have made many slips in his life, (else there were none virtuous, for, In many things we offend all,) also a comely man and lovely, though he have some warts upon his hand; yea, not only freckles upon his face, but also scars. No cause therefore why the word translated should be denied to be the word, or forbidden to be current, notwithstanding that some imperfections and blemishes may be noted in the setting forth of it. For whatever was perfect under the sun, where Apostles or apostolick men, that is, men endued with an extraordinary measure of God's Spirit, and privileged with the privilege of infallibility, had not their hand? The Romanists therefore in refusing to hear, and daring to burn the word translated, did no less than despite the Spirit of grace, from whom originally it proceeded, and whose sense and meaning, as well as man's weakness would enable, it did express. Judge by an example or two.

Plutarch writeth, that after that Rome had been burnt by the Gauls, they fell soon to build it again: but doing it in haste, they did not cast the streets, nor proportion the houses, in such comely fashion, as had been most sightly and convenient. Was Catiline therefore an honest man, or a good patriot, that sought to bring it to a combustion? or Nero a good Prince, that did indeed set it on fire? So by the story of Ezra and the prophecy of Haggai it may be gathered, that the temple built by Zerubbabel after the return from Babylon was by no means to be compared to the former built by Solomon: (for they that remembered the former wept when they considered the latter) notwithstanding might this latter either have been abhorred and forsaken by the Jews, or profaned by the Greeks? The like we are to think of translations. The translation of the Seventy dissenteth from the Original in many places, neither doth it come near it for perspicuity, gravity, majesty; yet which of the Apostles did condemn it? Condemn it? Nay, they used it, (as it is apparent, and as St Hierome and most learned men do confess) which they would not have done, nor by their example of using of it so grace and commend it to the Church, if it had been unworthy the appellation and name of the word of God. And whereas they urge for their second defence of their vilifying and abusing of the English Bibles, or some pieces thereof, which they meet with, for that Hereticks forsooth were the authors of the translations: (Hereticks they call us by the same right that they call themselves Catholicks, both being wrong) we marvel what divinity taught them so. We are sure Tertullian was of another mind: Ex personis probamus fidem, an ex fide personas? Do we try men's faith by their persons? We should try their persons by their faith. Also St Augustine was of another mind: for he, lighting upon certain rules made by Tychonius a Donatist for the better understanding of the Word, was not ashamed to make use of them, yea, to insert them into his own book, with giving commendation to them so far forth as they were worthy to be commended, as is to be seen in St Augustine's third book De Doctrina Christiana. To be short, Origen and the whole Church of God for certain hundred years, were of another mind: for they were so far from treading under foot (much more from burning) the translation of Aquila a proselyte, that is, one that had turned Jew, of Symmachus, and Theodotion, both Ebionites, that is, most vile hereticks, that they joined them together with the Hebrew original, and the translation of the Seventy, (as hath been before signified out of Epiphanius) and set them forth openly to be considered of and perused by all. But we weary the unlearned, who need not know so much; and trouble the learned, who know it already.

Yet before we end, we must answer a third cavil and objection of theirs against us, for altering and amending our translation so oft;

wherein truly they deal hardly and strangely with us. For to whom ever was it imputed for a fault (by such as were wise) to go over that which he had done, and to amend it where he saw cause? St Augustine was not afraid to exhort St Hierome to a Palinodia or recantation. The same St Augustine was not ashamed to retractate, we might say, revoke, many things that had passed him, and doth even glory that he seeth his infirmities. If we will be sons of the truth, we must consider what it speaketh, and trample upon our own credit, yea, and upon other men's too, if either be any way an hinderance to it. This to the cause. Then to the persons we say, that of all men they ought to be most silent in this case. For what varieties have they, and what alterations have they made, not only of their service books, portesses, and breviaries, but also of their Latin translation? The service book supposed to be made by St Ambrose (Officium Ambrosianum) was a great while in special use and request: but Pope Adrian, calling a council with the aid of Charles the Emperor, abolished it, yea, burnt it, and commanded the service book of St Gregory universally to be used. Well, Officium Gregorianum gets by this means to be in credit; but doth it continue without change or altering? No, the very Roman service was of two fashions; the new fashion, and the old, the one used in one Church, and the other in another; as is to be seen in Pamelius a Romanist his preface before Micrologus. The same Pamelius reporteth out of Radulphus de Rivo, that about the year of our Lord 1277 Pope Nicolas the third removed out of the churches of Rome the more ancient books (of service) and brought into use the missals of the Friers Minorites, and commanded them to be observed there; insomuch that about an hundred years after, when the above named Radulphus· happened to be at Rome, he found all the books to be new, of the new stamp. Neither was there this chopping and changing in the more ancient times only, but also of late. Pius Quintus himself confesseth, that every bishoprick almost had a peculiar kind of service, most unlike to that which others had; which moved him to abolish all other breviaries, though never so ancient, and privileged and published by Bishops in their Dioceses, and to establish and ratify that only which was of his own setting forth in the year 1568. Now when the Father of their Church, who gladly would heal the sore of the daughter of his people softly and slightly, and make the best of it, findeth so great fault with them for their odds and jarring; we hope the children have no great cause to vaunt of their uniformity. But the difference that appeareth between our translations, and our often correcting of them, is the thing that we are specially charged with; let us see therefore whether they themselves be without fault this way, (if it be to be counted a fault to correct) and whether they be fit men to throw stones at us: O tandem major parcas insane minori: They that are less sound themselves ought not to object infirmities to others. If we should tell them that Valla, Stapulensis, Erasmus, and Vives, found fault with their vulgar translation, and consequently wished the same to be mended, or a new one to be made; they would answer peradventure, that we produced their enemies for witnesses against them; albeit they were in no other sort enemies, than as St Paul was to the Galatians, for telling them the truth: and it were to be wished, that they had dared to tell it them plainlier and oftener. But what will they say to this, That Pope Leo the tenth allowed Erasmus's translation of the New Testament, so much different from the Vulgar, by his apostolick letter and bull? That the same Leo exhorted Pagnine to translate the whole Bible, and bare whatsoever charges was necessary for the work? Surely, as the Apostle reasoneth to the Hebrews, That if the former Law and Testament had been sufficient, there had been no need of the latter: so we may say, that if the old Vulgar had been at all points allowable, to small purpose had labour and charges been undergone about framing of a new. If they say, it was one Pope's private opinion, and that he consulted only himself; then we are able to go further with them, and to aver, that more of their chief men of all sorts, even their own Trent champions, Paiva and Vega, and their own inquisitor Hieronymus ab Oleastro, and their own Bishop Isidorus Clarius, and their own Cardinal Thomas a Vio Cajetan, do either make new translations themselves, or follow new ones of other men's making, or note the Vulgar interpreter for halting, none of them fear to dissent from him, nor yet to except against him. And call they this an uniform tenor of text and judgment about the text, so many of their worthies disclaiming the now received conceit? Nay, we will yet come nearer the quick. Doth not their Paris edition differ from the Louvain, and Hentenius's from them both, and yet all of them allowed by authority? Nay, doth not Sixtus Quintus confess, that certain Catholicks (he meaneth certain of his own side) were in such an humour of translating the Scriptures into Latin, that Satan taking occasion by them, though they thought of no such matter, did strive what he could, out of so uncertain and manifold a variety of translations, so to mingle all things, that nothing might seem to be left certain and firm in them? &c. Nay further, did not the same Sixtus ordain by an inviolable decree, and that with the counsel and consent of his Cardinals, that the Latin edition of the Old and New Testament, which the council of Trent would have to be authentick, is the same without controversy which he then set forth, being diligently corrected and printed in the printinghouse of Vatican? Thus Sixtus in his preface before his Bible. And yet Clement the eighth, his immediate successor, published another edition of the Bible, containing in it infinite differences from that of Sixtus, and many of them weighty and material; and yet this must be authentick by all means. What is to have the faith of our glorious Lord Jesus Christ with yea and nay, if this be not? Again, what is sweet harmony and consent, if this be? Therefore, as Demaratus of Corinth advised a great King, before he talked of the dissensions among the Grecians, to compose his domestick broils; (for at that time his queen and his son and heir were at deadly feud with him) so all the while that our adversaries do make so many and so various editions themselves, and do jar so much about the worth and authority of them, they can with no show of equity challenge us for changing and correcting.

The purpose of the Translators, with their number, furniture, care, &c.

But it is high time to leave them, and to shew in brief what we proposed to ourselves, and what course we held, in this our perusal and survey of the Bible. Truly, good Christian Reader, we never thought from the beginning that we should need to make a new translation, nor yet to make of a bad one a good one; (for then the imputation of Sixtus had been true in some sort, that our people had been fed with gall of dragons instead of wine, with whey instead of milk;) but to make a good one better, or out of many good ones one principal good one, not justly to be excepted against; that hath been our endeavour, that our mark. To that purpose there were many chosen, that were greater in other men's eyes than in their own, and that sought the truth rather than their own praise. Again, they came, or were thought to come, to the work, not exercendi causa, (as one saith) but exercitati, that is, learned, not to learn; for the chief overseer and ἐργοδιώκτης [taskmaster] under his Majesty, to whom not only we, but also our whole Church was much bound, knew by his wisdom, which thing also Nazianzen taught so long ago, that it is a preposterous order to teach first, and to learn after, yea that τὸ ἐν πίθῳ κεραμίαν μανθάνειν, to learn and practise together, is neither commendable for the workman, nor safe for the work. Therefore such were thought upon, as could say modestly with St Hierome, Et Hebraeum sermonem ex parte didicimus, et in Latino pene ab ipsis incunabulis, &c. detriti sumus; Both we have learned the Hebrew tongue in part, and in the Latin we

have been exercised almost from our very cradle. St Hierome maketh
no mention of the Greek tongue, wherein yet he did excel; because he
translated not the Old Testament out of Greek, but out of Hebrew.
And in what sort did these assemble? In the trust of their own knowledge, or of their sharpness of wit, or deepness of judgment, as it were
in an arm of flesh? At no hand. They trusted in him that hath the key
of David, opening, and no man shutting; they prayed to the Lord, the
Father of our Lord, to the effect that St Augustine did; O let thy
Scriptures be my pure delight; let me not be deceived in them, neither
let me deceive by them. In this confidence, and with this devotion, did
they assemble together; not too many, lest one should trouble another;
and yet many, lest many things haply might escape them. If you ask
what they had before them, truly it was the Hebrew text of the Old
Testament, the Greek of the New. These are the two golden pipes, or
rather conduits, wherethrough the olive branches empty themselves
into the gold. St Augustine calleth them precedent, or original, tongues;
St Hierome, fountains. The same St Hierome affirmeth, and Gratian
hath not spared to put it into his decree, That as the credit of the old
books (he meaneth of the Old Testament) is to be tried by the Hebrew
volumes; so of the New by the Greek tongue, he meaneth by the original Greek. If truth be to be tried by these tongues, then whence
should a translation be made, but out of them? These tongues therefore
(the Scriptures, we say, in those tongues) we set before us to translate,
being the tongues wherein God was pleased to speak to his Church by
his Prophets and Apostles. Neither did we run over the work with that
posting haste that the Septuagint did, if that be true which is reported
of them, that they finished it in seventy two days; neither were we
barred or hindered from going over it again, having once done it, like
St Hierome, if that be true which himself reporteth, that he could no
sooner write any thing, but presently it was caught from him, and published, and he could not have leave to mend it: neither, to be short,
were we the first that fell in hand with translating the Scripture into
English, and consequently destitute of former helps, as it is written
of Origen, that he was the first in a manner, that put his hand to write
commentaries upon the Scriptures, and therefore no marvel if he over-
shot himself many times. None of these things: The work hath not
been huddled up in seventy two days, but hath cost the workmen, as
light as it seemeth, the pains of twice seven times seventy two days,
and more. Matters of such weight and consequence are to be speeded
with maturity: for in a business of moment a man feareth not the
blame of convenient slackness. Neither did we think much to consult

the translators or commentators, Chaldee, Hebrew, Syrian, Greek, or
Latin; no, nor the Spanish, French, Italian, or Dutch; neither did we
disdain to revise that which we had done, and to bring back to the
anvil that which we had hammered: but having and using as great
helps as were needful, and fearing no reproach for slowness, nor
coveting praise for expedition, we have at the length, through the good
hand of the Lord upon us, brought the work to that pass that you see.

Reasons moving us to set diversity of senses in the
margin, where there is great probability for each

Some peradventure would have no variety of senses to be set in the
margin, lest the authority of the Scriptures for deciding of controversies
by that show of uncertainty should somewhat be shaken. But we hold
their judgment not to be so sound in this point. For though, Whatsoever things are necessary are manifest, as St Chrysostome saith; and,
as St Augustine, In those things that are plainly set down in the Scriptures all such matters are found that concern faith, hope, and charity:
yet for all that it cannot be dissembled, that partly to exercise and whet
our wits, partly to wean the curious from loathing of them for their
every where plainness, partly also to stir up our devotion to crave the
assistance of God's Spirit by prayer, and lastly, that we might be forward to seek aid of our brethren by conference, and never scorn those
that be not in all respects so complete as they should be, being to seek
in many things ourselves, it hath pleased God in his Divine Providence
here and there to scatter words and sentences of that difficulty and
doubtfulness, not in doctrinal points that concern salvation, (for in
such it hath been vouched that the Scriptures are plain) but in matters
of less moment, that fearfulness would better beseem us than confidence, and if we will resolve, to resolve upon modesty with St
Augustine, (though not in this same case altogether, yet upon the same
ground) Melius est dubitare de occultis, quam litigare de incertis: It is
better to make doubt of those things which are secret, than to strive
about those things that are uncertain. There be many words in the
Scriptures which be never found there but once, (having neither
brother nor neighbour, as the Hebrews speak) so that we cannot be
holpen by conference of places. Again, there be many rare names of
certain birds, beasts, and precious stones, &c. concerning which the
Hebrews themselves are so divided among themselves for judgment,
that they may seem to have defined this or that, rather because they
would say something, than because they were sure of that which they
said, as St Hierome somewhere saith of the Septuagint. Now in such

a case doth not a margin do well to admonish the Reader to seek further, and not to conclude or dogmatize upon this or that peremptorily? For as it is a fault of incredulity, to doubt of those things that are evident; so to determine of such things as the Spirit of God hath left (even in the judgment of the judicious) questionable, can be no less than presumption. Therefore as St Augustine saith, that variety of translations is profitable for the finding out of the sense of the Scriptures: so diversity of signification and sense in the margin, where the text is not so clear, must needs do good; yea, is necessary, as we are persuaded. We know that Sixtus Quintus expressly forbiddeth that any variety of readings of their Vulgar edition should be put in the margin; (which though it be not altogether the same thing to that we have in hand, yet it looketh that way;) but we think he hath not all of his own side his favourers for this conceit. They that are wise had rather have their judgments at liberty in differences of readings, than to be captivated to one, when it may be the other. If they were sure that their high priest had all laws shut up in his breast, as Paul the second bragged, and that he were as free from error by special privilege, as the dictators of Rome were made by law inviolable, it were another matter; then his word were an oracle, his opinion a decision. But the eyes of the world are now open, God be thanked, and have been a great while; they find that he is subject to the same affections and infirmities that others be, that his skin is penetrable, and therefore so much as he proveth, not as much as he claimeth, they grant and embrace.

Reasons inducing us not to stand curiously
upon an identity of phrasing

Another thing we think good to admonish thee of, gentle Reader, that we have not tied ourselves to an uniformity of phrasing, or to an identity of words, as some peradventure would wish that we had done, because they observe, that some learned men somewhere have been as exact as they could that way. Truly, that we might not vary from the sense of that which we had translated before, if the word signified the same thing in both places, (for there be some words that be not of the same sense every where) we were especially careful, and made a conscience, according to our duty. But that we should express the same notion in the same particular word; as for example, if we translate the Hebrew or Greek word once by 'purpose', never to call it 'intent'; if one where 'journeying', never 'travelling'; if one where 'think', never 'suppose'; if one where 'pain', never 'ache'; if one where 'joy', never 'gladness', &c. thus to mince the matter, we thought to savour more of

curiosity than wisdom, and that rather it would breed scorn in the
atheist, than bring profit to the godly reader. For is the kingdom of
God become words or syllables? Why should we be in bondage to
them, if we may be free? use one precisely, when we may use another
no less fit as commodiously? A godly Father in the primitive time
shewed himself greatly moved, that one of newfangledness called
κράββατον [cot, couch], σκίμπους [little couch, pallet], though the
difference be little or none; and another reporteth, that he was much
abused for turning 'cucurbita' [gourd] (to which reading the people
had been used) into 'hedera' [ivy plant]. Now if this happen in
better times, and upon so small occasions, we might justly fear hard
censure, if generally we should make verbal and unnecessary chang-
ings. We might also be charged (by scoffers) with some unequal
dealing towards a great number of good English words. For as it
is written of a certain great Philosopher, that he should say, that
those logs were happy that were made images to be worshipped;
for their fellows, as good as they, lay for blocks behind the fire: so
if we should say, as it were, unto certain words, Stand up higher,
have a place in the Bible always; and to others of like quality, Get
ye hence, be banished for ever; we might be taxed peradventure
with St James his words, namely, To be partial in ourselves, and
judges of evil thoughts. Add hereunto, that niceness in words was
always counted the next step to trifling; and so was to be curious
about names too: also that we cannot follow a better pattern for
elocution than God himself; therefore he using divers words in his
holy writ, and indifferently for one thing in nature; we, if we will not
be superstitious, may use the same liberty in our English versions out
of Hebrew and Greek, for that copy or store that he hath given us.
Lastly, we have on the one side avoided the scrupulosity of the
Puritans, who leave the old Ecclesiastical words, and betake them to
other, as when they put 'washing' for 'baptism', and 'congregation'
instead of 'church': as also on the other side we have shunned the
obscurity of the Papists, in their 'azymes', 'tunik', 'rational', 'holocausts',
'prepuce', 'pasche', and a number of such like, whereof their late
translation is full, and that of purpose to darken the sense, that
since they must needs translate the Bible, yet by the language thereof
it may be kept from being understood. But we desire that the Scripture may speak like itself, as in the language of Canaan, that it may
be understood even of the very vulgar.

Many other things we might give thee warning of, gentle Reader,
if we had not exceeded the measure of a preface already. It remaineth

that we commend thee to God, and to the Spirit of his grace, which is able to build further than we can ask or think. He removeth the scales from our eyes, the vail from our hearts, opening our wits that we may understand his word, enlarging our hearts, yea, correcting our affections, that we may love it above gold and silver, yea, that we may love it to the end. Ye are brought unto fountains of living water which ye digged not; do not cast earth into them, with the Philistines, neither prefer broken pits before them, with the wicked Jews. Others have laboured, and you may enter into their labours. O receive not so great things in vain: O despise not so great salvation. Be not like swine to tread under foot so precious things, neither yet like dogs to tear and abuse holy things. Say not to our Saviour with the Gergesites, Depart out of our coasts; neither yet with Esau sell your birthright for a mess of pottage. If light be come into the world, love not darkness more than light: if food, if clothing, be offered, go not naked, starve not yourselves. Remember the advice of Nazianzene, It is a grievous thing (or dangerous) to neglect a great fair, and to seek to make markets afterwards: also the encouragement of St Chrysostome, It is altogether impossible, that he that is sober (and watchful) should at any time be neglected: lastly, the admonition and menacing of St Augustine, They that despise God's will inviting them shall feel God's will taking vengeance of them. It is a fearful thing to fall into the hands of the living God; but a blessed thing it is, and will bring us to everlasting blessedness in the end, when God speaketh unto us, to hearken; when he setteth his word before us, to read it; when he stretcheth out his hand and calleth, to answer, Here am I, here we are to do thy will, O God. The Lord work a care and conscience in us to know him and serve him, that we may be acknowledged of him at the appearing of our Lord Jesus Christ, to whom with the Holy Ghost be all praise and thanksgiving. Amen.

The Dedication to King James I
(Cambridge University edition of 1950)

TO THE MOST HIGH AND MIGHTY PRINCE

JAMES

BY *THE GRACE OF GOD*

KING OF GREAT BRITAIN, FRANCE, AND IRELAND

DEFENDER OF THE FAITH, &c.

The Translators of the Bible wish Grace, Mercy, and Peace,

through JESUS CHRIST our Lord

Great and manifold were the blessings, most dread Sovereign, which Almighty God, the Father of all mercies, bestowed upon us the people of England, when first he sent Your Majesty's Royal Person to rule and reign over us. For whereas it was the expectation of many, who wished not well unto our Sion, that upon the setting of that bright Occidental Star, Queen Elizabeth of most happy memory, some thick and palpable clouds of darkness would so have over-shadowed this Land, that men should have been in doubt which way they were to walk; and that it should hardly be known, who was to direct the unsettled State; the appearance of Your Majesty, as of the Sun in his strength, instantly dispelled those supposed and surmised mists, and gave unto all that were well affected exceeding cause of comfort; especially when we beheld the Government established in Your Highness, and Your hopeful Seed, by an undoubted Title, and this also accompanied with peace and tranquillity at home and abroad.

But among all our joys, there was no one that more filled our hearts, than the blessed continuance of the preaching of God's sacred Word among us; which is that inestimable treasure, which excelleth all the riches of the earth; because the fruit thereof extendeth itself, not only to the time spent in this transitory world, but directeth and disposeth men unto that eternal happiness which is above in heaven.

Then not to suffer this to fall to the ground, but rather to take it up, and to continue it in that state, wherein the famous Predecessor of Your Highness did leave it: nay, to go forward with the confidence and resolution of a Man in maintaining the truth of Christ, and propagating it far and near, is that which hath so bound and firmly knit the hearts of all Your Majesty's loyal and religious people unto You, that Your very name is precious among them: their eye doth behold You with comfort, and they bless You in their hearts, as that sanctified Person, who, under God, is the immediate Author of their true happiness. And this their contentment doth not diminish or decay, but every day increaseth and taketh strength, when they observe, that the zeal of Your Majesty toward the house of God doth not slack or go backward, but is more and more kindled, manifesting itself abroad in the farthest parts of Christendom, by writing in defence of the Truth, (which hath given such a blow unto that man of sin, as will not be healed,) and every day at home, by religious and learned discourse, by frequenting the house of God, by hearing the Word preached, by cherishing the Teachers thereof, by caring for the Church, as a most tender and loving nursing Father.

There are infinite arguments of this right Christian and religious affection in Your Majesty; but none is more forcible to declare it to others than the vehement and perpetuated desire of accomplishing and publishing of this work, which now with all humility we present unto Your Majesty. For when Your Highness had once out of deep judgment apprehended how convenient it was, that out of the Original Sacred Tongues, together with comparing of the labours, both in our own, and other foreign Languages, of many worthy men who went before us, there should be one more exact Translation of the Holy Scriptures into the English Tongue; Your Majesty did never desist to urge and to excite those to whom it was commended, that the work might be hastened, and that the business might be expedited in so decent a manner, as a matter of such importance might justly require.

And now at last, by the mercy of God, and the continuance of our labours, it being brought unto such a conclusion, as that we have great hopes that the Church of England shall reap good fruit thereby; we hold it our duty to offer it to Your Majesty, not only as to our King and Sovereign, but as to the principal Mover and Author of the work: humbly craving of Your most Sacred Majesty, that since things of this quality have ever been subject to the censures of ill-meaning and discontented persons, it may receive approbation and patronage from so learned and judicious a Prince as Your Highness is, whose allowance and acceptance of our labours shall more honour and encourage us, than all the calumniations and hard interpretations of other men shall dismay us. So that if, on the one side, we shall be traduced by Popish Persons at home or abroad, who therefore will malign us, because we are poor instruments to make God's holy Truth to be yet more and more known unto the people, whom they desire still to keep in ignorance and darkness; or if, on the other side, we shall be maligned by selfconceited Brethren, who run their own ways, and give liking unto nothing, but what is framed by themselves, and hammered on their anvil; we may rest secure, supported within by the truth and innocency of a good conscience, having walked the ways of simplicity and integrity, as before the Lord; and sustained without by the powerful protection of Your Majesty's grace and favour, which will ever give countenance to honest and Christian endeavours against bitter censures and uncharitable imputations.

The Lord of heaven and earth bless Your Majesty with many and happy days, that, as his heavenly hand hath enriched Your Highness with many singular and extraordinary graces, so You may be the wonder of the world in this latter age for happiness and true felicity, to the honour of that great GOD, and the good of his Church, through Jesus Christ our Lord and only Saviour.

Kethib, Qere, and the Name "Jehovah"

The *Kethib-Qere* system can be illustrated best for the reader with a hypothetical example in English. Suppose you are a scribe with a manuscript containing the sentence, "He dedicated the monumental chapel." With the vowels added (in good Hebrew style) above or below the consonantal text, the sentence would appear as follows:

<pre>
              o
H ddctd th mnmntl chpl
 e eiae e ue a ae
</pre>

You wish to indicate a variant, however, because in checking some other copies of this passage you have found the reading, "He dedicated the memorial chapel." Your first step is to remove from the word "monumental" the vowels o-u-e-a. Then to the consonants *mnmntl*, which cannot be altered, are added the vowels e-o-i-a, the vowels of "memorial," while the consonants *mmrl* are placed in the margin. Placing a little circle at the beginning of the word in question, to inform the reader to consult the margin, your sentence would then read:

<pre>
              o
H ddctd th °mnmntl chpl   mmrl
 e eiae e e i a ae
</pre>

This would result in the strange, impossible word "menomintal" being in the text. All informed readers would ignore it, however, and take the vowels of the text (e-o-i-a) along with the consonants in the margin (*mmrl*) in order to reconstruct mentally the variant word "memorial."

While this ingenious system of the Masoretic scribes was devised to preserve variant readings and in some cases to correct what they considered to be erroneous readings in the consonantal text, it had another very interesting use throughout the whole Old Testament. The general term for deity was *Elohim*, translated "God," but the personal name of Israel's God was *Yahweh*, probably meaning "He causes (all things) to be." What an appropriate name this was to distinguish the God of Israel from the pagan gods of the surrounding nations! Again and again the prophets and psalmists refer to God as the one "who made heaven and earth."

After the Exile in Babylonia, however, the Jews came to conceive of God as being so other-worldly and holy his personal name could not be uttered in public. When reading the Scriptures they pronounced the word *'Adonay* "Lord, Master" every time they came to *Yahweh*. For centuries after the square script came into use this sense of awe was still manifested in some manuscripts by writing the personal name (which appeared as four consonants, YHWH, and so known now as the *"Tetragrammaton* = Four-letter") in the Old Hebrew script. A beautiful example is the Commentary on Habakkuk found among the Dead Sea Scrolls of Cave 1 (see Fig. 14 where the name, encircled for identification, occurs twice).

When vowels were added to the consonantal Hebrew texts the scribes decided to use the *Kethib-Qere* system with the name *Yahweh*. To the sacred consonants, YHWH, which had to remain in the text, were added the vowels of *'Adonay*. But due to the nature of the first consonant of *'Adonay* the first "a" became an "e" so that instead of the vowels a-o-a the scribes added e-o-a. Then the name in the text appeared as follows:

o
YHWH
e   a

The Jews knew that *YeHoWaH* was an artificial form and continued to pronounce the word *'Adonay*, ignoring the consonants in the text, but during the Middle Ages some Gentile scholars in the Church began to treat the artificial form as a real name. Because the language of these scholars transcribed "Y" as "J" and "w" as "v" the name *Yehowah* became *Jehovah*.

In the King James Version the personal name for God is normally translated "LORD," with small capital letters, to distinguish it from "Lord," the translation of *'Adonay* which always has lower case letters, but on seven occasions (for example, Ex. 6:3) the name appears as JEHOVAH. On the other hand, the American Standard Version, desiring to maintain a personal name for God, used "Jehovah" throughout the Old Testament, even though the translators knew it was an artificial form. Apparently they were not sure at that time that the name was to be pronounced *Yahweh*. Mistake or not, the term Jehovah has acquired special meaning for many because of its use in this translation and subsequent hymns and poems.

Actually, the idea of translating both *Yahweh* and *'Adonay* with the same word goes back to the Septuagint where the Greek word *Kurios* "Lord" was employed for both names. As the preface to the Revised Standard Version observes, "the use of any proper name for the one and only God, as though there were other gods from whom he had to be distinguished, was discontinued in Judaism before the Christian era and is entirely inappropriate for the universal faith of the Christian Church." The Revised Standard and Berkeley Versions, therefore, have returned to the King James Version use of "LORD" for the personal name. The distinction between small capital and lower case letters is a device to help the reader differentiate the two words, for at times knowledge as to which name is employed in the Hebrew adds significantly to the understanding of the passage.

Sometimes *'Adonay* and *Yahweh* occur together (in that order) in the Hebrew text. Rather than translate "Lord LORD," most of the versions have rendered "Lord GOD." This is true in Is. 7:7, for example, with the exception of the Berkeley Version which has "Lord God." However, the reader would interpret "God" as the translation of *Elohim*, not *Yahweh*. This complex use of names for God can be summarized in one rule: wherever in English translations a designation for God appears in small capital letters the reader knows that the Hebrew word back of it is *Yahweh*, the personal name for God.

More Recent Translations

When future historians describe the activities of the Church in the twentieth century, one outstanding feature of the story will be the boom of translations of Scripture. This phenomenon has brought new life and light to the Church, but it has resulted also in some confusion. Since most people can use only three or four translations effectively, they are often perplexed by the increasing number of available translations. All of them have some merits, but with time at a premium it is wise to read from those that best meet one's needs. In order to assist the reader in making his or her own evaluation the strong and weak points of the more recent translations will be discussed quite frankly.

THE NEW TESTAMENT IN PLAIN ENGLISH

This translation by Charles Kingsley Williams has been referred to in a number of the New Testament examples discussed earlier, but since it has been reprinted (Wm. B. Eerdmans Publishing Company, 1963) a more thorough consideration is in order. About 1935 it became apparent that the existing English translations were unsatisfactory for millions of people who read some English but whose native tongue was not English. The idea of preparing a simplified translation was conceived, and Mr. Williams, a Methodist minister with years of experience in teaching English overseas, was requested to undertake the task.

Plain English

The type of English is "plain" in that it is easily understood and yet neither "babyish" or "pidgin." Moreover, no obsolete words, forms, or word-groups appear. The standard vocabulary is the *Interim Report on Vocabulary Selection* (London: P. S. King and Son, 1936), a word list of about 2000 words "representing a foundation vocabulary for school use in the teaching of English to non-English-speaking pupils from twelve to eighteen years of age." A "Glossary" at the back of the translation lists an additional 167 words made up of special biblical words or ordinary words not included in the *Interim Report*.

Exclusive of proper names, the vocabulary of the Greek New Testament is about 4700 words. Accordingly, Mr. Williams had the difficult task of accurately reproducing the meaning of the biblical writers with less than half of their vocabulary. It is quite amazing how little effect this handicap had. Some traditional words and phrases acquire a new vividness: for example, "hardness of heart" becomes "stupidity" (Mark 3:5) and "hypocrites" are "double-dealers" (Mark 7:6).

The Greek word normally translated "righteousness" is a very complex term, and yet even in this instance a good deal of the original meaning has been preserved. Where the word is used as a technical theological term (as is often the case in Paul's letters) the translation "righteousness" is retained, but other words and phrases are employed elsewhere: for example, "that is right" (Matt. 3:15), "goodness" (Matt. 5:6,10,20; Luke 1:75; John 16:8,10; Acts 13:10;24:25), "good deeds" (Matt. 6:1), "way of doing right" (Matt. 6:33), "justice" (Acts 17:31; Rom. 3:5), "righteous action" (Rom. 1:17), "way of deliverance" (Rom. 3:21,22), and "deliverance" (1 Cor. 1:30).

Text and Style

Souter's edition of the Greek New Testament was, with few exceptions, the standard text for the translation. This edition (published by Oxford Press, 1910) attempted to reproduce the Greek text that lay behind the English Revised Version (1881). In one case (John 19:29) Williams ignores this text. A note explains, "The Greek here is *hyssopo*, which means, 'on hyssop.' But hyssop is a plant used in ceremonies for sprinkling; it is not a thing to put a sponge on. *Hysso* means 'on a spear,' which makes good sense. This is the only place in this translation where a word has been guessed." Although Williams thought this reading (accepted also in Moffatt, Goodspeed, Phillips, and the New English Bible) was a conjecture, it occurs in one Greek manuscript.

Unlike ERV and ASV (1901), Williams does not attempt a word-for-word translation of the Greek text. Furthermore, sentences are kept as short as possible. Whereas Eph. 1:3-14, which is one long sentence in Greek, is punctuated as one sentence in ERV and ASV, and as two sentences in KJV, Williams breaks it up into six sentences. The following examples will illustrate his simple, lucid style:

But we have these jewels in clay pots, that the wonderful greatness of the power may be not ours but God's. We are hard pressed on every side, but not cut off; in difficulty, but not in despair; persecuted, but not helpless; struck down, but not destroyed; everywhere we carry about in our bodies the dying of Jesus, that the life of Jesus may be seen in our bodies (2 Cor. 4:7-10).

You poor, foolish Galatians, who has bewitched you — you who saw Jesus Christ on his cross posted up before your very eyes? I wish to ask you only one thing: did you receive the Spirit because of works of law or because of hearing with faith? Are you so foolish? You began in the Spirit: are you ending now with the flesh? Has all your suffering gone for nothing — if it really is for nothing? (Gal. 3:1-4).

About this we have much to say, but it is hard to explain to you, because you have become dull of hearing. After all this time you ought to be teaching others; yet you need someone to teach you again the ABC of the truth of God; you need milk instead of solid food (Heb. 5:11-12).

Format

It has long been recognized that many passages in the New Testament are poetical in structure, but it is not always easy to determine the line between poetry and prose. Where the poetical nature of a passage is somewhat doubtful the translation appears in the regular paragraph format employed for prose. In the "Preface" Williams explains, "Most of the quotations from the Old Testament, the songs at the beginning of St. Luke, those parts of the teaching of Jesus Christ which are marked by strong rhythm, and the greater part of the Revelation of St. John are taken to be verse and are printed as verse." Luke 1:46-49 is typical:

And Mary said,
My soul gives praise to the Lord,
And my spirit rejoices in God my Saviour;
For he has looked with pity on his slave-girl in her humble place.
For, behold, from this day the people of all times shall call me happy.

For he that is mighty has done great things for me,
And his name is holy.

In order to facilitate reading, Williams omits all quotation marks. This practice has a further advantage, so he claims, in that "it is not necessary to decide where direct speech ends and narrative begins in those places where the Greek itself is not clear." On the other hand, there are places where the order of the Greek text indicates the extent of the quotation clearly and yet the English translation becomes ambiguous: for example, John 19:24, where "that the Scripture might come true" seems to be a part of the soldiers' statement. It would appear that the slight reduction of reading ease occasioned by quotation marks would be more than offset by the greater clarity of meaning. Difficult passages like John 3:15 could have been handled with a note, as in RSV, "Some interpreters hold that the quotation continues through verse 21." In fact, Williams follows this principle at times. Luke 7:29-30, for example, is enclosed within parentheses and a note reads, "Verses 29 and 30 may be the words of Jesus."

Notes

Instead of putting helps for the reader in the margin or at the foot of the page, they are inserted as a unit of "Notes" just prior to the "Glossary." An asterisk (*) in the text alerts the reader to consult the "Notes" for information concerning the word in question. The eleven pages of notes consist of three main types: (1) important differences of reading in the Greek, (2) important differences of meaning, and (3) difficult ideas or strange customs (including weights, measures, money, etc.). In some cases the reader will think the note is an alternative rendering when it is actually a variant Greek reading: for example, the note "Or: anger" (Mark 1:41) gives the impression that this is another meaning for "pity," but it represents another Greek word. A number of variant readings are prefaced with "Some authorities read," and this wording, instead of "Or," would have eliminated the ambiguity.

Conclusion

Mr. Williams explains the origin, nature, and purpose of his translation in an article published in *The Bible Translator* (April, 1952, pp. 61-66). He states that the language of his translation "is of such a kind that the foreigner, learning English as a second language, may take it as a model without being misled and confused." He also adds modestly, "I can think of many groups of readers whose mother-tongue is English to whom I should be willing to commend it." In fact, the translation is so smooth and lucid that only the more observant readers will be aware of the artful simplicity that Mr. Williams has built in. Notwithstanding some minor defects, *The New Testament in Plain English* can be highly recommended for all readers of English: natives or foreigners, educated or uneducated.

THE NEW TESTAMENT: AN EXPANDED TRANSLATION

The late Dr. Kenneth S. Wuest, Professor of New Testament Greek at Moody Bible Institute, intended his expansion as a companion translation to the KJV. He used as many words as he felt necessary to bring out the "richness of truth, force, and clarity of expression left behind in the Greek text" (Vol. 1, p. 11).

Merits of the Translation

Dr. Wuest selected a good Greek text (Nestle's Greek New Testament) as the basis for his translation. At times, however, he reverts to the Greek text back of the KJV without informing the reader that he has disregarded the Nestle text. Mark 16:9-20 is included in the text with no indication of the textual difficulty. The same is true of John 7:53-8:11. Even such doubtful passages as Luke 24:12 and John 5:3b-4 are included.

Another good feature is the deletion of the archaic pronouns ("thou," "thee," etc.), even in the case of Deity. In Matt. 16:16 Simon Peter replies, "As for you, you are the Christ, the Son of God, the living God." The context makes it quite clear that "you" (even without initial capital) is permeated with the sense of Deity.

Other obsolete forms and words from the KJV tradition have been omitted also. Single columns and paragraphs without verse numerals within the text make for easier reading.

In a number of passages Dr. Wuest has indicated more completely the meaning of the Greek, especially in connection with the imperfect and perfect tenses. The Greek imperfect tense denotes a continuous, customary, or repeated action in past time. Whereas most translations have "there went out" (Mark 1:5), Wuest translates "there kept on proceeding out." He has "customarily went" (Luke 2:41) while most translations have "went." The Greek perfect tense indicates a present result based on a past event. For the traditional translation "It is written" (Luke 4:4) Wuest has "It has been written and is now on record." Rom. 12:6-8 is an example of some passages where Wuest has expressed the meaning of the original language in a fresh, clear-cut way:

Having therefore gifts differing according to the grace given us, whether that of prophecy, prophesy according to the proportion of faith; or serving, exercise that gift within the sphere of service; or teaching, within the sphere of teaching; or he who exhorts, within the sphere of exhortation; the one who distributes of his earthly possessions, in the sphere of an unostentatious simplicity; the one who is placed in a position of authority, with intense eagerness and effort; the one who shows mercy, with a joyous abandon.

Defects in the Translation

The entire text is in a prose (paragraph) format, therefore the average reader will be unaware of the poetical passages. No attempt was made to provide such standard helps for readers as references, notes, and maps. Yet in some passages that Wuest considered crucial he incorporated interpretive notes within the text of his translation. Matt. 16:18, for example, reads, "You are Rock [*petros*, masculine in gender, a detached but large fragment of rock], and upon this massive rock [*petra*, feminine in gender, feminine demonstrative pronoun cannot go back to masculine *petros*; *petra*, a rocky peak, a massive rock] I will build my Church."

Brackets are also used to distinguish interpretive notes in Matt. 16:19, 23 and elsewhere in the Gospels, but in Acts 1:15, for example, the reader is likely to be confused because the side remark, which is part of the Greek text, appears within brackets. Because of this inconsistency caution is required where brackets appear.

Word-for-word Translation

The major defects of Wuest's expansion stem from faulty presuppositions. One major premise is that in "so far as a decent regard for good English will allow," a translator should follow "the Greek order of words in the sentence, placing the emphasis where the inspired writer put it" (Vol. 1, p. 13). It is true that at times the word order of the biblical writer is a clue to his meaning, but more often than not the way the writer expressed his idea was due to his training or cultural background. An instructive passage is Acts 28:8b, where Wuest has, "...into whose presence Paul having come and having prayed, having laid his hands upon him, he healed him." This translation points out certain features of style that are common to the biblical writers: (1)

the position of the subject varies considerably whereas in English it tends to come first; and (2) in describing a series of acts participles are used for all of them except the last, which is expressed by a regular verb form.

The important factor is the idea of the writer, not his Greek syntax. Accordingly, the correct principle of translation is to express the biblical idea in good English style. In order to achieve this equivalence of meaning it is often necessary to make a shift in word order and type of expression. The translation of Acts 28:8b by C. Kingsley Williams illustrates the point: "Paul went to see him, and prayed, and laid his hands on him and healed him."

One of Wuest's goals in his word-for-word approach was that the reader might "feel the pulse beat, understand the spirit of the times, sense the freshness, and breathe the exhilarating atmosphere of the original Greek manuscripts" (Vol. 1, p. 12). He even recreates Paul's cumbersome syntax of Eph. 1:3-14 by translating the material as one long sentence. In fact, he outdoes Paul by expanding his 202 Greek words into 338 English words. Where Williams translates, "Have salt in yourselves and be at peace one with another" (Mark 9:50), Wuest has "Be having salt in yourselves and be being at peace with one another." In Mark 2:9 Williams translates simply, "Stand up, take your stretcher, and go." Wuest produces a monstrosity: "Be arising and pick up your pallet at once and carry it away, and start walking and keep on walking." Such labored attempts at precision miss the mark. They do not really represent the "exhilarating atmosphere" of the Greek text and by no stretch of the imagination are they "good English."

Wuest defends his literalism further in that it "has the property of jogging the attention of the reader from his sleepy perusal of a version," thereby forcing him "to meditate over and think through what he is reading" (Vol. 1, p. 13). In an attempt to reproduce the Greek imperfect tense in Acts 27:18 he translates, "They began to be throwing the cargo overboard." This awkward English will certainly "jog" the reader, but will it help him meditate about the meaning? Moreover, the word "began" implies an event covering a period of time in the past, therefore the idea of the Greek could have been adequately expressed as C. Kingsley Williams has it, "They began to throw the cargo overboard."

Pure Translation

Another major defect in Wuest's translation is the assumption that in the vast majority of instances his expansion holds "very closely to the original in a pure translation without paraphrase or interpretation added" (Vol. 1, p. 32). In Acts 17:18 the single Greek word *spermologos* becomes "ignorant plagiarist, picking up scraps of information here and there, unrelated in his own thinking and passing them off as the result of his own mature thought." There are no brackets, therefore it is implied that Wuest considered his 27-word expansion as the equivalent of the single Greek word. But such a translation involves interpretation, and since this is the only occurrence of the word in the New Testament, it is extremely hazardous to be dogmatic about the precise meaning intended by Luke.

The Greek word *kērusso* has the core meaning "to proclaim, declare." In Matt. 3:1;10:7;11:1 Wuest expands this word to read "making a public proclamation with that formality, gravity, and authority which must be listened to and obeyed." In Matt. 4:17 he inserts "as a herald" after "proclamation." The same expansion occurs in Mark 1:4,14;3:14, except that "listened to" becomes "heeded." This elaboration, with its inner variants, is simply Wuest's interpretation. It is doubtful that Jesus and the biblical writers meant all of this in these passages. Wuest himself recognizes that this definition does not fit in other contexts and so elsewhere he translates "making a public proclamation," "publicly proclaim," "proclaimed," "preached," and "teaching."

The word "danced" in Matt. 14:6; Mark 6:22 becomes "performed (danced) a rapid-motion, leaping, lewd dance." In Luke 15:28 "he was angry" becomes "he flew into a rage that was the explosive outlet of a long-time resentment against his brother, a resentment that had been smouldering in his breast." Another illustrative passage is 1 John 3:12, where Cain's murder of Abel is discussed. Wuest expands the verb "slew" to "killed by severing his jugular vein." The Hebrew verb in Gen. 4:8 does not indicate the mode of the murder. Apparently Wuest interpreted Abel's death in the light of animal sacrifice, but there is no clear-cut evidence to justify this conclusion. Instead of being "pure translation" the expansion is really *wishful thinking*.

In contrast to these excessive paraphrases, some important and difficult words are passed over with no paraphrase or bracketed explanation: for example: "Korban" (Mark 7:11) and "Word" (John 1:1).

Within recent years it has become clear that there is always an element of interpretation in a translation. Where the Greek is ambiguous and alternative renderings are possible the theological position of the translator is usually the deciding factor. This element of subjectivity is magnified when a translator attempts to expand and interpret the Greek text. Time and again what Wuest calls "pure translation" is only his theological system superimposed on the biblical text. The odd translations "be having salt" and "be being at peace" (Mark 9:50) resulted from Wuest's desire to show that the Greek present tense indicates action in progess. In John 1:12 he translates the present tense as "those who place their trust." If Wuest had been consistently literal he would have translated "those who are placing their trust" or "those who continue to place their trust." The same is true in John 3:16 where "everyone who places his trust" should have been "everyone who continues to place his trust." It is quite apparent, whether Wuest realized it or not, that his theological point of view led him to violate one of his basic principles of translation.

Some of Wuest's solutions to translation problems stem from an oversimplified set of rules. This is especially true with respect to participles and conditional clauses, but his so-called "mathematical" precision is extended to other areas of Greek grammar. A prime example is his attempt to harmonize the contradiction between Acts 9:7 (where the men with Paul heard a voice) and Acts 22:9 (where they did not hear the voice). Wuest explains, "The word 'voice' in 9:7 is in the genitive case, which means that they heard the voice merely as a sound. In 22:9 it is in the accusative case, which means that they did not understand the words" (Vol. 1, p. 20). Accordingly, in 9:7 he translates "hearing a voice merely as a sound" and in 22:9 after the statement "they did not hear the voice" he adds the unbracketed explanation "so as to understand the words, but heard it merely as a sound."

Yet two verses previously (Acts 22:7) Paul tells how he "heard a voice" (genitive case). According to Wuest's own rule, then, Paul was saying that he heard the voice merely as a sound. But Wuest ignores the rule and translates simply "heard a voice." Since Paul recalls the words of the voice and since he repeats his answer to the question asked by the voice, it is quite evident that Paul heard with understanding. Moreover, in describing Paul's experience the text of Acts 9:4 states that he "heard a voice" (accusative case). The same is true in Acts 26:14 when Paul relates his experience the second time. If Wuest's rule stands, then Paul contradicts himself between Acts 22:7 and 26:14. Thus, while Wuest assures the reader that a problem has been solved, he has actually created another problem. However, the reader is blissfully unaware of the new difficulty because Wuest has translated "heard a voice" (without expansion) in 22:7 and 26:14.

Conclusion

Wuest's major purpose in making *An Expanded Translation* was to recreate for nonscholarly readers "the richness of truth, force, and clarity of expression in the Greek text." This goal will be partially achieved for those who can tolerate the awkward English constructions. On the other hand, Wuest ranges inconsistently from a minimal, literal translation all the way to exaggerated paraphrases. His theological bias and his faulty concepts of Greek grammar are woven throughout the translation.

Unfortunately the expansion is least trustworthy in the very details that were intended to distinguish it from the standard translations. Its supposed advantage becomes its detraction because the readers for whom it was designed will often be misinformed without realizing it. If a person really wants to "breathe the exhilarating atmosphere" of the Greek manuscripts he must learn Greek.

THE NEW ENGLISH BIBLE – NEW TESTAMENT

In 1946, the year that the RSV New Testament appeared, plans for the *New English Bible* (hereafter NEB) were set in motion. Membership on the Joint Committee was extended to include representatives from nine non-Roman communions in the British Isles, plus the British and Foreign Bible Society and the National Bible Society of Scotland. The University Presses of Oxford and Cambridge assumed the cost of the project and therefore they were awarded the copyright.

The Joint Committee, with Dr. C. H. Dodd as Director, assigned the actual work of translation to four panels: Old Testament, Apocrypha, New Testament, and literary advisers for the whole project. The translators were commissioned to make "a faithful rendering of the best available Greek text into the current speech of our own time, and a rendering which should harvest the gains of recent biblical scholarship" (p. vii). The Committee met regularly twice a year, mostly in the Jerusalem Chamber, Westminster Abbey. The New Testament appeared on March 14, 1961, and work continues on the Old Testament and the Apocrypha.

Design and Format

The NEB is a very attractive volume. Single columns with clear type and open spacing between lines make reading a pleasure. Prose is in paragraph format and poetry in poetic style with indented margins. Quotation marks are used, but alternative possibilities are seldom noted: for instance, the words of Jesus are extended through John 3:21 with no note that 3:16-21 may stem from the biblical writer. Verse numerals are along the outside margin of the page on the line where the verse begins. "Sometimes, however," the translators note, "successive verses are combined in a continuous English sentence, so that the precise point where a new verse begins cannot be fixed; occasionally in the interests of clarity the order of successive verses is reversed (e.g., at John 4:7,8)" (p. xiv).

Footnotes (indicated alphabetically beginning on each page) give alternative renderings, variant Greek readings, and explanations of interesting features in the text. The play on words in John 3:8, for example, is indicated by the note "A single Greek word with both meanings" on the words "wind" and "spirit." There are a few inconsistencies. An alternative rendering is noted for Matt. 23:28, but it is missing from the identical passage in Luke 13:35.

While there are no paragraph titles, there are well-chosen section titles. John has six: 'The Coming of Christ" (1:1-51); "Christ the Giver of Life" (2:1-6:71); "The Great Controversy" (7:1-10:39); "Victory over Death" (10:40-12:50); "Farewell Discourses" (13:1-17:26); and 'The Final Conflict" (18:1-21:25). Acts has five: "The Beginnings of the Church" (1:1-5:42); "The Church Moves Outwards" (6:1-12:25); "The Church Breaks Barriers" (13:1-15:35); "Paul Leads the Advance" (15:36-21:26); and "From Jerusalem to Rome" (21:27-28:31).

Text of the Translation

No one manuscript or edition of the Greek text was used as the basis for translation. Each textual problem was considered separately and the solution determined by vote of the Committee. Thus the NEB, like the RSV, represents an eclectic Greek text, but it tends to list more variant readings (NEB 275, RSV 243). This tendency is quite evident in John (33 to 14). The normal introductory phrase is "Some witnesses read (add, omit, or insert)." In some instances the simple formulation of the note does not indicate accurately the complexity of the textual problem: for example, Mark 8:26, where the translation "Do not tell anyone in the village" stems from an early Latin translation and not from the Greek, as the footnote would imply. In a few cases NEB ignores Greek readings with strong support and no footnote alerts the reader: Gal. 4:25, for instance. The text of RSV has "Now Hagar is Mount Sinai in Arabia," but a note indicates the variant, "For Sinai is a mountain in Arabia." While the text of NEB has "Sinai is a mountain in Arabia," there is no note listing the variant.

The NEB, like the majority of recent translations, notes the standard textual variants: for example, the Trinity passage (1 John 5:7-8) is deleted without a note; the two endings of Mark are set off by spaces within the text and notes explain the situation; and John 7:53-8:11 is placed at the end of the Gospel with a note and the section title "An Incident in the Temple." In John 19:29 the NEB has "javelin," with the note, "So one witness; the others read *on marjoram.*" It is thus the first committee translation to follow the lead of individual translators like Moffatt, Goodspeed, C. K. Williams, and Phillips. It is doubtful whether the technical term "marjoram" is an improvement over the traditional word "hyssop."

Translation and Paraphrase

The dilemma of every translator is trying to balance fidelity to the Greek text with intelligibility in current language. If faithfulness to the Greek includes word order, idioms, and sentence structure, then it will not appeal to the modern reader. On the other hand, if the translation is "modernized" too much the reader will get very little flavor of biblical times. The NEB translators attempted to combine both features, but as they state in the "Introduction" (p. xi), "No one who has not tried it can know how impossible an art translation is."

Because the translators were instructed to produce "a genuinely new translation" using "the idiom of contemporary English to convey the meaning of the Greek," the "overriding aims were accuracy and clarity." Thus a meaning-for-meaning approach was followed instead of the older word-for-word method.

But this approach invariably lays greater responsibility on the translator and it necessarily brings up the question of paraphrase. "Our intention," the translators state, "has been to offer a translation in the strict sense, and not a paraphrase, and we have not wished to encroach on the field of the commentator" (p. x). "But," they explain, "if the best commentary is a good translation, it is also true that every intelligent translation is in a sense a paraphrase. But if paraphrase means taking the liberty of introducing into a passage something which is not there, to elucidate the meaning which is there, it can be said that we have taken this liberty only with extreme caution, and in a very few passages, where without it we could see no way to attain our aim of making the meaning as clear as it could be made" (p. x). A good example is John 16:8-11:

When he comes, he will confute the world, and show where wrong and right and judgement lie. He will convict them of wrong, by their refusal to believe in me; he will convince them that right is on my side, by showing that I go to the Father when I pass from your sight; and he will convince them of divine judgement, by showing that the Prince of this world stands condemned.

In many cases the gap between what the Greek text says and what it means was bridged by considering the minds of those for whom the New Testament books were originally written. In general the biblical writers knew the people to whom they were writing and so they implied many things that are not in the experience and understanding of modern readers. How much of this lack should be filled by the translator? This is a very subjective matter indeed, and equally good scholars differ as to the answer. How the NEB translators handled the problem is shared with the reader: "There is probably no member of the panel who has not found himself compelled to give up, perhaps with lingering regret, a cherished view about the meaning of this or that difficult or doubtful passage. But each learned much from the others, and from the discipline of working towards a common mind. In the end we accept collective responsibility for the interpretation set forth in the text of our translation" (p. x).

A very simple illustration of NEB translation principles is John 10:30. The Greek text says literally, "I and the father one are." The RSV translation, "I and the Father are one," makes the minimal change necessary to express the meaning in good English. It was common practice in biblical times for the speaker to note himself first, and this ancient feature is preserved in the RSV. But when a modern reader comes to this idiom he tends to imply a spirit of boastfulness. The NEB translation, "My Father and I are one," removes the possibility of this false implication. Moreover, inasmuch as the Gospel of John has numerous examples of "the Father" and "the Father of me" used interchangeably and apparently with the same meaning, the NEB translators supplied the pronoun "My" at the same time they were inverting the word order. Good examples of more extensive interpretations are found in Rom. 3:20; 2 Cor. 1:24; Gal. 2:17; and Eph. 2:14.

When NEB inserts words not clearly implied by the Greek in order to clarify the meaning, such words are put in parentheses. The very difficult passage in Mark 4:12 begins "so that (as Scripture says) they may look and look, but see nothing." While this interpretation may be questioned, the important feature is that the reader understands that the words have been added. But in Mark 7:26 an explanation by Mark it put within parentheses. This inconsistency is sure to mislead readers because it is not always clearly apparent from the English whether the explanation derives from the biblical writer or from the translators.

Ambiguities of the Greek Text

In a number of instances the Greek text has two possible meanings. The translator can play it safe by reproducing this same ambiguity in his English translation, but the NEB, true to its aim of clarity, makes a choice in most of these situations. The translators explain, "There are passages where no one, in the present state of our knowledge, could say with absolute certainty which of two (or even more) meanings is intended. In such cases, after careful discussion, alternative meanings have been recorded in footnotes, but only where the difference was deemed of sufficient importance" (p. x).

Alternative translations for over 350 passages are given in the footnotes. In at least one instance (Luke 17:21) the Greek text was considered as having four valid translations. The one favored by the Committee appears in the text and the other three are in the notes. One could argue that a number of alternatives with "sufficient importance" have been left out, but this again is a matter of subjectivity.

In some cases NEB did not decide between alternative meanings, but included them both. In Phil. 3:1 and 4:4, for example, the same Greek word is translated "Farewell" and the other meaning "I wish you joy" follows immediately in the text.

Language and Style

The NEB translators define current English as "the natural vocabulary, constructions, and rhythms of contemporary speech" (p. x). At the same time they avoided those "transient modernisms" that are likely to pass out of style and become dated. Some examples of these "current," but "timeless," expressions are as follows: "took to their heels" (Mark 5:14); "more than we can stomach" (John 6:61); "I sponged on no one" (2 Cor. 11:9); and "fighting one another, tooth and nail" (Gal. 5:15).

Current "British English" is not necessarily the same as "American English," however, and so some expressions will seem strange: for example, "people rounded on them" (Matt. 20:31); "they fell foul of him" (Mark 6:4); and "trying to catch me out" (Mark 12:15). While the meaning of such expressions may not be very clear to American readers, the use of "corn," where the text means "grain," will actually mislead the modern American reader.

The aim of "clarity" has been achieved so completely that the meaning flows as easily as the style. This is quite apparent in Paul's letters: for example, Eph. 1:3-14, where Paul's long sentence is broken up into eight sentences. A good deal of credit for the smooth-flowing style is undoubtedly due the literary advisers. The following short passages will illustrate the aptness of expression: " 'Why are you such cowards?' he said; 'how little faith you have!' " (Matt. 8:26); "If your brother commits a sin, go and take the matter up with him, strictly between yourselves, and if he listens to you, you have won your brother over" (Matt. 18:15); "Then Judas spoke, the one who was to betray him. 'Rabbi,' he said, 'can you mean me?' Jesus replied, 'The words are yours'" (Matt. 26:25); "The words were still on his lips, when there came a cloud which cast a shadow over them" (Luke 9:34); "He said to them, 'You are the people who impress your fellowmen with your righteousness; but God sees through you; for what sets itself up to be admired by men is detestable in the sight of God'" (Luke 16:15); and "In a word, there are three things that last for ever: faith, hope, and love; but the greatest of them all is love" (1 Cor. 13:13).

Improved Understanding of the Text

In some cases NEB has gone beyond other committee translations in elucidating the meaning of the text. Whereas RSV follows tradition in translating "lead us not into temptation" (Matt. 6:13), NEB has "do not bring us to the test." No longer will the layman have to wrestle with the implication that God is in the business of tempting people.

In Matt. 7:11 KJV translates, "If ye then, being evil, know how to give good gifts unto your children, how much more shall your Father which is in heaven give good things to them that ask him?" RSV begins the verse, "If you then, who are evil." The word "evil" implies too much. Jesus recognized the sinfulness of man, but in this instance the concept of "depravity" is not foremost in his thinking. The contrast Jesus intended is made explicit when NEB translates, "If you, then, bad as you are, know how to give your children what is good for them, how much more will your heavenly Father give good things to those who ask him!"

Eleven times the KJV translates the Greek word meaning "robber" as "thief." Whereas a thief steals by stealth, a robber uses force. The caves of Palestine in Jesus' day swarmed with bandits and revolutionaries intent on robbery and the overthrow of the Roman government. The story of the good Samaritan (Luke 10:30-37) makes it clear that these "thieves" employed physical violence, but the reader misses an important fact when he does not recognize that Jesus was crucified with two robbers. KJV "den of thieves" (Matt. 21:13; Mark 11:17; and Luke 19:46) does not carry the impact of Jesus' accusation. RSV improves with "den of robbers," but NEB gives the actual meaning with "robbers' cave."

In the Old Testament period the priests, kings, and prophets were messiahs, that is, "anointed ones," because they were anointed with a special oil when they assumed their duties. Between the Old and New Testaments, however, the term "Messiah" came increasingly to be the title for the anticipated king who was to save Israel. In most places the New Testament writers translate the Hebrew word with the Greek term "Christ," but "Messiah" (transliterated into Greek letters) appears in the text of John 1:41 and 4:25 as a title with the explanation that it means "Christ." Therefore, wherever NEB thinks the designation "Christ" is used as a title, the term "Messiah" is substituted (for example, Matt. 1:16, 17, 18; and 2:4).

NEB has also attempted to be more precise in its handling of the term *ekklesia*, traditionally translated "church." In Matthew, Acts, and the Pauline letters "the church" refers to the Jerusalem church or the church universal (the body of Christ). Local groups outside Jerusalem are called "congregations" or "communities." On the other hand, the seven groups named in Rev. 1:11 are called "churches." Aside from this apparent inconsistency, many scholars doubt that the term *ekklesia* had such precise distinctions in first-century Christianity.

Conclusion

Over-all the NEB New Testament is an accurate, smooth-flowing translation with exceptional clarity. It interprets more extensively than RSV but much less than Phillips. On the other hand, NEB agrees with Phillips that "current English" is more important than any linguistic or stylistic ties to the King James tradition of translations. Thus NEB falls logically between RSV and Phillips as a combination of good features from both. In America it will become one of the standard translations for personal study and in time it may rival the KJV and RSV for a place in public worship.

THE TWENTIETH CENTURY NEW TESTAMENT

While *The Twentieth Century New Testament* (hereafter TCNT) was included in "Appendix A" of this book, it was not one of the translations consulted because its more famous contemporary, Weymouth's New Testament (1903), had been selected for illustrations. However, since the Moody Press has reprinted TCNT (1961) it is imperative that some consideration be given to this excellent translation.

Origin and Purpose

In 1933 one of the translators of the TCNT, perhaps the last survivor, entrusted the secretary's records to the safe keeping of The John Rylands Library. Without these papers we might have never known the adventurous story of this version and its courageous translators.

Sometime in 1890 Mrs. Mary Kingsland Higgs, wife of a Congregational minister and mother of four children, wrote to W. T. Stead, editor of *Review of Reviews,* expressing her concern that young people could not understand the traditional idioms found in the KJV and ERV. Elsewhere in England an engineer, Ernest Malan wrote to Mr. Stead expressing the same concern. After Malan and Higgs had been referred to each other they began collaborating on a translation of Mark.

In 1891 Stead printed an invitation for "co-workers in the task of translating the Gospels and the Acts of the Apostles into every-day speech." This appeal brought the Committee of translators up to twenty members. Malan, just 33, was the leader of the project and served as its secretary. Since the members had never met and had to keep in touch by mail, Malan insisted that each one send an autobiographical sketch as an introduction to the others. The fifteen sketches preserved reveal an amazingly disparate group. Their ages ranged from 19 to 63, their education varied greatly, they came from all sections of the British Isles, and their religious affiliations included the Church of England, Presbyterians, Congregationalists, Baptists, and Wesleyans. They were housewives, businessmen, schoolmasters, and ministers. Almost all of them had poor health at one time or another and most of them had large families. Their difficult lives gave them an empathy for the common man, therefore they were active in the social, political, and intellectual revolutions shaking Victorian England at the end of the nineteenth century.

Malan's plan of procedure was so well devised its basic features are still employed for group translations. The Committee was divided into five groups, each with an assigned section to translate. The group, in turn, divided its assignment among its members. Each translator circulated his work among members of the group in order to receive criticism from the others. The finished product of the groups was interchanged and criticized by the other groups. Each group selected one of its members as a Reviser to be its representative on the Revising Committee. The group translations were circulated among the Revisers and changes made only by two-thirds vote. An English Committee, chosen from the translators, reviewed the translation to improve the English idiom. Finally, in order to get the fullest criticism the New Testament circulated for a time in three parts before the definitive publication in one volume.

As the translation progressed, twelve more members were added to the Committee, but unfortunately their biographies were not requested. Since none of the thirty-two members was a recognized scholar, three reputable advisors were brought in. Prof. G. G. Findlay, Headingly College, Leeds, served for a while in 1892. Richard F. Weymouth, who retired as Headmaster of Mill Hill School in 1886 and began his own translation of the New Testament, worked closely with the Committee from 1895 to 1897. Prof. J. Rendell Harris, Clare College, Cambridge, assisted the project briefly in 1901.

Part I (Gospels and Acts) appeared in 1899 and by 1901 all three parts were in circulation. Before completing the publication of his own translation Weymouth died, but Ernest Hampden-Cook (one of the original twenty members of the TCNT) edited the version and had it published in 1903. Comparisons indicate that the Weymouth translation was directly responsible for a number of revisions in the tentative text of the TCNT.

The final edition of the TCNT appeared in 1904 with the subtitle *A Translation into Modern English*. The anonymous preface (dated September, 1904) was written by Edward D. Girdlestone, the translator who had proposed the title *The Twentieth Century New Testament*. The purpose of the translators was, as Girdlestone expressed it, "to enable Englishmen to read the most important part of their Bible in that form of their own language which they themselves use." In support of this appeal for the mother tongue he remarked, "The Greek used by the New Testament writers was not the Classical Greek of some centuries earlier, but the form of the language spoken in their own day." With this insight Girdlestone anticipated the conclusions reached by later scholars.

Format

In the 1904 edition each book of the New Testament is prefaced with an introduction, usually one page, giving background information such as date and authorship. The text of the translation is in paragraphs. In addition to titles for large units of a book (for example, there are five or six for each of the Gospels), many sectional titles highlight the contents for the reader. Verse numerals appear in the margin. Poetry is set off by indentation and smaller type. Quotation marks are used, but alternative possibilities are not indicated. The words of Jesus cease at John 3:15, for example, but there is no note (as in the RSV) that the quotation may extend through verse 21. Most of the footnotes deal with references or explanations. The books are rearranged according to the chronological order accepted by the final revisers. Thus Mark is the first Gospel and James follows immediately after Acts.

The Moody reprint modifies the format of the 1904 edition in some respects. Unfortunately, the excellent preface by Girdlestone has been replaced by a new, one-page preface. The books are rearranged in the traditional order and all introductions have been omitted. British terms like "gaol" and "shilling" are wisely revised. Luke 10:35 is confusing, however, because "four shillings" appears in the text while a footnote explains a "florin." Apparently the editor forgot to change "four shillings" to "two florin."

A good feature of the 1904 edition is the recognition that some nonbiblical books influenced the New Testament writers. References in the footnotes indicate that Jude 14-15 is a quotation from the Book of Enoch and that 2 Pet. 2:4 and Jude 4 and 6 are allusions to the same book. Except for editorial oversights (Enoch 40:5 at Luke 23:35 and Wisdom of Solomon 2:18 at Mark 15:39 and Luke 23:47), the Moody reprint deletes all references to nonbiblical books.

Text of the Translation

The merit of the TCNT stems in part from the fact that it was based on the excellent Greek text of Westcott and Hort. The two endings for Mark are included within square brackets under the headings "A Late Appendix" and "Another Appendix." The Moody reprint omits the headings. An asterisk (*) at John 8:12 refers the reader to the end of the Gospel where John 7:53-8:11 (with the title "A Passage about an Adulteress") appears after the explanation "Inserted in some manuscripts from an ancient source and found either after John 7:52, or after Luke 21:38." The reprint makes no changes, except that in the explanation 7:52 accidentally appears as 7:53. The Trinity passage in 1 John 5 is omitted and the numeral "7" is missing from the margin. Again Moody makes no revision.

Translation and Paraphrase

Girdlestone notes in the preface that the TCNT is not a revision of a previous version, but a new translation made directly from the Greek. While he denies that it is a paraphrase, he adds "Yet, on the other hand, our work is more than a verbal translation. No purely verbal rendering can ever adequately represent the thoughts conveyed in the idioms of another language. In this translation, not only has every word been carefully weighed, but also the emphasis placed upon every word, and the effort has been made to give the exact force and meaning in idiomatic modern English." These pioneers in modern translation techniques applied the principle of equivalent ideas with such a minimum of intepretation their achievement is still superior to some translations made since then.

Even so, a few passages have been revised in the reprint, apparently because they did not conform to (or would raise questions about) the theological views of Moody Press and its constituency. In Matt. 1:18, concerning Mary, "betrothed" becomes "engaged" and "before the marriage took place" is revised to read "while she was still a virgin." "Every Scripture is God-inspired and is helpful" (2 Tim. 3:16) has been substituted for "Everything that is written under divine inspiration is helpful." In all these revisions, however, a footnote indicates the reading found in the text of the 1904 edition.

Language and Style

"Our constant effort," writes Girdlestone, "has been to exclude all words and phrases not used in current English. We have, however, followed the modern practice of using an older phraseology in the rendering of poetical passages, and of quotations fom the Old Testament, and in the language of prayer." Thus, aside from the retention of "thou," for example, in poetry, quotations, and prayer, the TCNT is a marked contrast to the antiquated phraseology of the ERV and ASV. In Matt. 16:16 Peter answers, "You are the Christ, the Son of the Living God."

The overriding concern of Mary Higgs and Ernest Malan had been for a translation that their children could understand, and the Committee of translators continued the policy of clarity at all costs. The TCNT was the first committee translation to break away from many hallowed, but ambiguous or meaningless, expressions found in the KJV and perpetuated in the ERV and ASV.

The Greek text of Matt. 26:27 makes it quite clear that Jesus instructed all of his disciples to drink from the cup but, KJV, ERV, and ASV have the ambiguous translation "Drink ye all of it." While the translators knew what the Greek said, they did not put a comma after "all," therefore most readers have implied that "all" refers to the contents of the cup. The TCNT made a significant change by translating "Drink from it, all of you."

As noted previously (p. 83), Tyndale made a breakthrough in his 1525 translation by using "love" instead of "charity" in 1 Cor. 13. The second edition of the Bishops' Bible (1572) reverted to "charity," however, and the term was preserved in the KJV and ERV. The TCNT vindicated Tyndale's judgment by translating "love."

The translators took a courageous step by rendering "the darkness never overpowered it" in John 1:5. This correct insight (followed by the RSV and other modern versions) removed the obscurity of "comprehended it not" (KJV) and "apprehended it not" (ERV and ASV). For the ambiguous and half-accurate translation "They gave him audience unto this word" (Acts 22:22 in the KJV, ERV, and ASV), TCNT renders lucidly, "Up to this point the people had been listening to Paul."

In Acts 26:28 of the KJV and ERV Agrippa is reported to have said, "Almost thou persuadest me to be a Christian." The margin of ERV and the text of ASV suggest another meaning by translating "With but little persuasion thou wouldest fain make me a Christian." A footnote in the ASV suggests "In a little time thou, etc.," and the TCNT makes this alternative explicit by translating, "You are soon trying to make a Christian of me!"

The ERV and ASV improve the inaccurate KJV translation "For our conversation is in heaven" (Phil. 3:20) by rendering "For our citizenship is in heaven." However, the TCNT is even clearer: "But the State of which we are citizens is in Heaven." The KJV has Paul, who warns against slothfulness (Rom. 12:11), commanding the Philippians, "Be careful for nothing" (4:6). The TCNT expresses Paul's desire: "Do not be anxious about anything."

Conclusion

In our day the two primary criteria for evaluating a translation are accuracy and clarity. At this writing (1964), sixty years after the appearance of the final edition, the TCNT tests out remarkably well. In a Bible study class over a period of years, Dr. E. H. Robertson had occasion to compare the TCNT with other translations and he concluded that it was "the most faithful rendering of the Greek in nearly every difficult passage we encountered" (*The New Translations of the Bible*, p. 54).

The TCNT is equally as good in the realm of clarity. The most important factor was the translators' common spirit of independence. They were pioneers in other realms and this boldness led them to break with traditional concepts and phrases where these were outmoded. Moreover, they were always open to new ideas and ways of improving their own work.

In concluding his story and evaluation of the TCNT, Prof. Kenneth W. Clark is certainly correct when he states, "We are forced to conclude that the devotion to their task has made of them better scholars than they were at first. It is to their credit that they were always responsive to suggested revision, even to the last. Still it is amazing to find that the finest scholars of later years paid tribute to their work by adopting many of the same phrases and perceptive insights. Much of what we may say in praise of this version of 1904 may sound commonplace today, but under the conditions of half a century ago it was extraordinary. It shares with Weymouth's New Testament the honour of inaugurating the truly modern-speech versions" (*Bulletin of the John Rylands Library* [September, 1955] p. 81).

Not all reprints are worthy projects, but this excellent translation has deserved greater recognition and a wider reading. Now, thanks to the Moody Press, this honor can become a reality.

THE NEW JEWISH PUBLICATION SOCIETY VERSION

The Torah: The Five Books of Moses, published on January 28, 1963, is the first section of The New Jewish Publication Society Version (hereafter NJPSV). Whereas the Society's translation of 1917 was in the KJV tradition, this recent translation "is not a revision, but essentially a new translation."

The translation committee consisted of three eminent scholars (Dr. Harry M. Orlinsky, Dr. H. L. Ginsberg, and Dr. Ephraim A. Speiser), three learned rabbis, and the editor of the Society. Since Dr. Orlinsky, also a member of the Old Testament Committee for the RSV, had suggested the idea of a new translation, the Society asked him to serve as editor-in-chief. He "prepared a draft translation which was circulated among the seven working members, each of whom made comments and suggested changes. These were in turn circulated among the members who then, at periodic meetings, arrived at decisions by majority vote." An indication of the care taken is that it took eight years to prepare and publish the Pentateuch alone.

Format

One of the outstanding features of the NJPSV is its improved format. Single columns, paragraph units, unobtrusive verse and footnote indicators, light clear type, and well-spaced lines make for excellent readability. Moreover, fairly long excurses or scribal explanations in the Hebrew text are made explicit by indented units (for example, Deut. 2:1-12,20-23). Shorter intrusions (such as Deut. 3:9,11) appear in the regular text within parentheses.

The NJPSV follows the RSV principle of indicating all poetic passages in poetry format, but since there is often no clear distinction between prose and poetry in the Hebrew text the committee felt justified in carry the principle further (for example, Gen. 7:11;8:22;9:6; 12:2-3). One basic difference between the RSV and NJPSV is that the latter does not employ double indentation it its poetry format.

A decided improvement is the use of Arabic numbers instead of spelling out the numerals (for example, the genealogies in Gen. 5 and 11, and the census reports in Num. 1 and 26). Italics are employed only to transliterate certain doubtful or uncommon Hebrew words: "*hadar* trees" (Lev. 33:40); "*seraph* serpents" (Num. 21:6) instead of the normal translation "fiery serpents;" and measures or units like *kesitah* (Gen. 33:19), *omer* (Ex. 16:16), *ephah* (Ex. 16:36), etc. However, the monetary units "shekel" and "talent" appear in regular roman type.

Since the NJPSV is primarily for Jewish readers, the text indicates the 54 *parashim*, weekly Scripture lessons, which (according to the ancient Jewish tradition of Babylonia) permit the Pentateuch to be read through in one year. In some instances the translators ignore the traditional chapter and verse designations because these divisions are relatively late and at times do violence to the unity of the paragraph or sentence. Gen. 7:24 is coupled with 8:1, for example, following the precedent of Saadia Gaon, the great tenth-century Jewish scholar. Also Gen. 27:46 is joined with 28:1, as in the RSV. A variant versification is followed in the Ten Commandments: the verses Ex. 20:13-16 of most English translations are included under one verse (20:13), and Deut. 5:17-20 becomes 5:17.

In line with the KJV and the RSV, the NJPSV employs "LORD" to indicate "Yahweh," the personal name of Israel's God. In Ex. 6:3, where specific mention is made of the name, the four Hebrew letters (known as the Tetragrammaton) appear in the English text.

Letters of the alphabet are used to indicate footnotes, but instead of lettering consecutively through the alphabet, as in the RSV, the alphabet is begun with each chapter. One disadvantage of this system is that the letter "a" appears twice on some pages (for example, 11 and 17), but this is a minor difficulty.

Text of the Translation

The committee "undertook faithfully to follow the traditional (Masoretic) text." Words clearly implied in the Hebrew idioms are supplied in the English text with no distinguishing features. In some instances neither the Hebrew text nor the idiom warrants the words demanded by the context. In such cases the additional words appear within square brackets: for example, Gen. 1:30;14:11; Lev. 27:9.

Care is also taken to distinguish different Hebrew words with corresponding English terms. In Ex. 7:3, for example, the verb *qashah* is translated "harden," as in most translations, but *hazaq* (7:13) becomes "stiffen" rather than "harden." A distinction is made also between *peder* "suet" (Lev. 1:8) and *heleb* "fat" (Lev. 4:26).

Alternative Renderings

The text of the RSV for Gen. 1:1 begins with the traditional rendering "In the beginning God created," while the alternative translation "When God began to create" appears in a footnote. The NJPSV improves on the RSV by putting the alternative rendering up in the text. In order not to lose the traditional translation, it is placed in a footnote prefaced by "Or."

While the translators were convinced of the essential accuracy of the Masoretic text, they quite openly recognized difficulties and defects in the Hebrew text before them. A number of footnotes state, "Heb obscure," or "Meaning of Heb uncertain." When "an old rendering, no longer retained, was so well known that it would very likely be missed," the traditional translation was put in a footnote prefaced by "Others;" for example, Gen. 6:2, where "the divine beings" appears in the text and "the sons of God" in the note.

Revocalization of the Text

Although the vowels of the traditional text were supplied relatively late (after A.D. 600), the NJPSV committee followed the Masoretic vocalization wherever possible. In the KJV Gen. 10:10 reads, "And the beginning of his kingdom was Babel, and Erech, and Accad, and Calneh, in the land of Shinar." According to the best archaeological information the city "Calneh" was in Syria, not "Shinar," the ancient name for Babylonia. By supplying different vowels with the consonants of "Calneh," the RSV translators arrived at the rendering "The beginning of his kingdom was Babel, Erech, and Accad, all of them in the land of Shinar." The NJPSV retains "Calneh" in the text, but it explains in a footnote, "better vocalized *we-khullanah* 'all of them being.'"

In an attempt to solve the meaning of the enigmatic "Shiloh" (Gen. 49:10), the consonants were divided into two groups and revocalized as *shai loh,* meaning "tribute to him." A footnote on "So that tribute shall come to him" indicates the vowel change and then adds "following Midrash; cf. Isa. 18:7. Heb. obscure; lit. 'until he comes to Shiloh.'"

Readings from Related Passages

At times the translators recognized that the more probable reading was to be found in similar or correlated passages elsewhere in the Masoretic text. While "Dodanim" is retained in the text of Gen. 10:4, the footnote indicates that the preferred reading "Rodanim" occurs in 1 Chron. 1:7. At other times the committee was bold enough to depart from the traditional text. A good example is Gen. 10:5, where the statement "These are the sons of Japheth" appears in the text within square brackets. Since the justification lies in similar expressions connected with "Ham" (10:20) and "Shem" (10:31), a footnote reads, "Cf. vv. 20 and 31."

Another revision of the Masoretic text occurs in Gen. 10:14. The RSV, following the traditional text, translates "Pathrusim, Casluhim (whence came the Philistines), and Caphtorim." Amos 9:7 states that the Philistines came "from Caphtor," that is, the island of Crete. Accordingly, in Gen. 10:14 the NJPSV has, "the Pathrusim, the

Casluhim, and the Caphtorim, whence the Philistines came forth." A
note on "Caphtorim" reads, "I.e. the Cretans; moved up for the sake
of clarity; cf. Amos 9:6." According to the Kittel edition of the
Masoretic text, and all the English translations, the reference to
Caphtor occurs in Amos 9:7. Unless the translators were employing
some variant versification, the note should be corrected. In any case, a
related passage is used to revise the order of the Masoretic text.

It should be noted that the committee did not employ the RSV
footnote symbol "Cn" (Correction) to indicate a change in the consonantal Hebrew text. Rather, it chose to use explanatory notes, leaving
it to the reader to understand the extent of the textual change.

Variants from the Versions

Another means of improving faulty portions of the Masoretic text
was the use of textual variants "found in some of the ancient manuscripts or versions of the Bible." An interesting example is Gen. 4:8.
On the basis of the Samaritan Pentateuch, and the Greek (Septuagint)
and Syriac translations, the RSV includes "Let us go out to the field"
in the text. The NJPSV indicates its preference for this variant by the
footnote "Ancient versions, including the Targum, read 'Come, let us
go out into the field.'" Since adherence to the Masoretic Hebrew
seemed to bar the variant from the text, the committee got around the
difficulty by translating, "And Cain said to his brother Abel[e] ... and
when they were in the field, Cain set upon his brother Abel and killed
him." Footnote "[e]" supplies the missing words.

Further marginal references to textual variants are noted at Ex. 5:5;
Num. 24:17; and Deut. 11:14. The NJPSV translators show their
objectivity by preferring certain readings from the Samaritan Pentateuch, notwithstanding the long rivalry between the Samaritans and
the Jews that has tended to prevent traditionally oriented Jews from
considering any variants from this source.

It is clear, therefore, that in their references to textual variants the
NJPSV translators have actually employed an English version of the
Kethib-Qere system (see "Appendix E," p. 155) used by the Masoretic
scribes. Where adherence to the *Kethib* "written" text of the Masoretic
tradition excluded a reading from the *Kethib* of the English text, the
committee indicated its preference by a footnote, with the implication
that the marginal English translation was *Qere* "to be read."

One might dissent from some of the textual variants employed or
point out some apparent inconsistencies, but in general the NJPSV

translators have been very judicious in their handling of the text. Over-
all they are more faithful to the Masoretic text than the RSV, yet they
frankly admit that the Hebrew text is faulty in places. Moreover,
within the limitations prescribed for the translation they do not hesitate
to indicate the better reading.

Improved Renderings

One of the major objectives of the NJPSV translators was "accuracy"
and they were bold enough to utilize archaeological and linguistic ad-
vances of the last half-century by improving on many traditional
phrases and renderings. The text of Ex. 10:19 and 13:18, for example,
has "Sea of Reeds," while the note explains, "Traditionally, but in-
correctly, 'Red Sea.'" Thus the NJPSV corrects an ancient misunderstanding of which the RSV was cognizant but declined to handle. The
RSV text of Gen. 2:6 reads, "but a mist went up from the earth and
watered the whole face of the ground." A footnote on "mist" states,
"Or *flood.*" The NJPSV takes this preferable reading into the text by
translating, "but a flow would well up from the ground and water the
whole surface of the earth." Another advance over the RSV occurs in
Gen. 38:21, where instead of "harlot" the NJPSV has "cult prostitute,"
as in the RSV note.

The legal sections in Exodus and Leviticus have a number of improved translations made possible by recent knowledge about the
customs and thinking of the ancient Near East. The Society claims, "In
accuracy alone we believe this translation has improved on the first
JPS translation in literally hundreds of passages." One must concur,
and one might add that in many places it has improved on all existing
English translations of the Old Testament.

Language and Style

The RSV took a half step when it translated passages addressed
to Jesus Christ with "you" instead of "thou," but it retained the archaic
pronouns in all statements addressed to God because they were still
commonly used in prayer. The NJPSV takes the other half step by
eliminating all archaic personal pronouns. Not even the unpublished
Old Testament of the New English Bible plans to take this step. But
the effect in the NJPSV is somewhat dulled by the appearance of capital letters beginning *all* pronouns referring to Deity. While the use
of capitalized pronouns for Deity has been common in popular religious
writing, the practice has seldom been employed in the *major* English

translations of the Old Testament. Moreover, since the practice has been dying out, its use in the NJPSV would seem to be a reversion. The only reason for a pronoun with a capital letter is in the case of ambiguity, but seldom does the reader require such assistance. One example of "you" in lower case, occurs in Ex. 5:22, where Moses is addressing God. Would that all the other pronouns were like it!

The other major objective of the NJPSV translators was "clarity." Along with the RSV, they eliminate the Hebrew idiom "and it came to pass," but they go further in shortening other idioms where all the words are not necessary for an equivalent English expression. The particle *waw*, which was very common in ancient Hebrew style, is normally translated "and" in the KJV and ASV. The NJPSV, like the RSV, recognizes that the particle can be translated a number of ways, or left untranslated, depending on the sense required by the context. However, the NJPSV is even more true to English idiom in the variety of translation given *waw* and in the freedom with which it ignores the particle.

The NJPSV communicates with a new intensity because of its truly modern terms and idioms. Some may consider such modernity as bordering on sacrilege, but those without traditional fixations will benefit from it. The story of Balaam is an excellent example of the short, crisp style in the NJPSV: RSV "God's anger was kindled," NJPSV "God was incensed" (Num. 22:22); RSV "Balaam's anger was kindled," NJPSV "Balaam was furious" (22:27); and RSV "I wish I had a sword in my hand, for then I would kill you," NJPSV "If I had a sword in my hand, I'd kill you" (22:29). Other examples are: RSV "beguiled," NJPSV "duped" (Gen. 3:13); RSV "Make marriages," NJPSV "Intermarry" (Gen. 34:9); RSV "Let it suffice you; speak no more to me of this matter," NJPSV "Enough! Never speak to Me of this matter again" (Deut. 3:26); and RSV "fear," NJPSV "revere" (Deut. 10:12).

In giving precedence to clarity and equivalent English expressions the NJPSV is so modernized that the flavor of the Hebrew idiom is often lost. In a number of places, therefore, the translators have indicated the literal Hebrew or traditional rendering in a footnote. A prime example is Ex. 20:7, where the text reads, "You shall not swear falsely by the name of the LORD your God." This is a vast improvement over the traditional translation, found even in the RSV, because "take in vain" is commonly interpreted to mean "curse" by using God's name. The translation "ale" (Deut. 14:26) is a distinct advance over "strong drink," as in the KJV, ASV, and RSV, because the average reader takes this expression to mean distilled or hard liquors, something the ancient Hebrews never had. Where the RSV translates "valley of Siddim (that is, the Salt Sea)," the NJPSV reads, "Valley of Siddim, now the Dead Sea" (Gen. 14:3). Since the ancients tended to use the figures 5 and 10 as generalities, the NJPSV translates the Hebrew word "five" as "several" (Gen. 43:34) and "a few" (Gen 47:2). In Num. 14:22 "ten" is translated "many."

Explanatory Footnotes

The NJPSV makes common use of explanatory footnotes. In Gen. 2:7, for example, two notes indicate the relation of the word "man" (Heb *'adam*) to the word "earth" (Heb *'adamah*). Other plays-on-words not indicated by the RSV occur in Gen. 4:25;9:27;16:2; and 25:25. A note on "officers" (Ex. 14:7) states, "Heb *shalish*; originally 'third man on royal chariot'; hence 'adjutant,' 'officer.'" Where a specific event is referred to in the text a note gives the reference: for example, "the regular burnt offering instituted at Mount Sinai" (Num. 28:6) refers the reader to Ex. 29:38-41. A note at Ex. 38:24 states, "A talent here equals 3,000 shekels." A footnote for "Urim and Thummim" (Ex. 28:30) declares, "Meaning of these two words uncertain. They designate a kind of oracle: cf. Num. 27:21."

Theological Implications

Any attempt to achieve accuracy and clarity necessarily involves the theological aspects of the Hebrew text. In Gen. 1:2 the NJPSV speaks of "a wind from God sweeping over the water." The new translation is explained (in a brochure) as follows: "The Christian translation of this word (Heb *ruach*) has been 'spirit,' and this interpretation was adopted in the 1917 edition of the JPS Bible. But in the context *ruach* is used, as it is used in Genesis 8:1 when God causes a *ruach* to calm the Flood, 'wind' becomes the more accurate and acceptable translation. Moreover, the use of the word 'spirit' implies there was a secondary, or intermediary, power participating in the Creation — an implication totally unacceptable to Judaism." Although some Christians have taken affront at this statement, it must be acknowledged that the doctrine of the creative activity of Christ, the pre-incarnate Word, is a New Testament claim. One can believe the doctrine, notwithstanding Judaism's rejection of it, but that does not warrant reading the New

Testament concept back into the Old Testament. In all probability the writer of Genesis thought in terms of "the wind of (from) God."

A similar situation is found in Gen. 1:26, where the NJPSV translates, "And God said, 'I will make man in My image, after My likeness.'" A note explains, "Taking the Heb plural forms as plurals of majesty; cf. v.27." There is much justification for this change. *Elohim,* the Hebrew term for God, is a plural form, yet when the word is used for the God of Israel the singular form of the verb occurs. Moreover, as the note indicates, the Hebrew text of Gen. 1:27 clearly states, "And God created man in his image." Why the plural forms occur in 1:26 is impossible to determine. Another instance of the plural appears in Gen. 3:22, where the NJPSV and all other translations have "the man has become like one of us." Apparently the use of "one" prevented the NJPSV from rendering "the man has become like Myself." Even if one grants that Gen. 1:26 and 3:22 indicate a plurality in the Godhead, that plurality was not understood to be a Trinity, as many Christians claim, but as God addressing those of his royal court (see Ps. 82:1). Again great care must be taken not to read New Testament ideas back into the Old Testament text.

All in all, the NJPSV is as well suited for Christians as for Jews. It vindicates the publisher's claim that it "is the most accurate account of the true meaning of God's Word ever to appear in English." We can look forward with anticipation to the publication of the two remaining portions of the Old Testament: Second Section, "The Prophets," and Third Section, "The Sacred Writings."

FOUR PROPHETS: AMOS, HOSEA, FIRST ISAIAH, MICAH

Because of the great success of *The New Testament in Modern English* many hundreds urged J. B. Phillips to continue his good work through the Old Testament. He was "touched and pleased" by this confidence in him and so he accepted the challenge. But the Hebrew Old Testament is a far more difficult and complex problem than that of the Greek New Testament, and in the opening sentence of the "Translator's Preface" Phillips confesses, "Many times during the last few years I have found myself wondering why I ever agreed to attempt to translate four Old Testament prophets into the English of today!"

Phillips selected these four prophets "partly because the period of their ministry was such a crucial time in the history of God's chosen people, and partly because they pierce through a great many falsities (including religious falsities)."

Format

The text is single column with the same type for prose passages (in paragraphs) and for poetry (with indented lines). The "easy-to-read" quality of these pages is enhanced by many section titles or "cross-headings," as Phillips calls them. In his New Testament chapter and verse are indicated only at the beginning of each section or unit of text, but the difficulty of the text made this approach impossible in the Old Testament. Chapters are indicated by headings in capital letters (for example, "CHAPTER ONE"), while the verse numerals appear in the margin to the left of the text. Sometimes, as in the RSV and other translations, units of text ignore the chapter divisions.

The "Translator's Preface" is followed by "Historical Background," a chapter in which E. H. Robertson discusses the world-wide importance of the century 750-650 B.C. Phillips arranges the prophets in their chronological order (Amos, Hosea, Isaiah, and then Micah) rather than in traditional order of the English Bibles. An introduction to each book treats background and preliminary information under the headings "THE PROPHET" and "THE THEME." Since Isaiah closes with chapter 35, the heading "CHAPTERS THIRTY-SIX TO THIRTY-NINE" has the following explanation:

These chapters, which conclude the first part of the book of Isaiah, are paralleled almost exactly in 2 Kings 18:13-20:19. The chief differences in the two accounts are (a) the omission in the book of Isaiah of the story of Hezekiah's submission and payment of tribute (2 Kings 18:14-16); and (b) the addition of the psalm of thanksgiving, following Hezekiah's recovery from illness. This can be found in Isaiah 38:10-20, although most scholars do not consider this psalm to have been the work of Isaiah. The American Revised Standard Version provides a more accurate and intelligible version of the psalm than the familiar Authorised Version.

The reader is not informed about chapters 40-66, but the use of "First Isaiah" implies that these chapters will appear in another section under the title "Second Isaiah."

In Amos and Hosea, Phillips continues his New Testament practice of omitting all footnotes, but quite unexpectedly five notes appear in Isaiah (15:9;19:11;28:13;30:29-33; and 34:16). There are no notes in Micah. Quotation marks are not used for direct discourse and the

KJV-RSV practice of using "LORD" (with small capital letters) for
Yahweh is abandoned. Thus *'Adonay* (as in Isa. 6:1) and *Yahweh*
(Isa. 6:3) both appear as "Lord," with lower case letters.

Two maps ("The World Surrounding the Four Prophets" and "The
Land in the Time of the Four Prophets") are included at the end of
the translation.

Text of the Translation

Four Prophets has the subtitle *A Modern Translation from the
Hebrew*. But as Phillips acknowledges in his Preface, "Sometimes
the text is 'defective,' which means that some word or words are missing, and sometimes it is 'corrupt', which means that later hands have
altered, or made additions to, the original writing so that no one now
knows what it was." Thus four of the five notes in Isaiah deal with
problems of the text (for example, the note for 30:29-33 reads, "The
verses from here to the end of Ch. 30 are obviously out of order. I owe
this re-arrangement to the Interpreter's Bible."). It is strange that some
notes do not appear in Hosea, for (as Phillips notes in the introduction
to the book) the Hebrew text of chapters 4-14 "is sometimes unin-
telligible, and the messages themselves appear to be muddled and
repetitive." The numerous footnotes in the RSV testify to this fact.

Major shifts in the order of the text are clearly indicated by the verse
numerals in the margin: for example, 3a, 12, 3b and 11, 13 in chapter
12 of Hosea indicate that verse 12 has been inserted (as in Moffatt's
Old Testament) between the first and last parts of verse 3. It is impossible, however, for the average reader to detect smaller revisions and
deviations from the Hebrew text. Phillips' assumption is that the
reader must trust his judgment as to the best text.

At times Phillips turns to the Septuagint for help. With Moffatt,
American Translation (hereafter AT), and the RSV he has "Assyria"
in Amos 3:9, while the KJV and ASV retain the Hebrew reading
"Ashdod." In Isa. 1:20, however, Phillips omits "for the mouth of the
Lord has spoken," even though the Dead Sea Isaiah Scroll, the standard
Hebrew text, the Septuagint, and all the major English translations
contain the words. Phillips' primary concern for the meaning of a passage leads to some rather bold handling of the Hebrew text, but it is
questionable that this omission was intentional. A similar expression in
Mic. 4:4 is translated, "The Lord of hosts has declared this with his
own voice."

Translation and Paraphrase

In the "Translator's Preface" of *Letters to Young Churches* Phillips expresses the principles that governed his translation. "When necessary," he notes, "the translator should feel free to expand or explain, while preserving the original meaning as nearly as can be ascertained." This "translation (or in some cases, the paraphrase) should 'flow' and be easy to read." In *Four Prophets* Phillips claims, "I have said more than once that a translator is not a commentator; his job is communication. I have done my best to translate, not for the scholar but for the ordinary intelligent layman. I have tried, wherever possible, without distorting the Hebrew, to convey the Prophet's message as clearly as I can."

Phillips is absolutely correct in his claim that the only accurate translation of some passages is a paraphrase. The difficulty is determining when the paraphrase has crossed that fine line separating it from commentary on the text. In Amos 3:15, for example, the KJV, ASV, and RSV translate the Hebrew literally as "houses of ivory," but archaeology has shown that these ancient palaces were panelled with, not made of, ivory. The expression was not misunderstood originally because this fact was known. Phillips has prevented the modern reader from misinterpreting the Hebrew idiom by the expanded translation "ivory-panelled houses." The Hebrew text of Amos 4:1 is translated "Bring, and let us drink" (KJV and ASV) and "Bring, that we may drink" (RSV). Since Amos 6:6 makes it clear that the leaders in Samaria drank "wine in bowls," Phillips (following Moffatt's lead) expands the condensed Hebrew text of 4:1 to read "Bring us wine to drink."

The reviewer agrees that paraphrastic interpretations of this sort are valid and even necessary if the modern reader is to get the most accurate picture of the ancient situation. The only criticism would be instances in which the principle seems to be carried too far. In Isa. 3:4, for example, Phillips translates, "And I will make mischievous boys their leaders and let them be led by the nose," whereas the RSV (following the Hebrew text closely) has, "And I will make boys their princes, and babes shall rule over them." Does the context really imply that the boys will be "mischievous" and is the English idiom "led by the nose" the best way to reproduce the meaning of the Hebrew?

Phillips has a far more valid reinterpretation in Amos 6:5. The KJV and ASV agree in essence with the RSV translation, "Who sing idle songs to the sound of the harp, and like David invent for themselves

instruments of music." Since the first part of the verse deals with singing of songs, Phillips (following Moffatt and AT) interprets the general Hebrew word "instruments, equipment" as referring to musical
compositions. He translates accordingly, "Who croon to the music of
the harp, and compose melodies as though you were David himself!"
In Amos 7:12 Moffatt translates "O seer" as "You dreamer!" Phillips
heightens Amaziah's sarcasm by expanding the retort to read "you silly
dreamer!"

In Hos. 7:8 the RSV (following the Hebrew text closely) has,
"Ephraim mixes himself with the peoples; Ephraim is a cake not
turned." Phillips expands to read, "Israel has lost himself among
strangers, Ephraim is half-baked — scorched on one side and uncooked
on the other!" Phillips does not make a practice of using explanatory
notes and so he incorporates explanations in the text. By substituting
"Israel" for the first use of "Ephraim" he is following the inverted order
of Hos. 11:8, where "Ephraim" appears in the first line and "Israel"
in the second. Apparently Phillips is informing the reader that Hosea
employs "Ephraim," then the dominant northern tribe, as a symbol for
"Israel," the northern kingdom. In Isa. 7:3 "Shearjashub," the Hebrew
name of Isaiah's son, is followed by the English translation "(Return-of-
the-Remnant)." The reverse procedure is followed in Isa. 8:1, where
the text has *"Quick-pickings-Easy-prey* (Maher-shalal-hash-baz)."

Speaking of explanations, the name "Zoan" (Isa. 19:11) has the
footnote, "Egypt's summer capital, near the border of Palestine, and
therefore the court best known to Isaiah." It is difficult to account for
this unexpected note. It contradicts Phillips' practice and, furthermore,
there are numerous passages where explanatory notes are as necessary,
if not more so, than here.

Modernizing the Text

The long expansion in the last half of Hos. 7:8 is Phillips' attempt
to make the Hebrew idiom explicit to the reader. Closely related to the
matter of paraphrase is the question of how much of the ancient flavor
is to be preserved in a translation. As in the New Testament, Phillips'
primary concern is with the meaning of the text. He states, therefore,
"We should be able to know what the prophet meant, and, to some
extent, feel what he felt without being continuously and embarrassingly
aware of that gulf of 2,600 years. In other words, we must try to place
the emphasis on what is of eternal value and tone down the 'accidents'
of period and place."

Thus, for the Hebrew term "Sheol," meaning the gloomy place where the spirits of the dead reside, Phillips translates "the land of the Dead" (for example, Amos 9:2, where Moffatt has "Death-land," and Isa. 5:14). Yet in Hos. 13:14, where Moffatt has "Death-land," Phillips has "the power of Sheol." Apparently he rejected the expansion here because the line would have been very cumbersome and also it is clear from the text line that "the power of Sheol" means "death." In Isa. 14:9,11,15 Phillips, again following Moffatt's lead, translates "Sheol" as "the underworld," but the context will prevent the American reader from thinking in terms of professional gangsters.

The Hebrew idiom "cleanness of teeth," preserved in the KJV, ASV, and RSV of Amos 4:6, has nothing to do with dental hygiene, therefore Phillips translates "hungry mouths." Bible readers are so accustomed to Hebrew idioms carried over into English they do not realize how odd they sound to people reared outside the Church. Isaiah's accusation "your hands are full of blood" (1:15) does not mean what it literally says, and so Phillips rephrases, "Your hands are dripping with blood." Another example is the time-honored idiom "as the waters cover the sea" (Isa. 11:9). This literal translation of the Hebrew, found even in the RSV, is strange to modern ears. Moffatt catches the sense by rendering "as the ocean-bed is full of water." Similarly, Phillips translates "as the seas are filled with water."

The ASV and RSV retain the idiom to "strike hands" (Isa. 2:6), but Phillips explains the custom by translating "make bargains." It is interesting to note that the KJV translators attempted to modernize the idiom by translating "please themselves." The Hebrew idiom of Amos 1:3 is preserved by the RSV translation, "For three transgressions of Damascus, and for four, I will not revoke the punishment." This expression "three...and four," which occurs seven more times in the first two chapters, has the sense of "too much" or "more than enough." Moffatt has "After crime upon crime of Damascus I will not relent," and Phillips follows the suggestion by translating, "Because of outrage after outrage committed by Damascus I will not relent!"

Along with Moffatt and half the translators of AT, Phillips eliminates "im," the Hebrew masculine plural ending, by using English plural forms; for example, traditional "seraphim" (Isa. 6:6) becomes "seraphs." He also concurs with Moffatt's substitution of general terms for specific Hebrew words for weights, measures, etc. Where the RSV renders "that we may make the ephah small and the shekel great" (Amos 8:5), Moffatt has, "small you make your measures, large your weights."

Phillips improves by reading, "While you make your measure short and your price high." Isa. 5:10 in the RSV reads, "For ten acres of vineyard shall yield but one bath, and a homer of seed shall yield but an ephah." "Bath" is not our English word, but a transliteration of a Hebrew liquid measure, and since ten of the dry measure "ephah" equal a "homer," Moffatt translates, "For ten acres of vineyard shall yield but eight gallons, and the harvest shall only be a tenth of what is sown." Phillips reads similarly, "Ten acres of vineyard will produce only a few gallons, and the harvest of grain be but a tenth of the seed that is sown."

Over and above the modernization of idioms, Phillips converts intelligible terms into equivalent expressions that the author might have used had he written to communicate to our generation. A striking example, found only in Phillips, is "party dresses" where the RSV has "festal robes" (Isa. 3:22). In Isa. 5:27 "belt," as in Moffatt, replaces "waistcloth" (RSV) and "girdle" (KJV and ASV). Where the KJV, ASV, and RSV have "crush" (Amos 4:1), Phillips paraphrases "ride roughshod over." The traditional translation "How the faithful city has become a harlot!" (Isa. 1:21) regains some of its sting with Phillip's unique rendering, "See what a slut the city has become — she who was once so true!" A decided improvement theologically is "reverence" (Isa. 11:2), as in Moffatt, instead of the traditional term "fear."

One area where Phillips attempts to preserve the ancient flavor is with respect to the pun. In Amos 8:1-2 the Lord shows Amos a basket of "summer fruit" (Heb. *qayits*). When Amos acknowledges what he sees the Lord informs him that the "end" (Heb. *qets*) of Israel has come. The RSV indicates the pun by the transliterations in the footnotes, but with the one exception noted above Phillips does not use explanatory notes. Rather he accepts Moffatt's clever solution by using "ripe" to indicate the pun: "And he said, Amos what do you see: And I said, A basket full of ripe fruit. Then the Lord said to me, So are my people Israel ripe for destruction."

Mic. 1:10-15 contains a series of the prophet's puns on the names of towns taken or threatened by Sennacherib, the Assyrian king. Over this unit Phillips has the heading "The Prophet looks at the little towns and puns bitterly over their place-names." Taking his clue again from Moffatt, he makes the puns explicit by inserting an English translation of the root idea that the prophet saw in the Hebrew name of the town. In 1:10, for example, the RSV reads, "Tell it not in Gath, weep not at all; in Beth-le-aphrah roll yourselves in the dust." Phillips has, "So then, in Gath where tales are told, breathe not a word! In Acco, the town of Weeping, shed no tear! In Aphrah, the house of Dust, grovel in the dust!"

Language and Style

Phillips' ideal is to present the "Prophets' message" in "modern English." He succeeds very well, even for those who speak American English. British spellings such as "judgement" and "honour" are minor matters. Probably the most misleading expression is "corn" (for example, Amos 8:5 and Hos. 2:9), the British synonym for "wheat." Inasmuch as the Hebrew terms translated "corn" actually refer to a grain such as "wheat," use of the latter word should have eliminated from American minds the erroneous idea of "maize, Indian corn" while still communicating the accurate meaning in words understood by the British.

Phillips, like the NJPSV, goes beyond Moffatt, AT, and the standard translations by rejecting all archaic pronouns, even when addressing God. But in contrast with the NJPSV Phillips does not capitalize the pronouns referring to Deity. Isa. 12:1 reads, "I give thanks to you, Lord; for you were angry with me and now your anger is past and you have given me comfort." Another good example is Isa. 25:1, "O Lord, you are my God; I will glorify you, I will sing the praises of your name."

In his preface Phillips observes that the informal, down-to-earth style that he employs in *Letters to Young Churches* is "wildly unsuitable for the transferring into English of the dignified utterance or the passionate pleading of these ancient men of God. There is little hint in any of them of a conversational, let alone a colloquial, style. They were speaking in the name of the Lord and, like King James' translators . . . , both they and their later editors thought that only the highest language could do justice to the oracles of the Most High."

"But," as Phillips hastens to note, "no one could deny that the meaning of even the most beautiful passages is frequently obscure, and the sharp edge of what the prophets had to say is blunted by being enclosed in so beautiful a scabbard." He attempted, therefore, "a style at once more lofty than our common speech and yet not so far removed from us that our minds cease to receive the message as God's living Word and relegate it to the realm reserved for aesthetic appreciation. For the Bible was never designed to be read merely as literature."

The following samples are typical:

Alas for the complacent ones in Zion,
Who live on the heights of Samaria without a care,
Appointed by the whole house of Israel! (Amos 6:1)

But come home, Israel, come home to the Lord your God!
For it is your sins which have been your downfall. (Hos. 14:1)

The Lord has also said:
Because the daughters of Zion are high and mighty,
Walking with their noses in the air,
Flirting with their eyes,
Mincing along with jingling anklets,
The Lord shall strike their scalps with scabs
And uncover what they keep hidden. (Isa. 3:16-17)

Who is he trying to teach?
Who is he trying to instruct?
Are we just weaned,
Are we children just taken from the breast,
Do we have to learn that
The-law-is-the-law-is-the-law,
The-rule-is-the-rule-is-the-rule,
A little bit here, a little bit there? (Isa. 28:9-10)

But you, Bethlehem Ephratah,
Almost too small to be counted
Among the ranks of Judah,
From you shall come forth for me
The future Ruler of Israel!
He springs from a line of ancient times,
From the days of long ago. (Mic. 5:2)

You know well enough, Man, what is good!
For what does the Lord require from you,
But to be just, to love mercy,
And to walk humbly with your God? (Mic. 6:8)

Conclusion

James Moffatt blazed a trail in Old Testament translation method
with the appearance of his Bible in 1924. In some respects *An American
Translation* (1927) carried on this tradition. Phillips is in debt to both
of these translations, but especially to Moffatt. On the other hand,
Phillips makes his own contribution and in a number of places he
improves on his predecessors.

In any given passage one might dissent from Phillips' reconstruction
of the Hebrew text, his interpretation of that text, or his equivalent
English expression, but granting his purpose of translating "for the

ordinary intelligent layman," one must conclude that Phillips has been eminently successful. His first venture into the Old Testament had the same lucid and piercing qualities that characterized his work in the New Testament. The awe, authority, urgency, righteous indignation, compassion, and love that characterized the prophets are communicated with intensity. It is especially suited for those without a traditional or Church orientation, but it serves admirably as a supplemental translation to clarify many obscure and strange passages in the standard versions. It is hoped that Phillips will continue his task through the Old Testament.

THE AMPLIFIED BIBLE

The *Amplified Bible* (hereafter AB) is one of the projects completed under the auspices of The Lockman Foundation. The New Testament appeared in 1958, Part Two of the Old Testament (Job-Malachi) in 1962, and Part One (Genesis-Esther) in 1964. Mrs. Frances E. Siewert, Research Secretary and leading figure in preparation of the translation, wrote the introductions to the volumes.

The AB is designed to furnish (as far as the Greek and Hebrew texts legitimately permit) "multiple expressions for a richer, fuller and more revealing appreciation of the divine message. It is not a substitute for other versions. It is intended to supplement them, authentically, concisely and in convenient form." In selecting the multiple expressions for the New Testament, for example, "twenty-seven translations and versions... in whole or in part were assiduously examined and the greatest lexicographers of all times continuously consulted." The aims of the AB translators were: (1) to be true to the original text; (2) to be grammatically correct; (3) to be wholesomely readable and understandable to the masses, both young and old; and (4) to give the Lord Jesus Christ the place that Scripture gives to him.

Format

While the AB is in single column, it retains the KJV feature of indenting the text at the beginning of each verse. The New Testament uses Roman numerals to indicate chapters while the Old Testament has Arabic numerals. There are no section titles or other means of indicating units of material. Quotation marks have been omitted because in some cases they "require an arbitrary decision as to who is speaking and where his speech ends." References to events noted and passages quoted or alluded to are indicated within brackets at the end of the verse in question. Both *Yahweh* and *'Adonay* are translated "Lord."

In the New Testament there are some explanatory notes, but most of the notes indicate the version, lexicon, commentary, or author from which the text was derived. These sources (about sixty) are listed at the end of the New Testament. One of the most trusted sources is Kenneth S. Wuest, who has seven books referred to or quoted. There are fewer notes per page in the Old Testament, but they are usually much longer because they consist largely of explanatory and commentary on the text. Psalm 1, for example, has the prefatory note. "This has been called *The Preface Psalm*, because in some respects it may be considered 'the text upon which the whole of the Psalms make up a divine sermon.' It opens with a benediction, 'Blessed,' as does our Lord's Sermon on the Mount (Matt. 5:3)."

In the amplified text parentheses and dashes "signify additional phases of meaning included in the original word, phrase or clause." Brackets "contain justified clarifying words or comments, whether implied or not, which are not actually expressed in the immediate original text." Italics in the New Testament "indicate certain familiar words or passages found in the King James Version, but generally omitted now because they are not adequately supported by more recent scholarship." In the Old Testament italics may be substituted for brackets. Throughout the AB "and," "or," and other connectives in italics "indicate that the portions so connected are to be found in the same original word or expression." The application of these definitions is often a very subjective matter and at times the result is confusing and inaccurate. An example is Mark 8:35 "For whoever wants to save his [higher, spiritual, eternal] life, will lose [the lower, natural, temporal life which is lived (only) on earth]; and whoever gives up his life [which is lived (only) on earth], for My sake and the Gospel's will save [his higher, spiritual life in the eternal kingdom of God]." If the words in brackets are not in the original text, then how can the parentheses indicate another meaning of the original word? Moreover, the Greek text has "it" after "will lose" and "will save."

Text of the Translation

In an attempt to authenticate the scholarship back of the version the Preface to the New Testament states that the "Greek text of Westcott and Hort was pursued with meticulous care." An example is Matt. 5:22, where "without cause" is omitted from the text. But the claim of "meticulous care" is highly misleading because many familiar passages found in the KJV are retained in the text of the AB even though West-cott and Hort omit them. This is true in Col. 1:14, where "through His blood" appears in italics even though the textual evidence is less than that for "without cause." Similarly, Matt. 6:4,6, and 18 retain "openly" or "in the open" in italics when the meaning of the addition actually undercuts the idea Jesus is trying to communicate.

The Trinity passage in 1 John 1:7-8 is in italics so that the alert reader can discern that the words "are not adequately supported by more recent scholarship," but many readers will interpret the italics as emphasis. Mark 16:9 has the note "Verses 9 to 20 not in the two earliest manuscripts," and yet the passage is retained in the text without italics. The same is true of John 7:53 to 8:11 where a note explains, "John 7:53 to 8:11 is not found in the older manuscripts, but it sounds so like Christ that we accept it as authentic, and feel that to omit it would be most unfortunate." But to accept this story as an authentic event in the life of Jesus is no warrant for including it in the text with-out italics when the passage could have been retained as a footnote.

Another misleading aspect with respect to the text is the use of "Alternative reading" in the footnotes to indicate an alternative render-ing. The term "reading" is understood by scholars as referring to the Greek text. In Matt. 6:20, for example, the text has "nor rust *nor* worm," but "worm" is not based on another Greek word, as the footnote implies. Rather it is another way of rendering the word that is trans-lated "rust."

In the Old Testament the translation is "based primarily on the accepted Hebrew text," but readings from early translations, especially Septuagint, are not uncommon. Between Job 2:9 and 10, for example, a sixteen-line passage in italics is inserted on the basis of the Septuagint. Job's wife is called "Dinah" on the strength of the Chaldee (Aramaic) Version and Jonathan's (Aramaic) Targum is noted in Isaiah. Readings from the Dead Sea Scrolls are indicated in the text and footnotes of Isaiah and Habakkuk.

Language and Style

The AB makes "a determined effort to keep, as far as possible, the familiar wording of the earlier versions." On the other hand, it deletes the archaic forms of the pronouns and verbs. "You," for example, is used throughout the Bible even when addressing God in prayer, but all references to Deity, both God and Jesus Christ, are capitalized whether the speaker thought in such terms or not. In John 5:11, for example, the healed invalid answers, "The Man Who healed me *and* gave me back my strength, He Himself said to me, Pick up your bed and walk!" A note on "Man" reads, "Capitalized because of what He is, not what the speaker may have thought He was." In Isa. 9:2 the text has "Light" and a note explains, "Capitalized because the verse is quoted by Matthew as fulfilled when Jesus went into Galilee in the borders of Zebulun and Naphtali." Archaic pronouns and quotation marks are not used in the AB because the manuscripts neither employ special forms for Deity nor use marks to indicate the extent of a statement. But since the Greek and Hebrew texts do not employ capital letters to indicate references to Deity, is it true that this procedure gives "the Lord Jesus Christ His proper place, the place which the Word gives Him"?

The amplifications are an aid to clarity, but the variety of sources produces a cumbersome style that is designed primarily for study, not for easy reading. As Mrs. Siewert notes in the Introduction to the New Testament, "One does not expect literary beauty and finesse in a work which must give the plain, unchanged words of various authorities without embellishment."

Translation and Paraphrase

The basic principle of the AB is to amplify the text to the point where the key Greek and Hebrew words are given "their full equivalent in English." What is not stated is that certain areas of meaning included in the English words are not part of the message that the biblical writer intended to convey. Whereas a single English word seldom says all that the author intended, a multiplication of words usually says more than he wished to convey.

One Greek word in Matt. 5:3 is translated "Blessed — happy, to be envied, and spiritually prosperous [that is, with life-joy and satisfaction in God's favor and salvation, regardless of their outward conditions]." In the next verse the same Greek word becomes "Blessed *and* enviably [with a happiness produced by experience of God's favor and especially conditioned by the revelation of His matchless grace]." In fact, this word (which is the same in all the Beatitudes) is amplified in a slightly different way each time. These collections of comments and translations from various men imply more than the Greek word warrants.

The Greek text of 1 Cor. 10:13 has thirty words and the RSV translates the verse with 44 words. The AB, adding almost another 100 words, translates: "For no temptation — no trial regarded as enticing to sin [no matter how it comes or where it leads] — has overtaken you *and* laid hold on you that is not common to man — that is, no temptation or trial has come to you that is beyond human resistance and that is not adjusted and adapted and belonging to human experience, and such as man can bear. But God is faithful [to His Word and to His compassionate nature], and He [can be trusted] not to let you be tempted *and* tried *and* assayed beyond your ability *and* strength of resistance *and* power to endure, but with the temptation He will [always] also provide the way out — the means of escape to a landing place — that you may be capable *and* strong *and* powerful patiently to bear up under it."

Interpretation

The Introduction to Part Two states that the AB "is free from private interpretation and is independent of denominational prejudice." The implication of this claim is that the task of translation was approached with the intention of being as objective as possible. But perfect objectivity is not humanly possible and most recognized translators today readily acknowledge that translation necessitates interpretation. Since the translator must choose between various interpretations his choice necessarily involves "private interpretation." The fact that such a sweeping claim is made indicates how unconscious prejudice can be. A number of the interpretations incorporated in the AB are not limited to any one individual or one denomination, but they are prejudice just the same. In other words, the AB is not free from nondenominational prejudice.

It is interesting to note that whereas quotation marks are omitted because they "require an arbitrary decision as to who is speaking and where his speech ends," the AB does not hesitate to make arbitrary decisions in order to identify every speaker or person in the text. The Greek text of Matt. 3:16 and Mark 1:10 states clearly that Jesus, not John the Baptist, saw the Spirit descending. But since John 1:32 says the opposite the AB felt constrained to reinterpret the Greek text of Matthew and Mark by translating "he [John]...Him" and "he... Him." In Matt. 3:16 "John" is inserted to eliminate all possibility of ambiguity, whereas in Mark 1:10 the reader is to understand that "he" refers to John the Baptist and "Him" to Jesus. One wonders, however, how this mistranslation is being "true to the original Greek."

Interpretations of varying validity are incorporated in the text and footnotes. Some views expressed are needed correctives of popular, but erroneous, interpretations. The text of Isa. 14:12, for example, inserts "O blasphemous, satanic king of Babylon!" to make sure that the reader understands who is addressed. A long note explains that "Lucifer" (as in the KJV) is not used in the text of the AB because of the erroneous tradition that the name refers to Satan. In Isa. 7:14 the AB translates, "Behold, the young woman *who* is unmarried *and* a virgin shall conceive and bear a Son." The note on "Son" reads: "Very often in the Old Testament, prophecy has a double reference, an immediate, partial fulfillment and an ultimate one. Primarily the prophet may be giving King Ahaz a sign that is to be partially fulfilled in the immediate future, but that the ultimate reference is to Christ is obvious from Matthew 1:22, 23, though Isaiah himself may not have been aware of it." The recognition of a fulfillment in the immediate future is a step in the right direction.

In Dan. 9:25 the text has "anointed one" and a note reads, "Although the early English translators and many commentators have understood verses 25 and 26 to refer definitely to the Messiah and have so translated them, the use of the indefinite article ('an' instead of 'the') compels us to refrain from capitalizing the personal nouns. However, this does not preclude the probability that the Messiah is the person intended." Except for the last statement the note is objective and accurate. If this passage is an intended reference to "the Messiah," it is very strange that neither Jesus nor the New Testament writers quote or mention verses 25 and 26. Amplifications and notes in Daniel 11 acknowledge that the chapter refers to ancient history from the close of the Persian Empire down through the reign of Alexander the Great into the period of the Egyptian and Syrian kings.

Of very questionable nature are the notes that attempt to read later concepts back into the text. In the RSV the first part of Job 28:25 reads, "When he gave to the wind its weight." The AB amplifies by translating "When He gave to the wind [and atmosphere] weight *or* pressure. A note on "pressure" states, "Modern man did not become aware of atmospheric pressure until the seventeeth century, but He who inspired this book had known about it from the beginning. Without such 'weight' there could exist on the earth neither animal nor vegetable life."

An extreme example of dogmatic interpretation is the Song of Solomon. The book is prefaced with a note in italics extending for almost a page and a half. Part of the note reads as follows: "As is true in our Lord's parable of The Prodigal Son, there is not even a hint in the immediate text of this book of its spiritual significance. Yet Jesus Himself said to read the Old Testament Scriptures, for they testify of Him, and nowhere is that more obvious than in this precious book." As a logical result of this assumption the AB "finds in the story three principal characters: the Shepherd, representing Christ; the Shulammite, representing the individual Christian; and King Solomon, representing the world."

After translating the introductory verse (1:1) two more notes are added: "THE BACKGROUND" (29 lines) and "THE SETTING" (20 lines). The translation is resumed with 1:2 under the heading "THE NARRATIVE." Verse 1:4 is typical of the extended and highly subjective amplifications that swarm throughout the book: "[But Solomon is obviously about to make his choice, and there is a chorus of voices crying] Draw me! [Then as he selects one and is leaving the room, the others cry] We will run after you! [But the one chosen answers them] The king brings me into his apartments! [And the other women reply, addressing Solomon] We will be glad and rejoice in you! We will recall [other occasions when we were favored with] your love, more fragrant than wine. The upright [are not offended at your choice, but] sincerely love you." Verse 1:5 is prefaced with a nine-line explanation in italics. Between 1:6 and 7 are thirty lines of amplification in italics. Rev. 19:5,7-9 is inserted in small italics after 8:13 and Rev. 22:20 after 8:14.

One of the major purposes of the AB in the Old Testament is "to identify references to Christ wherever they are certain, and outstandingly fulfilled prophecies wherever they occur." The AB translation of Isa. 3:17 begins, "Therefore the Lord will smite with a scab the crown of the heads of the daughters of Zion (making them bald)." A note on "scab" reads, "Results of atomic warfare?" Isaiah's reference to "a highway out of Egypt to Assyria" (19:23) has the note: "This prediction, made more than 2600 years before, concerning a highway, had been accurately fulfilled by 1960 A.D. First an air highway was put in operation between Cairo in Egypt and Bagdad in Iraq or ancient Assyria. Later a rail highway was also established between Cairo, and Haifa in Palestine, and finally continued to Bagdad."

The prediction that Jerusalem would be rebuilt "from the tower of Hananel to the Corner Gate" (Jer. 31:38) has the note: "Many times after the days of the Old Testament, Jerusalem was destroyed. . . . Yet not only did God's word declare it would be rebuilt, but definitely and in detail drew a word map of the exact outline which the future city would follow — from a well-known tower to the gate at a certain corner, then on over a particular hill, coming now outside the wall of the original city and taking in a large area definitely shown by familiar landmarks. Eight details are unmistakably given here, and Zechariah adds another (Zech. 14:10). Moreover, the city's enlargement was to be in one general direction — to the northwest. Twenty-five hundred years later, in 1935 A.D., the prophecy had been fulfilled to the letter, as if indeed with God's 'measuring line' (verse 39). What a God, and what a Book! So unlikely seemed this prophecy's fulfillment that some commentators had said it should be interpreted spiritually!"

Conclusion

The popularity of the AB is beyond dispute. Between 1958 and 1962 more than 750,000 copies of the New Testament were printed and distributed. A major factor in its continuing success has been the "commentary" feature of the translation. Most human beings, Christians included, do not have the mental toughness to live with unresolved problems. They demand authoritative answers even when the evidence does not justify a definite conclusion. Thus a Bible with authoritative notes and explanations is more likely to succeed. This was true of the Geneva Bible and it also explains why the KJV did not become popular until 40-50 years after its publication.

One should not judge the AB and its translators in the light of the exaggerated claims of the sponsor and the publisher. Originally the claim was made that the New Testament restored "meaning to some 10,000 obscure words." By adding up all the variant amplifications one might arrive at the figure 10,000, but figures lie, even in religious circles. The clear implication of the claim is that previous translations were terribly inaccurate or that the AB is out of this world. In a number of instances, however, it is quite human. In Part Two Mrs. Siewert makes acknowledgments to many, including "all the notable English translators from Wycliffe in 1525 A.D. to the present." The date should be 1382 or else the name should be Tyndale. A note on Isa. 4:1 states, "Ezekiel here foresees a time when the ratio between marriageable men and women will be one to seven in Jerusalem."

Another overstatement is made in the Preface of the New Testament. After noting that Noah, Moses, Amos, Peter, and Paul were God's right servants for the right time of God's purpose, the following eulogy appears: "Frances E. Siewert, B.Lit., B.D., M.A. (with training extending far beyond the suggestion of these listed degrees), spent the major portion of a long life in humble, thorough preparation for such hallowed endeavor as this represents, memorizing chapter after chapter of the Greek text — translating, collating and correlating in an amazing display of ability and accomplishment." The Preface of Part Two adds, "But most of all we are grateful that the Lord has spared His servant, Frances E. Siewert, B.Lit., B.D., M.A., D.Lit., (with training and experience far beyond the suggestion of these listed degrees), to continue with the work as Research Secretary."

The AB is the product of Mrs. Siewert and her associates, and it evidences their love for God and zeal for his Word. It clarifies many obscure passages and God has undoubtedly used it to enlighten many others who love him, but the limited outlook (linguistically and theologically) of its translators, especially in the Old Testament, prevents the AB from accomplishing the potential that such a study translation has.

NEW AMERICAN STANDARD BIBLE

The *New American Standard Bible* (hereafter NASB), a revision of the ASV, is being produced and published by The Lockman Foundation and Press. The Gospel of John appeared in 1960, the four Gospels in 1962, and the entire New Testament in 1963. The project is continuing systematically and in due time the entire Bible will be published. The origin, purpose, and nature of this revision is set forth in the "Preface to the New American Standard Bible A.D. 1963."

The primary impetus for undertaking this task was the "disturbing awareness that the American Standard Version of 1901 was fast disappearing from the scene." The producers believe that the ASV "has been in a very real sense the standard for many translations" and that this "monumental product of applied scholarship, assiduous labor and thorough procedure" should be rescued "from an inevitable demise." An editorial board "composed of linguists, Greek scholars and pastors undertook the responsibilities of translation and revision." Its purpose was "to present to the modern reader a revision of the American Standard Version in clear and contemporary language."

Format

Unlike the ASV the text is in single column with each verse indented. Boldface numerals or letters appear in the NASB where the ASV has indented lines to indicate paragraphs. Section headings appear at the top of each page. Notes appear in a column on the outer edge of each page under the verse numbers to which they refer. Notes with raised letters of the alphabet "refer to cross references." Notes with raised numerals "refer to literal renderings, alternate translations, or explanations." The term "translations" includes both variant readings and alternative renderings. The following examples are typical of the explanatory notes: "ten thousand talents" (Matt. 18:24) has the remark "About $10,000,000 in silver content but worth much more in buying power"; and "denarii" (Matt. 18:28) has the explanation "The denarius was worth 18 cents in silver, equivalent to a day's wage."

Old Testament quotations are indicated by small capital letters and quotation marks are employed "in accordance with modern English usage." Italics in the text "indicate words which are not found in the original Greek but implied by it." The NASB is more literal in its use of italics than was the ASV. In Matt. 5:45 the NASB has, "for He causes His sun to rise on *the* evil and *the* good, and sends rain on *the* righteous and *the* unrighteous." The Greek adjectives are plural and mean literally "evil (ones)," etc. Thus they have the meaning of collective nouns even though the definite article is missing each time. The ASV translators decided that "evil (ones)" in Greek was the equivalent of "the evil" in English and so they did not put the article in italics. In Matt. 12:35 the NASB has "*his* good treasure" where the Greek has "the good treasure." The ASV interpreted "the good treasure" as a Greek idiom for "the good treasure (of him)," and when it translated the English equivalent, "his good treasure," the pronoun was not put in italics.

These examples illustrate how subtle the problem of italics can be. Unless the reader knows how to interpret the italics, the only value they have is to indicate the ways in which Greek idiom and syntax vary from English. Yet even this antiquarian feature is not completely trustworthy because the NASB (like the KJV and ASV) has inconsistencies and inaccuracies at times. In John 5:12, for example, "pallet" is in regular type even though the Greek text does not have the word and the ASV has "bed" in italics. The error probably arose because the eye of the translator or editor returned to 5:11 where the word "pallet, bed" does occur in the Geek text. Another inaccuracy is John 8:6, where "grounds" should be in italics. On the other hand, words have been put in italics when the Greek text has them: for example, *"He"* (John 1:43) and *"have"* (John 4:39). In the writer's opinion it is still doubtful that this difficult, outmoded practice is worth all the time and effort involved.

Text of the Translation

The Nestle Greek text was selected as the basis for revising the ASV text. "In most instances," the revisers state, "the 23rd edition . . . was followed." But the Doxology of the Lord's Prayer (Matt. 6:13) and three complete verses (Matt. 17:21; 18:11; 23:14) are included within brackets in the text even though these passages are in the margins of both the ASV and Nestle's text. Morover, the text of ASV (not Nestle) is preferred in Luke 24:12; John 5:2; and John 7:53-8:11.

Language and Style

The archaic forms "thou, thy, thee" are changed to "you" except "in the language of prayer when addressing Deity." In order to eliminate ambiguity "second person pronouns are marked 'you^s' or 'you^{pl}'" when it cannot be determined from the context whether they are singular or plural." Unlike the ASV, personal pronouns are capitalized "when pertaining to Deity." This is true irrespective of the speaker's attitude. For example, those who spat on Jesus and beat him with their fists are quoted as saying, "Prophesy to us, You Christ; who is the one who hit You?" (Matt. 26:68).

Many obsolete, ambiguous, and obscure words in the ASV have been modernized in the NASB: for example, Matt. 2:7 "privily/secretly;" 2:16 "wroth/enraged;" 3:4 "raiment/a garment" and "girdle/belt;" and 3:12 "garner/barn." Furthermore, many awkward constructions in the ASV have been revised to conform to modern English usage: "Take heed that ye do not your righteousness before men" (Matt. 6:1) is translated "Beware of practicing your righteousness before men," and "Then shall he answer them" (Matt. 25:45) becomes "Then He will answer them."

In revising the ASV the NASB made the attempt "to adhere to the original languages of the Holy Scriptures as closely as possible and at the same time to obtain a fluent and readable style according to current English usage." But in a number of instances devotion to the literal Greek text takes precedence over "current English usage." The traditional expression "And it came to pass" is revised to read "And it happened" (Matt. 9:10) or "And it came about" (Mark 1:9; Luke 7:11). While these expressions are quite understandable today, they are not idiomatic English. The RSV translators recognized that this Hebrew idiom (which was carried over into the New Testament) was unnecessary for conveying the meaning of the biblical writers and therefore they omitted it. The NASB has not increased its accuracy by retaining the idiom — it has only preserved some of the antique flavor of the biblical languages.

As a means of enlivening a narrative it was common for New Testament writers to use the present tense for the past, but they mixed tenses in the same sentence. In the NASB edition of the Gospels the revisers retained the ASV practice of translating the Greek present with the English present. John 1:43 reads, 'The next day *He* purposed to go forth into Galilee, and He finds Philip, and Jesus says to him, 'Follow Me.'" But the revisers recognized that the sudden shift in tenses ("purposed"..."finds"..."says") was jarring for readers thinking in English, therefore they reversed themselves by changing the historical presents into English past tenses. They indicate such forms with an asterisk, thus the verse in the New Testament edition reads, "The next day *He* purposed to go forth into Galilee, and He *found Philip, and Jesus *said to him, 'Follow Me.'" This translation is an improvement, but one still wonders why the literal Greek syntax was retained. The RSV really translates this verse in "contemporary language" by rendering: "The next day Jesus decided to go to Galilee. And he found Philip and said to him, 'Follow me.'"

An unnatural feature of the NASB that cannot be attributed to the ASV is the use of a double question (negative-positive) to translate Greek questions with *mê*, meaning "not." Since such questions expect a negative answer the traditional method of translating them has been to leave the negative untranslated. Thus the ASV and RSV have, "Can this be the Christ?" (John 4:29), while the NASB reads, "this is not the Christ, is it?" Another good example is John 6:67: RSV "Will you also go away?" and NASB "You do not want to go away also, do you?"

Translation and Interpretation

Although the NASB is dedicated to as literal a translation of the Greek as modern English will permit, it seeks for greater clarity than the ASV and thus it adds more words in italics. Where the ASV has "Fear not" (Luke 8:50), the NASB translates, "Do not be afraid *any longer.*" In John 18:12 the ASV has "the band," but the NASB expands to read, "the *Roman* Cohort."

Neither is the NASB averse to interpreting general expressions in more explicit terms. In John 1:17, for example, the ASV and RSV translate, "grace and truth came through Jesus Christ," while the NASB has "grace and truth were realized through Jesus Christ."

An area where the NASB combines fidelity to the Greek text with current English idiom is in its translation of the Greek imperfect tenses. The basic meaning of this tense is continuous action in past time. Thus, whereas the ASV has "Jesus went about all the cities" (Matt. 9:35), the NASB translates, "Jesus was going about all the cities." The inceptive use of the imperfect is translated "*started* on His way" (Luke 7:6) or "*began* to walk" (John 5:9), where the ASV has "went" and "walked." In the ASV the imperfect of Mark 6:20 is rendered "he heard him gladly," but the NASB translates it as a customary imperfect, "he used to enjoy listening to him."

Conclusion

The literal nature of the ASV has made it an excellent study guide for those who know little or no Greek and Hebrew and yet desire to do inductive study of the English Bible. Such students will welcome the NASB because in spite of its defects it reads with greater clarity and ease than the ASV.

Scriptural Index

Genesis				
10:4	36	11:34	96	1 Chronicles
12:14	106–107	14:14	85	1:7	36
20:6	59	Ruth		6:57	52–53
31:34	57	3:5	40	11:11	51–52
43:25	56	3:12	41	18:11–13	37
Exodus		1 Samuel		29:10–13	23
8:23	47	1:24–25	46–47	2 Chronicles
19:12	115–116	2:30	131–132	2:3	115
28:8	61	6:18	47	4:10	85
Leviticus		13:1–2	49–50	14:5	97
11:20, 21, 27, 42		13:19–21	7, 97	34:4, 7	97
	113	16:16	57	Nehemiah
23:39–43	26	17:22	61	13:26	60–61
26:30	97	2 Samuel		Job
Numbers		1:4	57	17:3	109–110
24:14	57	3:10	58	19:3	62
32:14	131	8:6	37	31:35	61
Deuteronomy		8:11–14	36–37	37:7	48
2:4, 18	113	8:14	80	Psalms
2:22, 23	113	13:39	50–51	24:6	48
21:23	44	23:8	51–52	60 Title	37
24:11	57	1 Kings		68:11	58
Joshua		10:28–29	92–94	84:6	42
21:13–14	52–53	11:1	60	90:10	76–77
Judges		13:27	112	96:10	44
8:2	141	2 Kings		113–118	27
		8:17	50	118:25	27

SCRIPTURAL INDEX

210

119   43
119:4 (LXX 118:4)   126
119:147   60
145:13   43, 46
Proverbs
4:18   84
9:9   116
26:23   94
Ecclesiastes
1:9   131
7:1   113–114
Song of Solomon
5:4   4, 88
Isaiah
4:5–6   38
7:7   157
8:20   132
17:8   97
21:8   42
27:9   97
29:11   134
32:8   59
33:8   2, 3, 36, 41
35:1–2   77
35:9–10   78–79
38:11   38
38:19–20   38
38:21–22   38
43:13   59
49:17   42
51:10–11   78–79
53   48
59:4   85–86
Jeremiah
2:23–24   86–87
31:27, 31, 38   41
43:4–7   45
Ezekiel
6:4, 6   97
20:41   114
42:16   37, 40
Nahum
3:19   56
Habakkuk
1:2   101
2:4   100–101
Matthew
5:18   126

6:1–18   11
6:1   10–11
6:2   11
6:5   11
6:9   80
6:9–13   30
6:13   22–24
6:16   11
9:15   5
11:28–30   55
13:20   61
16:13   80
16:16   65–66
16:23   65
22:29   132
23:27   111
25:1   112
26:27   4
27:54   102–103
27:65   99, 102
Mark
2:19   5
6:14   57–58
6:15   58
6:25   61
10:14   59
16:8   28–29
16:9–20   27–29
Luke
5:34   5
5:39   79
7:12   95–96
7:36–37   110
8:42   95, 97
9:17   89
9:38   95
11:2–4   30
12:20   108–109
17:9   56
17:27   114
17:29   114
21:38   25
22:31–32   64
24:25   132
John
1:9   8
1:14   5, 95, 97
1:18   2, 95
3:16   95–97

3:18   95–96
5:39   102, 132
7:36   25
7:37   26
7:46   25
7:52   25
7:53–8:11   24–27
8:2   27
8:12   27
8:31–32   8
11:21–22   65
17:1   80
17:13   80
21:24   25
Acts
7:51   131
8:28–29   132
11:16   80
17:11   132
17:23   62
Romans
1:13   4, 59
1:17   101
8:28   12, 16–17
1 Corinthians
5:16   80
7   88
7:36–38   90–92
13   83–84
14:11   134
2 Corinthians
6   88
6:12–13   87–88
8   88
8:1   56–57
8:4   20
8:14   Figs. 12, 13
9:15   59
Galatians
3:11   101
3:13   44
6:2, 5   6–7
Ephesians
1:3–14   5
1:7   29–30
Philippians
1:7   62
2   88
3:20–21   60

Colossians		Titus			I John	
1:14	29–30	I		88	3:1	9–10
I Thessalonians		Philemon			4:8	83
4	88	20		88	4:9	95
4:15	4, 60	Hebrews			5:6–8	18–22, 25
5:14	6	3:3		114	5:18	12
2 Thessalonians		8:3		114	Revelation	
3:6, 7, 11	6	9:13		13	9:1–2	124
2 Timothy		10:36, 38		101	22:16–21	20
3:15	132	11:5		58	22:18–19	30–31
		11:17		95–97		

ADDITIONS TO SCRIPTURAL INDEX

Genesis					Deuteronomy	
1:1	181	34:9	185		2:1–12	180
1:2	186	34:21	184		2:20–23	180
1:26, 27	187	43:34	186		3:9	180
1:30	181	47:2	186		3:11	180
2:6	183	49:10	182		3:26	185
2:7	186	Exodus			5:17–20	181
3:13	185	5:22	185		10:12	185
3:22	187	7:3	181		11:14	183
4:8	165, 183	7:13	181		14:26	185
4:25	186	14:7	186		II Kings	
5	180	16:16	180		18:13–20:19	188
6:2	182	16:36	180		I Chronicles	
7:11	180	20:7	185		1:7	182
7:24	181	20:13	181		Job	
8:1	181, 186	20:13–16	181		2:9, 10	198
8:22	180	28:30	186		28:25	201
9:6	180	29:38–41	186		Psalms	
9:27	186	38:24	186		82:1	187
10:4, 5	182	Leviticus			Song of Solomon	
10:10	182	1:8	181		1:1, 2	202
10:14	182	4:26	181		1:4–7	202
10:20	182	27:9	181		8:13, 14	202
10:31	182	33:40	180		Isaiah	
11	180	Numbers			1:15	192
12:2–3	180	1	180		1:20	189
14:3	186	21:6	180		1:21	193
14:11	181	22:22	185		2:6	192
14:22	186	22:27	185		3:4	190
16:2	186	22:29	185		3:16–17	195
25:25	186	24:17	183		3:17	202
27:46	181	26	180		3:22	193
28:1	181	27:21	186		4:1	203
33:19	180	28:6	186		4–14	189

5:10	193	4:6	192	11:1	165
5:27	193	6:1	194	12:35	205
6:1	189	6:5, 6	190	14:6	165
6:3	189	7:12	191	16:16	162, 177
6:6	192	8:1–2	193	16:18, 19	163
7:3	191	8:5	192, 194	16:23	163
7-14	201	9:2	192	17:21	206
8:1	191	9:6	183	18:11	206
9:2	199	9:7	182, 183	18:15	172
9:18–21	188	Micah		18:24	205
10:1–4	188	1:10–15	193	18:28	205
11:2	193	4:4	189	20:31	171
11:9	192	5:2	195	21:13	173
12:1	194	6:8	195	23:14	206
14:9	192	Zechariah		23:28	168
14:11	192	14:10	203	25:45	206
14:12	201	14:39	203	26:25	172
14:15	192	Matthew		26:27	178
15:9	188	1:16	173	26:68	206
18:7	182	1:17	173	Mark	
19:11	188, 191	1:18	173, 177	1:5	162
19:23	202	1:22, 23	201	1:9	207
25:1	194	2:4	173	1:10	200
28:9–10	195	2:7	206	1:14	165
28:13	188	2:16	206	1:41	161
30:29–33	188, 189	3:1	165	2:9	164
34:16	188	3:4	206	3:5	159
35	188	3:12	206	3:14	165
36–39	188	3:15	159	4:12	170
38:10–20	188	3:16	200	5:14	171
40–66	188	4:17	165	6:4	171
51:14	192	5:3	197, 199	6:20	208
Jeremiah		5:6	159	6:22	165
31:38	202	5:10	159	7:6	159
Daniel		5:20	159	7:11	165
9:25, 26	201	5:22	197	7:26	171
11	201	5:45	205	8:26	168
Hosea		6:1	159, 206	8:35	197
2:9	194	6:4	198	9:50	164, 166
7:8	191	6:6	198	11:17	173
11:8	191	6:13	172, 206	12:15	171
12:3	189	6:18	198	15:39	176
12:11, 12, 13	189	6:20	198	16:9	198
13:14	192	6:33	159	16:9-20	162
14:1	195	7:11	172	Luke	
Amos		8:26	172	1:46–49	160
3:9	189	9:10	207	1:75	159
3:15	190	9:35	208	2:41	162
4:1	190, 193	10:7	165	4:4	163

7:6	208	7:52	176	10:13	199
7:11	207	7:53 8:11	162, 169,	13	178
7:29–30	161		176, 198, 206	13:13	172
8:50	207	8:12	176	II Corinthians	
9:34	172	10:30	170	1:24	170
10:30–37	173	10:40–12:50	168	4:7–10	160
13:35	168	13:1–17:26	168	11:9	171
15:28	165	16:8	159	Galatians	
16:15	172	16:8–11	170	2:17	170
17:21	171	16:10	159	3:1–4	160
19:46	173	18:1–21:25	168	4:25	168
21:38	176	18:12	208	5:15	171
23:35	176	19:24	161	Ephesians	
23:47	176	19:29	159, 169	1:3-14	160, 164, 172
24:12	162, 206	Acts		2:14	170
John		1:1–5:42	168	Philippians	
1:1	165	1:15	163	3:1	171
1:1–51	168	6:1–12:25	168	3:20	178
1:5	178	9:4	166	4:4	171
1:12	166	9:7	166	Colossians	
1:17	208	13:1–15:35	168	1:14	198
1:32	200	13:10	159	II Timothy	
1:41	173	15:36–21:26	168	3:16	177
1:43	206, 207	17:31	159	Hebrews	
2:1–6:71	168	21:27–28:31	168	5:11–12	160
3:8	168	22:7	166	II Peter	
3:15	161, 176	22:9	166	2:4	176
3:16	166	22:22	178	I John	
3:16–21	168	24:25	159	1:7–8	198
3:21	168	26:14	166	3:12	165
4:7	168	26:28	178	5	177
4:8	168	27:18	164	5:7–8	169 ᵛ
4:25	173	28:8b	163f	Jude	
4:29	207	Romans		4	176
4:39	206	1:17	159	6	176
5:2	206	3:5	159	14–15	176
5:3b–4	162	3:20	170	Revelation	
5:9	208	3:21, 22	159	1:11	173
5:11	199, 205	4:6	178	19:5	202
5:12	205	12:6–8	163	19:7–9	202
6:61	171	12:11	178	22:20	202
6:67	207	I Corinthians			
7:1–10:39	168	1:30	159		

General Index

The index includes, in addition to proper names and major subjects, key words from Biblical passages discussed in detail in the text; these appear below in *italic* type (Greek or Hebrew original) or in quotation marks (English translation).

Aaron, 52–53
'abel, 47
Abiezer, 141
Abraham, 95–96, 107
"abroad," 57
Absalom, 50
Accuracy of texts: Greek, 32; Hebrew, 45, 54
Acrostic, 43, 46
Acts, 21, 71, 87
Additions to Scripture, warning against, 30
'adonay, 42, 156–157
'adoniy, 42
Adrian I, Pope, 144
Adulterous woman, 24–27
Adverb, 108
Adverbial clause, 108
"advertize thee," 57
Africa, 135; North, 18
"against Joseph came," 56

agapao, 83
agape, 83
Age of manuscripts as textual criterion, 13, 15–16, 21
Ahab, 92
Albertus Magnus, 125
Albright, William F., 45
aleph, 15
Alexandria, Egypt, 15, 31
Alexandrinus, Codex A, 15–16
Alfonsus a Castro, 137
Alfred (Alured) the Great, 138
Alms(giving), 11, 83
Alternative translations: lack of, 103; opposition to, 100; validity of, 99–100
Ambiguous expressions and words: "abroad," 57; "advertize thee," 57; "company," 58; "cunning," 57; "furniture," 57; "liberal," 58–59; "perfect day," 84; "published," 58;

"translate," 58; "unspeakable," 59; "you," 64
Ambiguous meaning of italics, 112
Ambiguous syntax, 5
Ambiguous verb forms, 99–100
Ambrose, 24, 144
America, see United States
American Standard Version: alternative translations, 7, 99, 101, 103–104; archaistic features of, 57, 59, 62–63, 107, 157; clarity of, 89; criticism of, 62–63, 69–70, 106; explanatory footnotes, 23, 26, 28, 37, 47, 49; explanatory footnotes, omission of when text changed, 21, 29, 37, 47; failure to recognize language change, 63–64, 69; hopes of acceptance shattered, 70, 106; improvements in, 4, 11, 32, 60; inconsistency of, 96; italics, omission of, 108, 115, 116, use of, 3, 53, 108, 114; reconstruction of Hebrew text, 49, 50–51; revision of verse numbers, 21–22; translations, use of other, 47; variant readings in footnotes, Greek, 12, 23, Hebrew, 41
American Translation (see also Goodspeed New Testament): alternative translations, lack of, 103; explanatory footnotes, omission of when text changed, 37, 47, 48; footnotes, lack of, 53, 103; improvements in, 101, 107; italics, lack of, 53; reconstruction of Hebrew text, 41; translations, use of other, 47–48; vowel changes made in Hebrew text, 92
Amos, the prophet, 92
"And it came to pass," 107
Anglo-Saxon (Old English), 67–68, 138
"anon," 61
Antioch, 22, 31
Apocalypse (Revelation), 20, 31, 87
Apocrypha, 13, 87
Apostles' Creed, 96
Aqiba, Rabbi, 39–40, 105
Aquila, 105–106, 135, 143
Arabic, 138
Arabs (Bedouin), 3, 14

Aram, 37
Aramaic language: importance of, 35; part of Old Testament in, 34; spoken by Jesus, 22, 112
Aramaic (square) script, 35–36
Aramaic translations, 43, 48
Archaeology, 6, 94
Archaic pronouns, 61–66
'arim, 3, 41
Aristotle, 140–141
Arlington Cemetery, 111
Armenians, 137
Article, definite, 102–103, 109
Artistic style and the truth, 81–83, 89
Asia Minor, 19, 27, 31, 92–94
Assyrian Empire, 35; kings of, 3, 92
atakteo, 6
ataktos, 6
Athanasius, 22
Athenian, 134
Athos, Mt., 28
Augustine, 24, 100, 132–133, 136, 140, 143–144, 147–149, 151
Authorized Version (see also King James Version), 75
Autographs (see also Original text), 10, 17, 25, 34
auton, 12

Babylonian Empire, 35
Babylonian Exile, 35, 143, 156
Babylonian text-tradition, 39, 46
Babylonians (Chaldeans), 101
banayik, 42
Barnabas, Epistle of, 14
baros, 7
Baruch, 45
Basil of Caesarea, 132, 133
Beatty, Chester, Papyri of, 16, 24
Beauty (see also Literary qualities), 76, 77, 79, 82, 85, 87
Bede, Venerable, 67, 138
Bedouin (Arabs), 3, 14
Beget, 96
Belief, 8, 26
ben Asher text-tradition, 39–40
ben Naphtali text-tradition, 39–40
beracoth, 42

berecoth, 42

Berkeley Version (see also Verkuyl New Testament): alternative translations, lack of, 103; explanatory footnotes, 46, 49, 92, 93, 94; explanatory footnotes, omission of when text changed, 37, 47, 48, 51, 53, 116; improvements in, 93, 107, 157; inconsistency of, 97; interpretive footnotes, 101, 103; italics, lack of, 53; mistranslations of, 157; reconstruction of Hebrew text, 50, 51, 52, 53, 92–93; translations, use of other, 47, 48; vowel changes made in Hebrew text, 92

Bethel, prophet of, 112

Beza, Theodore, 21, Greek text-tradition of, 21, 31, Latin New Testament of, 112

Bezae, Codex D, 21, 25, 27

Bezer, 52

Bible (Scripture): authority of, 99, 100, 119, 148; clarity (perspicuity) of, 99, 100; customs in, 109–111; delight in, 147; for standard reference, 104, 118; fullness of, 133; importance of, ix; lands, 6; necessity of indicating difficult passages with theological issues, 100, 115, 116, 148; praise of, 132–134; reading of, 81, 88–89, 103; sanctity of, 82; Societies, United, 72; terms, new meanings of, 2, 6, 7, 91–98, 148; Translators, International Conference of, 72; without theological notes, 103; writers of, 10, 35, 70, 73, 74, 80, 82, 105, 112, 133, 135, 136, 147, 156

Bibliothèque Nationale, 16

Bilingual manuscripts, 21, 25

Bishops' Bible, 21, 68, 75, 83, 113, 117

Blayney, Benjamin, 114

Bodmer Library, 24

Bodmer II, 2, 24

Bomberg edition of the Hebrew, 62

bonayik, 42

"book," 61

Book of Common Prayer (Communion), 79, 142

Booths, Feast of, 26–27

"bowels," 4, 88

Bowie, Walter R., 117

British, 70, Museum of, 15

"bruit," 56

Butterworth, Charles C., 74–79, 87

"by-and-by," 61

Byzantine text-tradition, 31

Byzantium, 31

Cadence (see also Literary qualities), 76, 83, 87

Caesarea, 15, 31

Caesarean text-tradition, 32

Cairensis, Codex, 34

Cairo, 14, 25

Cajetan, Cardinal Thomas, 145

Calendar, 130

Calumniation: of the best things, 128–130; of the highest personages, 130–131; of King James I, 131–132

Calvin, John, ix, 21

Cambridge University, 113, editions of King James Version by, 113, 128

Canaan, 6, 135, 150

Canaanite (Old Hebrew) script, 35

Canon law, 125

Canterbury Tales, 67

Capital letters: in English Bible, 65, 102; in Greek texts, 13, 19

caritas, 83

"carriage," 61

Carthage, 18

Cave 1, Dead Sea (Qumran) Scrolls, 3, 36, 45, 156

Cave 4, Dead Sea Scrolls, 45

Centenary (Montgomery) New Testament, 122

Centurion, 102–103

Chaldeans (Babylonians), 101

Chaldee (Aramaic), 48, 148

Chariots, 93–94

"charity," 83–84

Charles I, the Great (Charlemagne), 144

Charles V, the Wise, 138

Chaucer, Geoffrey, 67

"children of the bridechamber," 5

Christ, see Jesus Christ

Christians, 23, 68, 103, 137

Chrysostom, 137, 148, 151

Church Fathers (see also Greek, and Latin Fathers), 34, 81, 112, 132, 133, 139

Church history, 118, 128

"Church language" (see also "language of devotion"), 63, 69, 72

Church, Protestant (see also Protestant Christianity): addressing God as "you," 66; members of denied counsel of King James Version translators, 100; language change ignored by, 63, 69, 72

Church, Roman Catholic, see Roman Catholic Church

Cilicia, 92–93

Clarendon Press, 114

Clarity (see also Literary qualities), 5, 75–76, 83, 87, 89, 117

Classical Greek, 74

Clement VIII, Pope (see also Vulgate, Clementine edition), 139, 146

Clement of Alexandria, 28

Coa, 92

Codex, 13

Codices, Greek minuscule: Codex 1, 25; Codex 13, 25; Codex 61, 19; Codex 69, 25; Codex 88, 19; Codex 124, 25; Codex 225, 25; Codex 346, 25; Codex 579, 28; Codex 629, 19

Codices, Greek uncial: Codex A, Alexandrinus, 15, 16, 17; Codex Aleph, Sinaiticus, 13–15, 16, 24, 28; Codex B, Vaticanus, 13, 15, 16, 17, 24, 28; Codex C, Ephraemi Rescriptus, 15–16, 27; Codex D, Bezae, 21, 25, 27; Codex L, Regius, 27, 28; Codex Psi, Mt. Athos, 28; Codex Theta, Koridethi, 27; Codex W, Washington, 25, 27; Codex p46, Beatty Papyri, 16, 24; Codex p66, Bodmer II, 2, 24; Codex 099, 28; Codex 0112, 28

Codices, Hebrew, Codex Cairensis, 34

Codices, Latin, Codex "k," 28

Codices, Syriac: Harklean, 28, 29; Palestinian, 24; Peshitto, 23, 27; Sinaitic, 28

Common people, 62, 63, 67, 69, 71, 72

Common people, language of, see "mother tongue"

Common Prayer, Book of, 79

Communion Book, 142

"company," 58

Confraternity New Testament, 122

Confraternity Old Testament, 122

"conjectural emendation," 49–53

Consonantal text, see Hebrew consonantal text

Consonants, Hebrew: as vowels, 36, 39; confusion of, 3, 36, 47, 50; inversion of, 37, 40, 52

Constantine, Emperor, 15, 19, 132

Constantinople, 15, 31, 134

Convert (proselyte), 105, 143

Correction of manuscripts, see Textual criticism, New Testament, and Old Testament

Courtroom, 85

Coverdale Bible, 68, 75, 77, 81

Coverdale, Miles, 75, 77, 79

Cranmer (Great) Bible, 68, 75, 79, 112

Cromwell, Lord, 138

"cubits," 37

"cunning player," 57

"curious girdle," 61

Customs: basic elements of, 110; Biblical, 109–111

Cyril of Alexandria, 132

Cyril of Jerusalem, 133

Daniel, book of, 34

Daughter, 90–92

David, 23, 36, 37, 50, 51, 52, 130, 147

Dead Sea (area), 3

Dead Sea (Qumran) Scrolls, 3, 16, 34, 36, 42; Isaiah Scroll, 3, 36, 38; Habakkuk Commentary, 156

Decoration (illumination) of manuscripts, 19, 81

Dedication to King James I, 62–63, 69, 152–154

Defiled, 111

de' Medici family, 16

Detroit, 25

Deuteronomy, 45

Dictionary, 105

Didache, 22, 23
dikaiosunen, 11
Disbelief (unbelief), 26, 30
Dispersion, 43
Dittography, 38, 93
Division of verses, 21, 22, 38
Division of words, 19, 35; lack of, 13, 35
Douay (Rheims) Bible, 23, 58, 75–76, 87
Double writing, see *Dittography*
"do you to wit," 56–57
Doxology, 22–24
"droves," 92, 94
Duns Scotus, 124
Dutch language, 142, translations in, 48, 138, 148

'*eben*, 47
Ebionites, 143
echete, 99, 102
'*edim*, 3, 41
Edinburgh Review, 106
Edom, 36, 37
Efnard, 138
Egypt, 13, 14, 16, 25, 31, 43, 45, 92–94, 107, 135
Egyptian text-tradition: Greek, 32; Hebrew, 45–46
eleemosunen, 11
Eli, 46
Elias (Elijah), 58
Elizabeth, Queen of England, 140, 152
Elohim, 156–157
Elzevir text-tradition, 31
Emendation of Hebrew text, 49–53
'*emunah*, 101
England, 67, 70, 71, 106, 126; Church(es) of, 117, 154; kings of 15, 138, 152
English Bible: for standard reference, 104, 118; history of, ix, study of, 106
English language, changes in, 2, 5, 67, 68, 71: ambiguous words, 57–59; misleading words, 4, 59–61; obsolete words, 56–57; pronouns "thou" and "you," in early English versions, 61–

63, in modern English versions, 64–66, in worship, 66; spelling, 56
English language, grammar (idiom) of, 64, 80, 102–103, 107–111, 112, 116
English language, styles of (see also Literary style), 5, 73, 74–82, 84–88
English language, syntax of, 5, 109, inverted word order, 4, 80
English language, types of: Anglo-Saxon (Old English), 67, 68, 138; Middle English (language of Wyclif), 62, 67–68; language of Tyndale, 62, 63, 68, 69; language of Shakespeare and 1611, 62, 63, 69; Modern English, 64, 70–72, 80
English literature, 81
English Revised Version: alternative translations, 103–104; archaistic features of, 56, 57, 58, 59, 60, 62, 63, 69; criticism of, 62–63, 69–70, 106; failure to recognize language change, 63, 64, 69; hopes of acceptance shattered, 70, 106; improvements in, 32; reconstruction of Hebrew text, 50–51; translations, use of other, 47
English translations, see American Standard Version, etc.
English vernacular (see also "mother tongue"), 66
Ephesus, 27
Ephraem of Syria, 15
Ephraemi Rescriptus, Codex C, 15–16, 27
Epiphanius of Cyprus, 136, 140, 143
Equivalence of meaning, 105, 107–111, 112–118
Erasmus, 20, 125, 137, text-tradition of, 20, 21, 31, translation of, 145
ereunate, 102
Esau, 151
Eshtemoa, 52
Esther, book of, 45
Estienne, Robert, see Stephanus
Ethiopians, 137, language of, 138
Euphony (see also Literary qualities), 83
Europe, 135
Eusebius, 15, 24, 28, 132

Evangelical zeal and translation, 118
Exodus, book of, 45
Ezekiel, book of, 97
Ezra, the priest, 46, 143; book of, 34

Faith(fulness), 101–102
Familiar use of pronouns, 63
"Family 13," 25
Fasting, 11
Ferrar, 25
Fiancée, 90–91
Footnotes (marginal notes), 19, 20: interpretive, 101, 103; lack of, 53–54, 103; opposition to, 100, 149; use of, 41, 89, 104; validity of, 2, 20, 40, 100, 148
Form, 110, 111
France, 152
Freedom of truth, 8
Freer, Charles L., 25, Art Gallery of, 25
French language, 67, 142; translations in, 48, 138, 148
Full spelling, Hebrew, 36
Function, 110, 111
"furniture," 57

Galatians, 145
gameo, 91
gamizo, 90–91
Genesis, 13, 123
Geneva Bible (see also Whittingham New Testament), 49, 75, 77, 103, 113
Geneva, Switzerland, 21, 24
Gentiles, 43, 135, 156
Gergesites, 151
ge'ulim, 78–79
Gezer Calendar, 35
Gideon, 134
Glosses, interlinear, 67
"go ahead of," 4
God, 20, 63, 80: as love, 83; Israel rebuked by, 86–87; personal name of, 156–157; providence of, 17, 80, 119, 148; revelation of, 39, 80, 81, 118; wisdom of, 66
Golan, 52
Goodspeed, Edgar, 1, 71

Goodspeed New Testament (see also American Translation): alternative translations, lack of, 103; explanatory footnotes, omission of when text changed, 21, 23, 26, 29; footnotes, lack of, 103; improvements in, 59, 102; "mother tongue," use of, 70, 71; revision of verse numbers, 21
Gospel according to the Hebrews, 24, 25
Gospels, 21, 25, 30, 67, 74, 87, 112, 138
Gothic, 138
Great (Cranmer) Bible, 68, 75, 79, 112
Great Britain, see England
Grecians, 137
Greek Bible (see also Apocrypha, Greek New Testament, and Greek Old Testament), 13, 15
Greek codices, see Codices, Greek
Greek Fathers, 25, 136: Athanasius, 22; Basil of Caesarea, 132, 133; Chrysostom, 137, 148, 151; Clement of Alexandria, 28; Cyril of Alexandria, 132; Cyril of Jerusalem, 133; Epiphanius, 136, 140, 143; Eusebius, 15, 24, 28, 132; Gregory Nazianzen, 146, 151; Irenaeus, 27, 139; Justin Martyr, 27, 44, 132; Origen, 28, 136, 147; Papias, 24, 25
Greek language, 21, 28, 125, 134: extent of use of, 43, 135; grammar (idiom) of, 64, 102–103, 108–109, 110–111; style of, 5, 26, 28, 71, 74, 80; syntax of, 8, 100, 106, 108–109; vocabulary of, 26
Greek language, types of: classical, 74; Koine, 71, 74; Septuagint (Hellenistic), 43
Greek manuscripts, decoration (illumination) of, 19
Greek manuscripts, materials of: papyrus, 6; parchment, 13; vellum, 13, 15
Greek manuscripts, 34; minuscule, 19, 20; uncial, 13, 35
Greek New Testament: accuracy of, 32; as basis for translation, 18, 21,

31, 32; correction of, 10, 12, 16, 17, 22, 23, 25, 27, 29, 32, 33, 56; direct-ness of, 74; Gospels of as translation, 112; marginal notes in, 20, 25; ori-gin of, 10; transmission of, 10, 16, 17, 19, 31, 32; variant readings of, 2, 9–10, 11, 12, 16, 17, 18, 22, 25, 27, 28, 29

Greek Old Testament, 13, 43; Aquila's translation of, 105–106, 135, 143; Theodotion's translation of, 135, 143; Symmachus' translation of, 135, 143

Greek Old Testament, Septuagint (LXX), 14, 43, 58, 92, 96, 101, 106, 135–136, 147, 157; accuracy of, 135, 148; correction of, 135; divergence from Hebrew text, 44, 143; origin of, 43, 135; rejection of by Jews, 44; textual value of, 43–46; transmission of, 43; use of by apostles and early Church, 44, 101, 135–136, 143; use of by King James Version, 47, 48; use of by modern translators, 37, 46, 47

Greek script: uncial, 13, 19; minuscule, 19

Greek text-traditions: Beza, 21, 31; Byzantine, 31; Caesarean, 32; Egyptian, 32; Elzevir, 31; Erasmus, 20, 21, 31; Koine, 31; Neutral, 32; Received, 31, 32, 33, 54; Stephanus, 21, 31; Westcott and Hort, 32, 33; Western, 32

Gregory the Great, 144
Gregory Nazianzen, 146, 151

Habakkuk Commentary, 156
Habakkuk, the prophet, 101
Haggai, book of, 143
ḥamman, 97
Hampton Court, 142
Haplography, 10, 38
Harklean Syriac, 28–29
Harmonization, 29, 30
heauton, 12
Hebraica veritas, 44
Hebrew alphabet: aleph, 15; nun, 43, 46; yod, 35, 36; waw, 36, 42

Hebrew consonantal text, 35; accuracy of, 45, 54; correction of by emenda-tion, 49–53; correction of by variant Hebrew readings, 3, 36–42; correc-tion of by variant readings from translations, 43–49; correction of by vowel changes, 42–43; Kethib-Qere, 40, 41, 155, 156; obscurity of, 7, 94; sacredness of, 39, 40; standardization of, 38–40, 105; transmission of, 39, 45, 46, 49, 54

Hebrew consonants: as vowels, 36, 39; confusion of, 3, 36, 47, 50; inversion of, 37, 40, 52

Hebrew customs, 109–111
Hebrew inscriptions: Gezer Calendar, 35; Lachish Ostraca, 35; Mesha (Moabite) Stone, 35; Ostraca of Sa-maria, 35; Siloam Inscription, 35

Hebrew language, 34, 134, 135, 146; grammar (idiom) of, 64, 94, 107, 108, 113, 114, 116; style of, 73–74; syntax of, 106, 107, 108

Hebrew manuscripts, 34; codices, 34; scrolls, 3, 34, 35

Hebrew manuscripts, materials of: leather (parchment), 3, 34; papyrus, 34; ostraca, 35

Hebrews, book of, 71, 101, 145

Hebrew script: Old Hebrew (Ca-naanite), 35, 36, 156; square (Ara-maic), 35, 36, 156

Hebrew spelling: full (plene), 36; short (defective), 36

Hebrew text-traditions: Aqiba, 39, 40; Babylonian, 39, 46; ben Asher, 39, 40; ben Naphtali, 39, 40; Bomberg, 62; Egyptian, 45, 46; Kittel, 40, 62; Masoretic, 38–41, 45–47, 49, 113, 115, 116; Palestinian, 46

Hebrew vowels: correction of, 42, 43; insertion (pointing) of, 39–41, 155, 156; lack of, 3, 35, 37; oral trans-mission of, 39; textual value of, 42

Hebron, 52
Heresy, 124, 125
Heretics, 123, 132, 143
Hermas, Pastor or Shepherd of, 14

Hermogenes, 132
Hesychius, 137
Hexapla of Origen, 136
Hierome (Hieronymus), see Jerome
"hinder," 4, 59
Hippo, 18
Holland, 72
Holy Spirit, 20, 126, 133, 135, 136
Homoeoteleuton, 10, 38
Horses, 92–94
Hort, F. J. A. (see also Westcott and
   Hort), 32, 33
Hosanna, The Day of the Great, 27
hoshianna, 27
hoti, 58
Hymns, 24, 157
Hypocrites, 111, 123, 126

Idioms, English, Greek, and Hebrew,
   107–111
Illumination (decoration) of manu-
   scripts, 19, 81
Imperative mood, 99, 102
Incarnation, 82, 97
"incense altars," 97
Indians, 137
Indicative mood, 99, 102
Inquisitors, 139
Insertion of Hebrew vowels, 39, 40,
   41, 155, 156
Inscriptions, see Hebrew inscriptions
Intelligibility of translations (see also
   Literary qualities), 2, 5, 6, 75–76,
   83, 87, 89, 117
Interlinear translation (glosses), 67,
   106
International Conference of Bible
   Translators, 72
Interpretations: improvements in, 2, 8,
   102; subjectivity of, 100, 103, 116
Ireland, 152
Irenaeus, 27, 139
Isaac, 96–97
Isaiah, the prophet, 73; 134; book of,
   3, 14, 97; scrolls of, 3, 36, 38, 42
Ishmael, 96
Isocrates, 125
Israel, 134; God of, 156; king of, 130;
   rebuked by God, 86–87

Istanbul, 31
Italian language, 142, translations in,
   48, 148
Italics as emphasis in modern usage,
   112
Italics in the Bible, 47, 112; defended,
   112; impracticality of, 113; inaccuracy of, 53, 108, 113–114; indicating reconstruction of Hebrew
   text, 47, 50–51, 53; misleading aspect of, 115–116; origin of, 112–
   113; purpose of achieved by footnotes, 116; uselessness of, 115; validity of, 114–115
Italy, 31
Ithacius, 19

Jacob, 134
Jairus, daughter of, 97
James I, King of England, see King
   James I
Jattir, 52
Jehoram, 50
Jehovah, 40, 156–157
Jephthah, 96
Jeremiah, the prophet, 45; book of,
   14, 45
Jerome, 18, 19, 44, 92, 96, 97, 132,
   133, 134, 136, 137, 140, 141, 144,
   146, 147, 148
Jerusalem, 45, 50, 139
Jesus Christ: death of, 44, 102–103;
   deity of, 2, 65, 66, 102–103; lan-
   guage of, 22; Light of world, 27;
   Lord, ix; Savior, ix, 8, 11, 12; Son
   of God, 8, 96, 135; Water of life,
   26, 27; Word, 8, 20
Jew(ish), 35, 38, 39, 40, 43, 44, 82,
   105, 111, 135, 139, 141, 143, 151,
   156
Jewish Publication Society of Amer-
   ica, translation of, 52
Job, 109, book of, 45
John, the Apostle, 9, 12, 26, 83; Gos-
   pel of, 2, 8, 24, 25, 67
John, the Baptist, 58, 135
Jonathan, 7
Jordan River, 52
Josephus, 43

Joshua, book of, 45
"jot," 35
Judaism, 43, 44, 157
Judas, 65
Jude, book of, 87
Judges, book of, 45
Julian of Eclanum, 132
Justin Martyr, 27, 44, 132
Justinian the Emperor, 136

Karkar, 92
katakeimai, 110
kataklino, 110
Kedesh, 52
kesapsigim, 94
Kethib-Qere, 40, 41, 155-156
Kidron, Brook, 27
King James I, 21, Dedication to, 62-63, 69, 152-154
King James Version: alternative translations defended, 100, 148-149; alternative translations noted, 104; Apocrypha included, 87; archaisms of, 4, 56-63, 87; as standard translation, 80-81, 84; assumed as original text, 31; beauty of, 76, 77, 79, 81, 82, 89; criticism of, 79, 87; dedication of, 62-63, 69, 152-154; dependence on Geneva Bible, 75; dependence on Tyndale, 68, 74; failure to recognize language change, 63; faulty italics of, 53, 108, 113-114, and caption for Fig. 13; Greek text used, 9, 10, 21, 31, 32, 80; harmonization of parallel passages, 51; inconsistency of, 83-84, 113-114; marginal notes of, 48, 62, 100, 148-149; mistranslations of, 11, 47, 89, 114; omission of italics in, 114; opposition to, 2, 100, 139-146; preface to, 2, 6, 48, 67, 78-79, 100, 117, 128-151; Qere, use of, 41; rapturous quality of, 77, 81; reconstruction of Hebrew text by, 47, 50, 51, 53; superiority of, 2, 70, 74, 76, 157; title page of, 48; use of other translations by, 47, 48, 49, 58; use of "you," 62; variety in wording, 78-79, 149-150; veneration of, 117;

vowel changes in Hebrew text by, 42; word order inverted, 4, 80
King James Version, editions of: 1611, 55, 113, 114; 1612 edition, 113; Cambridge editions of 1629 and 1638, 113; Cambridge (Paris) edition of 1762, 113-114; Oxford (Blayney) edition of 1769, 114
King James Version, translators: companies of, 76, 87; humility of, 117, 147; purposes of, 5, 6, 68, 117, 146; rules for translating, 21; rules disregarded by, 58, 75; skill of, 76, 77, 79, 146-147; textual methods of, 16, 47-51, 53, 58, 147-148; wisdom of, 100, 117, 118, 148
Kings, books of, 45
Kittel, Rudolf, 40, 62
Kleist, James, 122
Knox, Ronald, New and Old Testament translations of, 122
Koine Greek, 71, 74
Koine Greek text-tradition, 31
Koridethi Gospels, Codex Theta, 27
Kue (Que), 92-93
Kurios, 157

Laban, 134
Lachish Ostraca, 35
Lack of Hebrew vowels, 3, 35, 37
Language change, ignored by Protestant Church, 63, 72
"language of devotion" (see also "Church language"), 63, 65, 66
Latin codices, see Codices, Latin
Latin Fathers: Ambrose, 24, 144; Augustine, 24, 100, 132, 133, 136, 140, 143, 144, 147, 148, 149, 151; Ithacius, 19; Jerome, 18, 19, 24, 44, 92, 96, 97, 132, 133, 134, 136, 137, 140, 141, 144, 146, 147, 148; Priscillianus, 19; Tertullian, 132, 139, 141
Latin language, 21, 125, 134, 142, 146; extent of use of, 18, 136; importance of, 18, 67; influence on English, 4, 58, 60, 83
Latin text-traditions: Old Latin, 18, 22, 24, 27, 28, 96; Vulgate, 18-20,

23, 24, 44, 47, 48, 49, 81, 92, 96,
147, Clementine edition of, 19, 146,
Sixtine edition of, 19, 145–146
Latin translations, 43, 48: accuracy of,
18, 19, 136; as basis for English
translations, 23, 47, 48–49, 67, 112;
divergence of, 18, 136, 145; influence
on Greek manuscripts, 19, 20, 25;
influence on King James Version,
47, 48, 49; origin of, 18, 136; trans-
mission of, 18; value of, 34, 136
Law of Moses, 39, 43
Leather, 3
Leghorn, Italy, 13
Leipzig, 14
Leningrad, 15
Leo X, Pope, 145
"let," 4, 59
Levites, 27
Leviticus, 97
Lewis, Agnes S., 28
Lewis, C. S., 72, 81–82, 83
"liberal," 58–59
Libnah, 52
Lilly, Joseph, 122
"linen yarn," 92, 94
Literal sense, 124
Literary qualities: beauty, 76, 77, 79,
82, 85, 87; cadence, 76, 83, 87;
clarity (intelligibility, perspicuity),
2, 5, 75–76, 83, 87, 89, 117;
euphony, 83; rhythm, 76, 83, 85,
87
Literary style: in early English ver-
sions, 74–76; in Greek, 5, 71, 74; in
Hebrew, 73, 74; in King James
Version, 5, 76–82; in modern Eng-
lish versions, 5, 79, 83, 84–89
Literary tastes, variety of, 79, 81
Liturgy, 22, 23
London, 16, 125, 126, Bishop of, 125
Lord, 156–157
LORD, 156–157
Lord's Prayer, 23
"love," 83–84
Lucar, Cyril, 15
Lucian, 137
Luke, book of, 71
Lupset, Thomas, 83

Luther, Martin, ix
LXX (Septuagint), see Greek Old
Testament
Lyndewode, William, 125
Lyons, Gaul, 27

Maimonides, 40
Manuscripts, materials of: leather
(parchment), 3, 13, 34; ostraca, 35;
papyrus, 6, 34; vellum, 13, 15
Manuscripts, types of, see Greek, and
Hebrew manuscripts
Marginal notes, see Footnotes
Masoretes, 39, 40, 41
Masoretic text, 38–41, 45–47, 49, 113,
115, 116
Matthew Bible, 68, 75
Matthew, book of, 25
matres lectionis, 36
Meaning, equivalence of, 105, 107–
111, 112–118
Meaning of Biblical terms, 2, 6, 7, 91–
98, 148
Mediterranean, 94
Meek, Theophile J., 97
"menomintal," 155
Mesha (Moabite) Stone, 35
Messiah, 82, 103
Methodius, 138
Micah, 73
Michmash, 7
Minuscule manuscripts, see Codices,
Greek minuscule
Minuscule script, 19
miqweh, 92
Misleading expressions or words:
"anon," 61; "book," 61; "bowels,"
4, 88; "by-and-by," 61; "carriage,"
61; "curious girdle," 61; "let," 4,
59; "outlandish," 60–61; "prevent,"
4, 60; "strange," 60; "suffer," 59;
"vile," 60
misraim, 92
Moabite (Mesha) Stone, 35
Moffatt, James, 1
Moffatt Bible: explanatory footnotes,
26, 29; explanatory footnotes, omission of when text changed, 21, 23,
29, 37, 47; footnotes, lack of, 53;

improvements in, 58, 70, 101, 107; italics, lack of, 53; reconstruction of Hebrew text, 52, 92, 93; revision of verse numbers, 21; translations, use of other, 46, 47; variant Greek readings in text, 12; vowel changes made in Hebrew text, 42, 43, 92

Monastery of St. Catherine, 13, 14

monogenes, 95–96

Montgomery, Helen, Centenary New Testament of, 122

Mood: imperative, 99, 102; indicative, 99, 102

Moses, 39, 131

"mother tongue," opposition to Scriptures in, 67, 123, 124, 138–139; translations in, 6, 66, 67, 68, 137–138

"mothers of reading," 36

Mt. Athos, 28

Mt. Sinai, 13, 14, 28, 39

Munster, Sebastian, 112–113, Latin Old Testament translation of, 112

Muṣri (Muzri), 92–93

Nain, widow of, 96

Napoleon, 13

Nazianzen, Gregory, 146, 151

Nehemiah, the Governor, 46, 139

Neutral Greek text-tradition, 32

Nicaea: Council of, 19; Creed of, 22, 96

Normans, 67

nun, 43, 46

Obsolete expressions and words: "against Joseph came," 56; "bruit," 56; "do you to wit," 56–57; "trow," 56

Old English (Anglo-Saxon), 67–68, 138

Old Hebrew (Canaanite) script, 35, 36

Old Latin translations, 18, 22, 24, 27, 28, 96

Old Syriac, 23, 28

Omissions from Scripture, warning against, 30

on dit, 109

"only begotten Son," 95

Origen, 28, 136, 147

Original text, 10, 16, 17, 19, 22, 25, 30, 31, 39, 46, 49, 50, 112, 133

Orlinsky, Harry M., 45

Ornamentation, 13

Ostraca, Lachish, 35

Ostraca of Samaria, 35

"outlandish," 60–61

Oxford University editions of King James Version, 114

Palestine, 3, 31, 35, 38, 39, 44, 46

Palestinian Hebrew text-tradition, 46

Palestinian Syriac, 24

Palimpsest, 15

Papias, 24, 25

Papyri, 16, 24, 91

Papyri, Chester Beatty, 16, 24

papyrus, 6, 16, 34

Parchment (see also Leather, and Vellum), 13, 34

Paris, city of, 13, 16, 21, 27

Paris, Thomas, 113–114

Passive voice, 109

Passover, Feast of, 111

Paul II, Pope, 149

Paul, the Apostle, 93, 119; instructions of, 6, 7, 83, 101–102, 145; letters of, 5, 16, 17, 20, 30, 87; use of Septuagint by, 44; writing style of, 5

peduye, 79

Pentateuch (Torah), 43, 45, Tyndale's translation of, 121, 123

"perfect day," 84

"permit," 4, 59

Persian Empire, 35

Persians, 137

Peshitto, 23, 27

Peter, 28, 65

Petrograd, 15

Pharisees, 110, 111

Philistines, 7, 151

Phillips, J. B., 1, 74

Phillips New Testament: alternative translations, lack of, 103; explanatory footnotes, 26; explanatory footnotes, omission of when text changed, 21, 23, 29; footnotes, lack of, 103; improvements in, 59; "mother tongue," use of, 72; variant Greek readings in text, 12

Philo, 43

phortion, 7

Pilate, 99

pim, 7, 97

Pius, IV, 139

Plutarch, 142

"pointing" of Hebrew text, 39–41, 155–156

Polite use of pronouns, 63

Pope(s), 81, 100, 144, 145, 149

Potsherds, 94

Pottery: inscriptions on (see also Ostraca), 35; silver dross on, 94

Prayer, 11, 22, 23, 24, 27, 66

"prevent," 4, 60

Priests, 27, 67, 125

Priscillianus, 19

Private reading (worship), 89, 103, 118

Proselyte (convert), 105, 143

Protestant Christianity (see also Church, Protestant), ix, 23, 24

Protestant Reformation, ix, 1, 44

Protestant Scriptures (see also Bible), 13, 81, 100

Psalms (Psalter), 13, 27, 67, 74, 79, 138

Psi, Codex, 28

Ptolemy (Philadelphus) II, 135, 140

Public worship, 22, 81, 88–89, 116–117

"published," 58

Punctuation, 19, lack of, 13

Puritans, 142, 150

Qere, see *Kethib-Qere*

Quality of manuscripts as textual criterion, 16, 17, 21

Quantity of manuscripts as textual criterion, 16, 17

Que (Kue), 92–93

Qumran, 45, 46

Qumran Scrolls, see Dead Sea Scrolls

Quotations of Old Testament in the New, 44

Rachel, 57

Ras Shamra, 94

Received text, 31, 32, 33

Reformation (Protestant), ix, 1, 44

Regius, Codex L, 27, 28

Religion, 105, 131

Revelation (Apocalypse), 20, 31, 87

Revelation, of God, 39, 80, 81

Revised Standard Version: alternative translations, 89, 99, 101, 102, 104; clarity of, 89, 117; conservative feature of, 89; criticism of, 79, 84; explanatory footnotes, 23, 26, 28, 47, 48, 49, 50, 64; explanatory footnotes, omission of when text changed, 21, 29, 37; improvements in, 4, 6, 37, 54, 59, 102, 107, 110, 157; italics, lack of, 54, 116; "mother tongue," use of, 71; reconstruction of Hebrew text, 49, 54; revision of verse numbers, 21; style of, 79, 88–89; translations, use of other, 37, 46, 47, 48, 50; variant Greek readings in footnotes, 23, 28; variant Greek readings in text, 12; variant Hebrew readings in text, 3, 42; vowel changes made in Hebrew text, 42, 92

Revision of translations, necessity of, 1, 2, 68, 71, 72

Revision of verse numbers, 21–22

Rheims (Douay) New Testament, 23, 58, 75–76, 87

Rhythm (see also Literary qualities), 76, 83, 85, 87

Richard II, King of England, 138

Rieu, E. V., translation of the Gospels, 122

Robertson, A. T., 15

Rogers, John, 68

Rolle, Richard, 74

Roman armies, 3

Roman Catholic Church, 23, 80, 129, 138, 140, 144, 145, 146, 150

Roman Catholic translations: Confraternity, 122; Douay-Rheims, 23, 58, 75–76, 87; Kleist-Lilly, 122; Knox, Ronald, 122

Roman centurion, 102–103

Roman Emperor, 130

Roman Empire, 18, 137
Roman police, 82
Roman Senate, 134, 137
Roman soldiers, 103
Roman type, 112–113
Romans, 137, book of, 87
Rome, 13, 18, 31, 137, 142, 149
Russia, Emperor of, 14, 15

Sacredness of Hebrew consonantal text, 39, 40
St. Catherine, Monastery of, 13, 14
St. Petersburg, 15
Samuel, books of, 45, 130
Sanballat, 139, 141
Sarah, 96
Satan, 65, 145
Saul, 7, 49
Sauromatians, 137
Saxony, 14
Schaff, Philip, 106
Scofield Bible, 103
Scotland, 71
Scribal mistakes, 31; intentional, 2, 18, 23, 28, 29, 30, 44; unintentional, 18, 20, 23, 29, *dittography*, 38, 93, errors of eye, 10, 11, 12, 36, 37, 92, errors of mind, 11, 29, *haplography*, 10, 38
Script, see Greek, and Hebrew script
Script, Ugaritic, 94
Scripture, see Bible
Scrivener, F. H. A., 79, 114–115
Scrolls, Hebrew, 3, 34, 35
Scythians, 134, 137
Semitic language (see also Aramaic, Hebrew, and Syriac), 34
Seneca, 139
Septuagint (Hellenistic) Greek, 43
Septuagint (LXX), see Greek Old Testament
Sermons, 15, 24
Shakespeare, William, 62
Shalmaneser III, 92
Shechem, 52
Shekel, 7
"shibboleths," 66
Shiloh, 46
Short spelling, Hebrew, 36

Siewert, Frances E., 122
Siloam Inscription, 35
Siloam, Pool of, 27
Silver dross, 94
Similar ending, see *Homoeoteleuton*
Sinai, Mt., 13, 14, 28, 39
Sinaitic Syriac, 28
Sinaiticus, Codex Aleph, 13–15, 16, 24, 28
Single writing, see *Haplography*
Sixtus Quintus, Pope (see also Vulgate, Sixtine edition), 145, 146, 149
Sixtus Senensis, 137
Slavonian (Sclavonian), 138
Smith, Miles, 117
Solomon, 92–94, 130, 143
Spain, 20, 40
Spanish translation, 48, 148
Spiritual bride, 90–91
Spurgeon, Charles, 106
Square script, 35, 36
Standardization of Hebrew text, 38, 39, 40, 105
Stapulensis, 145
Stephanus, Robert (Estienne), 21; text-tradition of, 21, 31
Stephen, 131
"strange," 60
"strike hands with me," 109–110
Study of English Bible, 106
Style, literary, see Literary style
"suffer," 59
"sun-images," 97
"sun-pillars," 97
Symmachus, 135, 143
Syntax: English, 4, 5, 80, 109; Greek, 8, 100, 106, 108–109; Hebrew, 106, 107, 108
Syria, 15, 23, 36, 37, 94; Church of, 15, 23; kings of, 92, 130
Syriac codices, see Codices, Syriac
Syriac language: extent of use of, 23; importance of, 23; relation to Aramaic, 22
Syriac script, 138
Syriac text-traditions: Old Syriac, 23; Palestinian Syriac, 24; Peshitto, 23, 27; Sinaitic, 28

Syriac translations, 43, 48, 138, 148; origin of, 22, 23; transmission of, 23; value of, 34
Syriac vowels, addition of, 39
Syrians, 137

Tabernacles, Feast of, 26, 27
Tarsus, 93
Teaching of the Apostles: Greek text, 22; Syriac text, 24
Tekoa, 92
Temple, 27, 45, 130, 143
Tertullian, 132, 139, 141
Tetragrammaton, 156
Text-traditions, see Greek, Hebrew, Latin, and Syriac text-traditions
Textual criticism, New Testament: age of manuscripts, 13, 15, 16, 21; quality of manuscripts, 16, 17, 21; quantity of manuscripts, 16, 17; variant readings from translations, 19
Textual criticism, Old Testament: conjectural emendation of Hebrew consonantal text, 49–53; variant readings from Hebrew manuscripts, 36–42; variant readings from translations, 43–49; vowel changes, 42–43
Textual value of the Septuagint, 43–46
Textus Receptus (see also Received text), 31
Theodoret, 137
Theodotion, 135, 143
Theological bias, question of, 22, 30, 97
Theological notes, 103
Theological students, ix, 106
Theta, 27
"The Translators to the Reader," 2, 6, 48, 69, 78–79, 100, 117, 128–151
"Thou" and "you": alternation impossible, 65; in early English versions, 61–63; in modern English versions, 64–66; in worship, 66
Tiberias, 39
Tiflis, U.S.S.R., 27
Tischendorf, Lobegott Konstantine, 13–16

Tishri, 26
Tobiah, 141
Tomb, 111
Tomb of the Unknown Soldier, 111
Torah (Pentateuch), 43, 45
Traditionalists, 66
"translate," 58
Translation: and evangelical zeal, 118; into "mother tongue," opposition to, 67, 123, 124, 138–139; principles (essential features) of, 33, 54, 69, 70–71, 89, 98, 100, 103–104, 110, 115, 118; purpose of, 8, 105, 137
Translations: alternative, lack of, 103, opposition to, 100, validity of, 99–100; as God's Word, 118, 142; committee, 70, 71; desire for, 1, 70; for standard reference, 104; freedom to choose from, 118; increase of, 1, 118, 137–138; individual, 70; intelligibility of, 2, 5, 6; necessity of, 2, 134, 142; necessity of revision of, 1, 2, 68, 71, 72, 144–146; superiority of modern translations; 33, 54, 69, 70–72, 84–88, 96–98; word-for-word, 67, 69, 85, 104, 105–107
Translators, International Conference of Bible, 72
Translators, King James Version, see King James Version translators
Translators, question of theological bias, 22, 30
Translators, validity of textual changes of, 31
Transmission of Greek text, 10, 16, 17, 19, 31, 32
Transmission of Hebrew text, 39, 45, 46, 49, 54
Trent, Council of, 18, 145
Trevisa, John, 138
Trial, 109
Trieste, 14
Trinity College, 113
Trinity, doctrine of, 19, 22, 96
Trinity passage, 18–22, 25
Troilus and Criseyde, 67
"trow," 56
Truth: artistic style and the, 81–83, 89; blasphemy of, 124; communi-

cation of, 8, 81, 87, 132, 145, 154; defense of, 146, 153; enemies of, 124; freedom of, 8; rebuke of, 124

Twentieth Century New Testament, 121

Tyndale New Testament: archaistic features of, 56, 62, 89; improvements in, 58, 95–96; mistranslations of, 11, 102; "mother tongue," use of, 68; new expressions and words, 56, 59, 60; opposition to, 124–126; purpose of translation, 68, 124; style of, 74, 75; superiority of, 68, 70, 75, 81; translation from Greek, 83; use of "love," 83; word order inverted, 80

Tyndale Pentateuch and Jonah, 121

Tyndale, William, 56, 59, 62, 68, 74; "To the Reder," 68; "W.T. To the Reader," 68, 123–127

Ugaritic, 94

Ulfilas (Ulpilas), 138

Ultraviolet ray, 15

Unbelief (disbelief), 26, 30

Uncial manuscripts, see Codices, Greek uncial

Uncial script, 13, 19

unicus, 96

unigenitus, 96

United Bible Societies, 72

United States, 57, 64, 70, 71, 100, 106

"unspeakable," 59

Valdus, 138

Valla, 145

Variant readings (see also Greek New Testament, and Hebrew consonantal text), 25, 32, 40; necessity of noting, 2; validity of, 16, 17

Vatican Library, 13

Vaticanus, Codex B, 13, 15, 16, 17, 24, 28

Vellum (see also Parchment), 13, 15

Verkuyl, Gerrit, 1, 71

Verkuyl New Testament (see also Berkeley Version): archaistic features of 21, 23, 29, 65; conservative fea-

ture of, 97; explanatory foonotes, 21, 23, 26, 28, 65, 97; *Koine* Greek readings in text, 21, 23, 29; "mother tongue," belief in use of, 71; use of "you," 65; variant Greek readings in text, 12

Verse division, 21, 22, 38; revision of, 21, 22

"vile," 60

"virgin," 90–91

Vives, 145

Vocabulary, 26, 76

Vulgar (common, mother) tongue, 6, 82, 134, 137–138, 141, 150

Vulgate of Jerome, 18, 19, 20, 23, 44, 47, 48, 49, 81, 92, 96, 147; Clementine edition, 19, 29, 146; Sixtine edition, 19, 145, 146

Washington Codex, 25, 27, 111

Washington, D.C., 25

waw, 36, 42

Wesley, John, ix; New Testament translation of, 121

Westcott and Hort text-tradition, 32, 33

Westcott, B. F., 48

Western text-tradition, 32

Westminster New Testament, 122

Weymouth New Testament: alternative translations, 99, 104; explanatory footnotes, 21, 23, 26, 28; explanatory footnotes, omission of when text changed, 29; improvements in, 12, 59; "mother tongue," use of, 70; variant Greek readings, in text, 12, in footnotes, 23

Weymouth, Richard, 1, 70

"which," 80

"whited sepulchres," 111

"whitewashed," 111

Whittingham New Testament (see also Geneva Bible), 60, 95–96, 103, 112

Williams, Charles B., 1, 71

Williams, C. B., New Testament: alternative translations, lack of, 103–104; explanatory footnotes, 21, 26, 28; explanatory footnotes, omission of when text changed, 23, 29; inconsistency of, 96; "mother tongue," use of, 71; paraphrase in, 91–92; variant Greek readings in text, 12

Williams, C. Kingsley, 1

Williams, Kingsley, New Testament: alternative translations, 99, 104; explanatory footnotes, 26; explanatory footnotes, omission of when text changed, 21, 23, 29; improvements in, 102; revision of verse numbers, 21; variant Greek readings in text, 12

Wine, 27

"Word," see Jesus Christ

Word division, 19, 35; lack of, 13, 35

Word-for-word translations, 67, 69, 85, 104, 105, 106, 107

Word order, see Syntax, English, Greek, and Hebrew

Worship, private, 89, 103, 118; public, 22, 81, 88–89, 116–117

Wuest, Kenneth S., New Testament of, 122

Wyclif Bible: archaistic features of, 62; clarity of, 56, 57, 59, 60; "mother tongue," use of, 67; style of, 74; translation from Latin, 18, 83

Wyclif, John, 67, 74

Ximenes, Cardinal, 20

yaḥid, 96
Yahweh, 156–157
yod, 35, 36
"you," ambiguity of, 64

Zerubbabel, 46, 143

ADDITIONS TO GENERAL INDEX

Ambiguity in Greek text, 171

American Translation, 189, 191, 192, 194

American Standard Version, 160, 177, 178, 185, 186, 189, 192, 193, 204, 205, 206, 207, 208

Amplified Bible, 196–204

Archaic pronouns, 162, 177, 184f., 206

Bible Translator, The, 160

Brackets, use of in translating, 163

Capitalization of pronouns referring to Deity, 184

Clark, Kenneth W., 179

"corn," 194

Dodd, C. H., 167

ekklesia, 173
Elohim, 187

English Revised Version, 159, 160, 174, 177, 178

Findlay, G. G., 175

Four Prophets: Amos, Hosea, First Isaiah, Micah, 187–196

Ginsberg, H. L., 180

Girdlestone, Edward D., 175, 176, 177

Goodspeed, Edgar, 160, 169

Hampden-Cook, Ernest, 175

Harris J. Rendell, 175

Higgs, Mary Kingsland, 174, 178

hysso, 159
hyssopo, 159

Interim Report on Vocabulary Selection, 159

kêrusso, 165

King James Version, 160, 162, 172, 173, 174, 178, 181, 182, 185, 186, 189, 192, 193, 196, 198, 201, 203, 205

Kittel, Rudolf, 183

Letters to Young Churches, 190, 194

Literalism in translating, 163, 164

Malan, Ernest, 174, 178
Masoretic text, 181, 182, 183, 184
Moffatt, James, 160, 169, 189, 190, 191, 192, 193, 194, 195

Nestle's Greek New Testament, 162, 206
New American Standard Bible, 204–208
New English Bible, 160, 167–173, 184
New Jewish Publication Society Version, 179
New Testament: An Expanded Translation, The, 162–167
New Testament in Modern English, The, 187
New Testament in Plain English, The 158–162

Obsolete words, 159, 162
Orlinsky, Harry M., 180

Paraphrase in translating, 165, 169ff., 177, 190f., 199f.
Paragraph titles, 168
Parentheses in translating, 170f.
petra, 163
petros, 163
Phillips, J. B., 160, 169, 187–196
Plain English, 159
Poetical passages in Scripture, 160, 163, 168, 176, 177, 180, 188

Quotation marks, use of in translating, 161, 168, 176
quayits, 193

Revised Standard Version, 161, 167, 168, 170, 172, 173, 176, 178, 180, 181, 184, 185, 186, 189, 192, 193, 199, 201, 207, 208
Robertson, E. H., 179, 188

Septuagint, 189, 198
"Sheol," 192
Siewert, Frances E., 196, 199, 203f.
Souter's Greek New Testament, 159
Speiser, Ephraim A., 180
spermologos, 165
Stead, W. T., 174
Subjectivity, problem of in translating, 165

Titles for units of books, 176
Torah: The Five Books of Moses, The, 179
Twentieth Century New Testament, 174–179
Tyndale, William, 178

Westcott and Hort Greek text, 177, 197f.
Weymouth, Richard F., 174, 175
Williams, Charles Kingsley, 158–162, 164, 169
Word-for-word approach, 163f.
Word order in translating, 163f.
Wuest, Kenneth S., 162–167, 197